Language and literacy

Routledge Education Books

Advisory editor: John Eggleston
Professor of Education
University of Keele

Language and literacy
The sociolinguistics of reading
and writing

Michael Stubbs

Department of Linguistics
University of Nottingham

Routledge & Kegan Paul

London, Boston and Henley

First published in 1980
by Routledge & Kegan Paul Ltd
30 Store Street, London WC1E 7DD,
Broadway House, Newtown Road,
Henley-on-Thames, Oxon RG9 1EN and
9 Park Street, Boston, Mass. 02108, USA
Set in IBM Press Roman by
Hope Services
Abingdon, Oxon
and printed in Great Britain by
St Edmundsbury Press,
Bury St Edmunds, Suffolk
Reprinted in 1981

British Library Cataloguing in Publication Data

Stubbs, Michael, b. 1947

Language and literacy – (Routledge education
books).
1. Illiteracy – Social aspects
I. Title
301.2'1   LC149   79-41331

ISBN 0 7100 0426 5
ISBN 0 7100 0499 0 Pbk

Contents

v

Contents

Contents

Preface

On the one hand, books on reading and writing proliferate, and it requires some hesitation before adding yet another one. On the other hand, the literature on literacy is so vast and inconclusive, and still contains so many basic confusions and unanswered questions, that there is a clear need for books which attempt to make some sense of the state of the art.

I suspect that what may be required in work on literacy is not so much yet more basic research on small and isolated topics; but rather attempts to evaluate and integrate the incoherent masses of findings, and attempts to relate reading and writing to the communicative functions that written language serves in our society. There is nothing even approaching a coherent theory of reading or literacy. One reason for this is that there is also nothing approaching a coherent theory about the relations between reading and writing, or between written and spoken language, or about the place of written language in society and the purposes it serves. As a result, research on reading, although vast and stretching back over some seventy-five years of concentrated work, is unintegrated and inconclusive. In addition, this work is often unrelated to relevant research on language and on the uses of language in different social situations.

This book therefore attempts to provide the basis for such a theory, and to place reading within a discussion of the formal and functional characteristics of language in use in social settings. In some areas the argument will not be able to progress further than common-sense observations. For whilst some subjects are now quite well understood (such as the relation between the English spelling system and spoken English, or the problems of setting up a writing system for a previously unwritten language), in other areas the basic research has not yet been done. One such area, which would require concentrated analyses of a large corpus of written and spoken texts, is the formal differences in vocabulary and grammar between written and spoken English.

I hope the argument will be of interest to educationalists, especially those concerned with teaching reading and writing, and more generally with problems of language in education. It should also be of interest to students on courses of language study or linguistics, who require a discussion of the relation between spoken and written language and of the place of written language in society. The argument assumes that the reader has no previous knowledge of linguistics, and should therefore be accessible to students in most related disciplines, including English, linguistics, sociology, psychology and education, and to students in teacher-training. A peculiar feature of printed and published material is that the author never knows precisely who will read it: books are written for ill-defined, mythical social groups, such as 'student teachers' or 'second-year sociology students'. Since reading and writing are skills demanded of almost everyone in modern urbanized societies, this book may also interest the 'intelligent layman', if such a group of readers exists.

So the book is mainly intended as an introduction to the subject, a discussion of the state of the art, and a textbook, and is written so that non-linguists can read it. I would not have been entirely sanguine about writing it, however, if it had been merely a review of the field. But in preparing the material, I have constantly come up against problems which linguists have not yet solved, often because most linguists have simply ignored them for many years. This makes me hope that the book may also be of interest to those who are primarily interested in language.

Linguists often use the powerful research strategy of studying language apart from its social contexts of use, and therefore of ignoring its different realizations in speech and writing. There is no doubt whatsoever that this quite deliberate idealization has brought about enormous advances in our understanding of language structure, particularly in phonology (sound structure) and grammar. But there is equally no doubt that the strategy simply conceals certain types of linguistic phenomena, including the interaction between different realizations of language (spoken and written), the differences in form and function between speech and writing, the relation between written language and ways of thinking, and so on. Some of these topics concern predominantly social issues of language planning or initial literacy, but others raise problems of interest to the professional theoretical linguist, such as the parallelism between phonemes and graphemes, the relation of different writing systems to different levels of language (phonemic, lexical and grammatical), how literacy affects the rate of language change, and the possibility of identifying various linguistic universals.

There is a separate point which linguists might consider. Linguists are often reluctant to become involved in educational debates. They argue that it is their job to describe and explain language, but not to encroach on other people's professional territory by making statements about education. This is often due to admirable modesty and caution. Linguists are rightly unwilling, for example, to tell teachers how to behave in the classroom, and are clearly unqualified to do so merely by virtue of being linguists. In addition, the relation between linguistic theory (or psychology or sociological theory, for that matter) and classroom practice is seldom obvious. On the other hand, only linguists with a full-time professional interest in language could possibly hope to assimilate a large amount of contemporary linguistic theory and sift out from it those bits which are likely to be relevant to education. No educationalists, starting from scratch, could be expected to do this, since linguistics is now such a large area of study, much of which is clearly of no immediate interest to educationalists. It does seem then that linguists have the responsibility of trying to present in a helpful way those parts of the subject which could be of use to others. A great deal is now known about language which is of immediate use to teachers, if only it can be made accessible. A lot of detailed work has now been done, for example, on: the English spelling system, and writing systems in general; the nature of language standardization; children's language acquisition; the nature of an adult's knowledge of his native language; regional and social variation in language; and so on. All these are areas in which teachers need basic information, and linguistics can supply some of it.

Precisely how this information affects classroom teaching is a separate pedagogical problem; although linguists doubtless have their own personal ideas about it, they do not have any particular professional expertise to offer. Just one example, for the present. A lot is now known about English spelling, which turns out to be much more highly organized than many people think, but very complex (see Chapter 3). It seems clear that, ideally, all teachers of reading should have a sophisticated and up-to-date understanding of what is known about English spelling. But it is not at all obvious just how this knowledge ought to inform the teaching of reading, and how this knowledge ought to be presented, if at all, to children. The idea behind the Initial Teaching Alphabet (ITA), for example, is initially to protect children from the complexities of the system, until they have gained confidence and understood some of the principles. This might be an excellent pedagogical strategy, but it neither follows from nor contradicts the linguistic findings about English spelling.

It seems, in fact, that Sir James Pitman, the inventor of ITA, seriously misunderstands how English spelling works as a linguistic system. He wrongly believes, for example, that it is grossly 'inconsistent' and 'illogical' (Pitman and St John, 1969, pp. 41-4). The question of whether ITA is a good teaching medium seems, however, to a large extent independent of our understanding of the writing system. ITA might be based on a seriously defective theory of English spelling, and yet still work as a teaching strategy, since so many other factors come into teaching: not least the child's confidence. In general, then, the relation between linguistic theory and educational practice will be indirect.

Only relatively few linguists have made contributions in these areas. There are, for example, substantial discussions of different topics by Josef Vachek, W. Haas and K. H. Albrow, and important contributions by Dwight Bolinger, Martin Joos and others, as well as by the many sociolinguists primarily interested in language planning, standardization and literacy, including Kenneth Pike, Charles A. Ferguson, Joshua A. Fishman, Jack Berry, Eugene A. Nida and Sarah Gudschinsky. I have necessarily drawn on much of this work in preparing this book. Throughout, these sources are acknowledged in the normal way, but I would like to mention one influence in particular. I first discovered K. H. Albrow's short book on the English writing system some years ago, and for the first time realized that the English spelling system was (a) more interesting than I had thought, and (b) not as odd as I had thought. I had, in fact, never seriously thought about it, never having realized that it could be an interesting subject. I recommend this book (Albrow, 1972) to anyone interested in the area; having read it, I understood something for the first time about how English spelling works. My students are now often astonished when I point out to them some regularity in English spelling which they had never noticed and which I first discovered in Albrow's book.

Nottingham

Acknowledgments

I have received helpful comments on draft chapters and useful material from several people, including Margaret Berry, Christopher Brumfit, Andrew Crompton, John Gordon, Christopher Kennedy, Lesley Milroy and Bernadette Robinson. Ian Malcolm of Mount Lawley College of Advanced Education, Western Australia, and Susan Kaldor, of the University of Western Australia, very kindly supplied me with material, much of it unpublished, on problems of language and education in Australia. James R. D. Milroy, of Queen's University, Belfast, very kindly read the whole typescript in its final stages and made many useful points which have been incorporated in the text. Deirdre Burton, of the University of Birmingham, encouraged me to write the book and discussed it with me over two years: she remains sceptical, possibly rightly, of my account of the relation of written and spoken language. Hazel Hanlon typed the whole manuscript impeccably, demonstrating as she did so the powerful role of secretaries in normalizing and standardizing the printed word (see 4.6) by correcting some of my mistakes. All these people deserve much thanks; and no blame for the gaps and errors which remain.

Part one

The state of the art

Chapter 1

The state of the art and some definitions

It is generally agreed that we do not understand the process of reading, or what happens when a child does or does not learn to read. (Labov, 1970)

. . . the incredibly confused and inconclusive state of reading research . . . (Smith, 1973, p. 5)

Very little of the great mass published on the subject (of the teaching of reading) is significant in contributing to a theory of literacy. Indeed much of it reflects the absence of a theory, and the absence of any awareness of the need for a theory. (Mackay *et al.*, 1970, p. 78)

One reason why the literature on reading is so vast and unintegrated is that topics have been approached from different directions from within different disciplines, including psychology, education and linguistics. Often these approaches have been largely self-contained, making little reference to work within other approaches, and, in fact, putting forward contradictory definitions of *reading* and *literacy*. Furthermore, research on reading has been dominated by experimental psychology, which has seen reading as primarily a perceptual process. Until relatively recently, reading has been regarded only peripherally as a process of handling written *language* or as an activity with particular *social functions*. Certainly, the vast majority of research has concentrated on the psychological processes of reading in the individual reader, and therefore on the internal relations between perceptual processes, orthographic systems and, to a lesser extent, the reader's knowledge of his own language. But it has neglected the relation of reading to writing, the place written language plays in different societies, and so on.

As a result, we know quite a lot about reading as a psychological process, although findings tend to remain unintegrated, sometimes

3

contradictory, and often unrelated to linguistic and sociological approaches to reading and writing. But we know relatively little about reading and writing as linguistic processes, and even less about the social functions of reading and writing.

Research on reading has been carried on in a concentrated fashion since the beginning of the twentieth century. Compulsory education, with the minimum requirement of literacy for all, was introduced by the Education Acts of 1870 in England and Wales and of 1872 in Scotland, and systematic research was underway by the 1900s. The discovery that the eyes move in a jerky fashion during reading, fixing on a span of words or letters, then moving on rapidly to another fixation point, was made as early as 1879 by Javal. The term 'congenital word blindness' was first used by Morgan (1896) in an article in the *British Medical Journal*. And as early as 1897, Pillsbury had shown the importance of expectation on the perception of words: he presented words with deliberate typographical errors for very short periods by tachistoscope. Subjects were often certain they saw letters which were not present. The Armed Forces revealed high levels of illiteracy during the First World War and this provided fresh impetus for research. And National Reading Surveys have been carried out since 1940 (Morris, 1972). But despite seventy-five years or more of research, there is still nothing approaching a coherent theory. In a recent major book, Smith (1973) declares simply that reading research is 'incredibly confused and inconclusive'. A fashionable disclaimer at present is that we have not learned much more about the psychology of reading than is set out in Huey's classic book of 1908 (e.g., see Gibson, 1972, in Kavanagh and Maddingley, 1972; Kolers, 1968, cited by Gudschinsky, 1976, p. 9). Often, in fact, researchers appear to have despaired and relapsed into a mystic belief that it is all too complex to describe and involves the whole man. One finds unhelpful statements such as: 'Perhaps reading, like mystery, can only be described and evoked.... Reading must engage the total organism' (Jenkinson, 1969, p. 107). It is probably unfair to pick out this particular quote, as any one of so many might have been quoted in its place.

It will be useful to begin with a simple list of some of the potential confusions that will have to be borne in mind as the argument proceeds. Many of these distinctions appear obvious enough once they are pointed out, but they are often not made explicit in the literature.

1.1 Some potential confusions

Definitions of reading and writing

There is, first of all, still no general agreement on what is meant by *reading* and *literacy*. (See 1.2 below.) Most collections of articles on reading contain papers with titles such as 'What is reading?', 'The nature of reading', or even 'Reading: is there such a thing?' (see, for example, Melnik and Merritt, 1972b). The basic debate has been between those who hold that reading means essentially the 'mechanics' of reading, that is, the ability to decode written words into spoken words; and those who maintain that reading essentially involves understanding. There has been no agreement on this since Thorndike raised the issue very clearly in a now classic article published in 1917. In this article he argued that reading is 'understanding the meaning of printed words', and he himself took the extreme view that reading is 'reasoning' and that 'understanding a paragraph is like solving a problem in mathematics'. Whether one agrees with Thorndike or not, he did pose the alternatives very clearly; but there is still no consensus on the answer.

In order to begin to decide this question in a principled way, we must know whether writing systems do, in fact, relate written symbols to sounds, and, if so, how. Incredibly, however, one thing which is missing from many discussions of reading in English is a sophisticated understanding of how the English spelling system words. It has been suggested at intervals since the sixteenth century that English spelling and its 'irregularities' are a cause of reading failure. And various regular-ized writing systems have been proposed, either as permanent reforms or as aids in the initial stages of teaching reading. The most recent and best known in the latter category is the Initial Teaching Alphabet (ITA). For various reasons which do not concern us directly here, linguists have only recently shown much interest in English spelling. But there are now several illuminating and important studies of English spelling (including Albrow, 1972; C. Chomsky, 1970; Venezky, 1970), and this work will have to be discussed in detail below (see Chapter 3). It is essential that such an understanding should form a basis of a dis-cussion of reading, because one can never understand how something is learned, without a proper understanding of what is learned. Neither, of course, can one hope to understand the causes of reading failure, until one knows what it is that a child has failed to do.

This lacuna is part of a more general failure, in much of the experi-mental psychological literature, to regard reading and writing as *linguistic* processes. Reading has often been seen predominantly as a matter of visual processing, involving characteristic eye-movements, perceptual span, letter shapes, word gestalts, and so on. As a result, it has often been ignored that what people read is linguistically organized and meaningful material.

Another confusion, potentially right at the heart of the matter, is between *reading* and *writing*. It is often assumed tacitly that reading and writing are symmetrical mirror-images of each other, and that whatever is said of one is, *mutatis mutandis*, true of the other. But reading and writing are not symmetrically related (Smith, 1973, pp. 117ff.). For example: one may be able to read a word at sight and understand it, but not be able to spell it correctly or use it appropriately. In general, it is always easier passively to recognize a shape (letter, face, etc.) than to reproduce it actively. Readers do not therefore have to know every word they come across, but writers do; even, or perhaps especially, fluent readers have a much larger sight vocabulary than an active vocabulary that they themselves use. Writing involves motor skills which may be an added problem to beginners who have not mastered them; and so on. Also, reading and writing are not functionally symmetrical: many people read a great deal and rarely write anything; only a few people write much; and very few people, if any, write a lot but read little. In general, if someone can write, this implies that he can read; but to say someone can read, does not imply that he can write. I can, for example, read German printed in Gothic script without any difficulty, but I am quite unable to write Gothic script.

Any writing system has to compromise between the requirements of writers and readers. In terms of the greatest good for the greatest number, the needs of readers ought to take precedence, since there are many more readers than writers, and the majority of people who do much writing are professionals, and ought therefore to be able to tackle a few more problems. This principle is maintained in ITA, which is explicitly biased in favour of readers, so that teachers are not even required to be able to write it, except for notices in the classroom (Pitman and St John, 1969, pp. 138-9). Similarly, the gap between a child's ability to read a word and write it is recognized by the *Breakthrough to Literacy* materials (Mackay *et al.*, 1970), which provide children with printed words on cards which can be slotted into a sentence maker. The child can therefore create new sentences without being held up by the inability to spell individual words, or, more simply, by the lack of manual dexterity in using a pencil.

Other potential identifications are not clear either. For example, is it the case that listening and reading comprehension are essentially similar and differ only in the input medium, aural versus visual? (The answer to this question would affect one's definition of reading.) Are written and spoken language essentially similar, in lexis and syntax, or do they differ to an extent which could cause problems for learners? There is no real consensus, in fact, about the relations between reading, writing, speaking, listening and comprehension.

Eclectic theories

One crucial source of confusion is between *theories* of reading (what goes on in the head) and instructional *techniques* (what goes on in classrooms): although any teacher knows that what he teaches is only indirectly related to what pupils learn! A theory of reading may, of course, suggest a teaching strategy. But partial theories proliferate, and so do techniques, not to say gimmicks. In any case, it is usually impossible to show that a particular technique causes children to learn. For example, the phonic method (technique) clearly does work for most children. But this does not prove that children read phonically (theory), that is, by decoding from letters to sounds. They may, for example, learn by gaining confidence that the system is phonic and regular, proceed on this assumption, and end up by learning and reading in some other way, say in whole words and phrases. This is, after all, how fluent adults end up reading. (Cf. Smith, 1973, p. 6.) In fact, any method appears to work with most children. The consensus view at present appears to be that exclusive reliance on any single technique is a mistake. After waves of enthusiasm and disillusionment for different approaches to the teaching of reading, the consensus now seems to be that there is no single best way to teach reading, and one comes across regular pleas for an eclectic approach. (E.g., see Rauch, 1968; Goodacre, 1971; Stauffer, 1971.) But the use of terms such as 'eclectic approach' or 'mixed method' amounts to a tacit admission that there is no coherent theory that works, so that practitioners should not put all their eggs in one basket and may as well proceed in an *ad hoc* manner.

This same eclecticism necessarily pervades the literature on reading failure, where the overwhelming impression is that each individual case must be taken on its merits. Every logically conceivable type of explanation has been proposed (see 7.1). There are only a restricted number of possibilities: that there is something wrong with the learner, either medical (e.g., 'word blindness') or psychological (e.g., emotional disturbance), or with the learner's language (a language 'deficit' view); that there is something wrong with the learner's family background (a social pathology or social deprivation view); that there is something wrong with the teacher (e.g., the learner is not being sufficiently motivated); that there is something wrong with the method (hence the phonic-versus-whole word debate); that there is something wrong with the materials (e.g., they do not match the learner's interests, experience, etc.); or that there is something wrong with the medium, that is with the spelling system (hence ITA and similar schemes). There is, logically, nowhere else the explanation could lie: it has to be in the pupil, the teacher, the materials, the method, the medium or the pupil's background. Most likely there is some truth in all of these explanations, and that different pupils have difficulties deriving from a mixture of causes. That is, we have no coherent theory.

There is a simple but important overall worry. Despite all the research over the past eighty years or so, the vast body of findings still does not satisfactorily explain cases of reading failure. And the suspicion remains that the psychological and psycholinguistic factors, on which the bulk of research has been done, are quite easily swamped by much more powerful social and cultural effects such as the learner's motivation, the value which the community places on literacy or on education as a whole, or simply the skill of individual teachers.

Children and adults

Related to the confusion between how readers actually read (theory) and how they ought to be taught to read (technique) is a confusion between children and adults, or between fluent readers and learners. Many studies have not distinguished sharply enough between what fluent readers do, and what children learning to read do. But these may be quite different. As one writer put it, the best way of learning to dive may not be to start from the ten-metre board. The distinction is, of course, quite clear in many places: for example, it is the basic rationale behind ITA. Nevertheless, it may be that children are confused with adults in quite fundamental ways. It is now currently fashionable to assert that children of four or five years have awesome mastery of complex aspects of their native language; and this is true. The knowledge which an average five-year-old has of the phonology, morphology and syntax of English is so complex that linguists have not yet succeeded in describing and accounting for it in any satisfactory way. But there are differences between the phonological and morphological knowledge of five-year-olds and the knowledge of educated adults, and those differences may be crucial to someone learning the English writing system in particular.

For example, to understand fully how English spelling works, readers have to appreciate the identity between the roots of semantically related pairs of words which differ in sound, such as *medicine/medical, paradigm/paradigmatic, bomb/bombardier*. But many of these pairs are likely to be known only by educated speakers who are already fluent readers (see 3.6). Also, there is considerable debate about how and when young children acquire the ability to segment the speech continuum into phonemes (minimal sound units, see 2.6). And it has been suggested that syllables are a more salient linguistic feature for children. This would crucially affect our knowledge of the best methods of teaching reading, and also our theories about the relation between spoken and written language. Therefore, statements such as 'at the age of entering school, children have acquired a mastery of the complex phonological patterns of their native language' require to be interpreted with care. They certainly know most of the systems tacitly. But an alphabetic writing system requires not only tacit, unconscious knowledge, but analytic knowledge, the ability to segment the sound continuum into, say, phonemes, and that is a very different matter. There is the danger, then, of confusing unconscious knowledge with explicit, analytic knowledge (cf. Haas, 1970, p. 37).

Along with an understandable concentration on beginners in reading, there has also been an inevitable focus on reading failures, and therefore possibly a limited concept of what reading involves.

Theories and planning

The history of research on reading, and attitudes towards reading methods, tends to have been a series of reactions and counter-reactions: phonic methods abandoned in favour of whole-word methods, only to regain favour again later; the view that reading is decoding letters into sounds has been attacked on the grounds that reading is a 'psycholinguistic guessing game' which uses syntactic and semantic information (Smith, 1973); and so on. But reactions tend to be over-reactions. It is clear that the English writing system is basically alphabetic and phonemic; it is equally clear that this is not the whole story, and that the spelling relates partly to lexis and grammar. It is clear that readers use knowledge of syntax and context in order to guess words; it is equally clear that reading involves the ability to identify individual words isolated from context. It is clear that English spelling works basically from left to right; but it is equally clear that there are many exceptions to this, and that reading is not a purely left-to-right linear processing. Thus many statements in books and articles must be read with an eye to their context: what they are statements against. The tendency towards over-reaction and over-statement is partly due to the fact that reading problems are such an emotive subject to many people: the person who cannot read is likely to be socially stigmatized in our society; and technical reports of trends in reading standards are reported in the national press. Literacy is news.

Conclusions

Anyone approaching the literature on literacy is therefore faced with mutually incompatible disciplinary perspectives, nothing even approaching an integrated theory, and indeed quite contradictory definitions of reading and literacy, many studies which do not take account of the linguistic nature of the material that is being read, a confused relationship

9

between partial theories and practice, a mixture of meticulous research and outright polemic, and a socially very sensitive area about which almost everyone holds strong views.

Unfortunately, reading and writing processes appear to be almost opaque to introspection. Few people have any very useful memories about learning to read (I have none whatsoever), and we therefore find it very difficult to imagine the problems non-readers may have in learning. Fluent readers usually have no idea whether they process words linearly, letter-by-letter, or recognize them globally, whether they process written material subconsciously via the spoken word or whether they proceed direct to meaning, and so on. If readers did have any substantial intuitions about such matters, they would not be major topics in many research articles and conferences. At this level reading appears rather like riding a bicycle: those who can do it, cannot explain how they do it, because they do not know how they do it. It may even be that, in reading and in riding bicycles, the ability to perform well necessarily conflicts with knowledge about what we are doing, and that self-consciousness impedes the performance.

1.2   A note on definitions of reading and literacy

As I noted briefly in the previous section, there are still no widely agreed definitions of reading or literacy despite some seventy years of concentrated research. The suspicion must arise that the concepts are simply not definable. One reason might be that they refer to a cluster of rather different skills, and not to one single skill. Different professional groups may therefore tend to concentrate exclusively on different aspects of those skills, according to their professional interests. And it does rather seem as if experts looking at reading are sometimes like the blind men investigating the elephant: the one who felt a leg thought it was a tree, and the one who felt the tail thought it was a rope, and the one who felt the trunk thought it was a snake. Reading is partly a perceptual psychological skill involving eye-span and recognition of shapes; but it is also partly a linguistic skill involving, amongst other things, knowledge of the sequential probability of words and letters; and it is also partly a social skill with particular social uses.

A further problem in defining reading is that people use different reading skills under different conditions; for example, according to the difficulty or interest of the material, and also depending on their purposes in reading. It is not clear, therefore, that there is any single, non-trivial characteristic which is essential to all instances of what we would call reading. Apart from anything else, it is useful to remember that both *read* and *literate* are simply ambiguous in everyday English, as is clear from usages such as:

He read it but did not understand it.
He could not read his own writing.
He read the whole of James Joyce in six months.
To be fully literate, you have to know the classics.
Students are not literate these days: they can't spell.

Further confusion may be due to not distinguishing between what fluent readers can do if required (for example, as part of a psychological test), what they normally do, and what (if anything) is an essential feature of reading. For example, people can read nonsense syllables, but the normal use of reading implies understanding. It does not solve the problem, of course, to insist that there ought to be a well-defined sense of the term *reading* for use in scientific studies, for, in order to isolate a well-defined concept, we may simply be focusing on one aspect of reading and ignoring the others. We are then back where we started, having destroyed the object of study in our attempt to define it by simplifying it.

One way to illustrate these points is to take different definitions of reading and literacy and to comment on their implications. I will comment briefly on the three major types of definition which regard reading as:

(a) essentially a process of relating written symbols to sound units,
(b) essentially a process of understanding meaning, and
(c) essentially a process related to the social uses to which it is put.

Chall (1967) provides a major review of the 'great debate' between look-and-say and phonic methods of teaching reading. She proposes that reading methods can be classified according to whether they emphasize the meaning of the material being read or the code being read. Different terms have been used for these two views. For example, reading for meaning has also been called a global method; and a code/phonic method is often referred to as the 'mechanics of reading'. The debate over these two broadly opposed views of reading has existed over a long period of time, and the studies of reading instruction in fourteen countries in Downing (1973) show that the same debate, over what reading 'really' is, is carried out world-wide. The swings of fashion between phonic methods and reading for meaning certainly characterize the history of reading instruction in twentieth-century Britain and the USA. At present, in the USA, code methods appear to be in the ascendent, as a reaction against a previous fashion for global methods. (Flesch, 1955, provides the most famous polemic statement attacking whole-word methods and recommending phonics.) But it is probable that reading for meaning is about to come to the fore again, most likely in the guise of reading as a 'psycholinguistic guessing game', under the influence of the theories of Goodman and Smith.

Reading as decoding to spoken language

One possible statement of a decoding-to-sound definition is: Reading is the process of relating written symbols to units of spoken language. The assumption is that readers decode from visual symbols to sound symbols. One version of this view would assume that readers decode from letters to phonemes (see 2.6) but the definition above is wider and allows that one might decode at the level of syllables, morphemes or words. The definition attributes priority to the spoken language, in that it implies that written language is processed only via spoken language; it therefore denies that written language has a degree of autonomy. (See Chapter 2.) If the definition implies that readers always decode to spoken language, then it is too narrow, since it excludes rapid silent reading. The definition may apply particularly to beginners, but not necessarily to fluent readers. It is neutral as regards comprehension and would allow such statements as: 'He read it, but didn't understand it'.

Evidence about whether readers do, in fact, normally decode from written to spoken language ought to come from experiments into whether sub-vocal speech occurs when people are reading. The evidence is complex, and beyond the scope of the argument here, but the basic facts appear to be as follows (Lunzer and Harrison summarize the evidence fully). If sensitive recording apparatus is used to monitor muscular and nervous activity in and around the larynx while a person is reading, there is often evidence of sub-vocal speech. But this activity can be restricted or eliminated by training; for example, by taking a course in speed reading. There is much evidence that decoding to speech often occurs, then, but it is not necessary. Speech is much slower than even an average adult reading speed (*c.* 250-400 words per minute), so not everything can be decoded to speech. Again, children and learners have to be distinguished from adult readers.

Reading as decoding to meaning

A famous definition of reading as a meaningful activity is: 'Reading (is) understanding the meaning of printed words.... Understanding a paragraph is like solving a problem in mathematics.' This is Thorndike's view in his classic article on 'Reading as reasoning' (1917), and it has been said (e.g., by Otto, 1971) that much of the debate about definitions of reading consists of agreeing or disagreeing with Thorndike. Thorndike takes the view that reading essentially involves understanding, and that this involves reasoning, problem-solving and high-level inference. On the one hand, one wants to recognize that in reading one normally does draw on one's understanding of the language of the text and of the world. On the other hand, one wants to allow that comprehension is not specific to reading, but that the same problems of understanding may apply to spoken language.

Suppose I have a legal document and am not certain how to interpret it. I ring up my solicitor and he asks me to read out the relevant parts to him over the telephone. He considers it and explains it to me. I think we would have to say that I read it, although I did not understand it. The reason we have to take reading in this sense is that the same problems of understanding would arise whether the material had been written or spoken. I could understand it in neither case; the solicitor could understand it in both cases. This is not to say that there are not, in addition, different problems of comprehension which may arise with speech and writing; and spoken and written materials are characteristically organized in different ways to compensate for this. Also, readers and listeners have different, but overlapping, problems: listeners have to understand in real time, but readers can refer backward and forwards in the text (see Chapter 5).

The following useful and careful definition is by someone with a life-long involvement in organizing literacy programmes in developing countries:

> That person is literate who, in a language he speaks, can read with understanding anything he would have understood if it had been spoken to him; and can write, so that it can be read, anything he can say (Gudschinsky, 1976, p. 3).

This specifies that one can be literate only in a language one speaks. This is not as tautologous as it sounds, since in many countries children are initially taught to read in a foreign language. Ferguson (1971a) provides case studies of such situations for several countries in the Middle East. Gudschinsky's definition also makes literacy relative to the reader's command of spoken language, and therefore recognizes the spoken language as primary (see Chapter 2); but it remains uncommitted as to whether reading necessarily involves decoding to speech or not.

Summary

We would only admit that someone can read English fluently if they can, when required, both sound out nonsense syllables and understand most of what they read. But it seems that neither of these features is necessary to a particular act of reading, since it is possible both to read (and understand) a text without decoding to spoken language, and also to read words without understanding them. The term *read* is, as we have noted, ambiguous, and we have to distinguish between the ability to read ('Johnny can read') and the act of reading a particular text ('Johnny read *Ulysses* last month'); and to distinguish between what learners do and what fluent readers generally do.

Functional literacy

The two types of definition discussed so far are concerned with the ability of an individual and make no reference to what ability is expected of individuals in different societies. Clearly such expectations differ. It makes sense to say, 'Johnny is three years old and can't read yet', but it does not make much sense to say, 'Johnny is three years old and is illiterate', since, in our society, literacy is not expected of three-year-olds.

Functional literacy is a term coined by Gray (1956), and is used particularly in connection with literacy programmes organized in developing countries by Unesco. It defines literacy as relative to the requirements of an individual within a particular society: it is the degree of literacy required for effective functioning in a particular community. Since a Brazilian peasant requires a different kind of literacy from an American urban dweller, there is no single definition of functional literacy for all the world's population. And since it essentially involves the functions of literacy in a society, it also involves such notions as good citizenship: 'literacy should be regarded as a way of preparing man for a social, civic and economic role' (Report of World Conference of Ministers of Education on the Eradication of Illiteracy, Teheran, October 1965; cited by Bowers, 1968).

Pilliner and Reid (1972) point out that the term *literate* is a relative one even in its everyday uses. The purposes to which written language are put are so varied that no one has competence in them all, and the norm therefore shifts up and down over a wide range. The term is therefore open to use to mean 'as literate as someone else expects one ought to be'. Since *literate* is also used as a term of praise, meaning cultured or widely read, the term *illiterate* is used also in everyday speech to refer, for example, to university students' essays which are badly spelled or stylistically poor. In everyday usage, the term *literate* therefore has at least two main uses, one referring to the ability to read and write, one referring to wideness of education, and both these uses are relative to cultural expectations.

14

1.3 The sociolinguistics of literacy

The approach which will now be taken in this book is as follows. Reading and writing are linguistic activities. We do not normally read meaningless material, although we can do so if required, for example, as part of a psycholinguistic experiment. We normally read material which is linguistically organized at different levels, phonological (sound structure), morphological (word structure), syntactic (grammar) and semantic (meaning). There are situations in which children learn to read a language they do not speak (Ferguson, 1971b), but generally learners have a great deal of complex knowledge about how to speak the language, and they inevitably draw on this knowledge in reading.

Writing systems are related to spoken language, but different relations are possible (see Chapters 2 and 3), and the relation between the English writing system and spoken English is not straightforward. If it was straightforward, there would not have been centuries of still unresolved debate about revised spelling system, phonic-versus-whole word instruction methods, and so on. At the basis of a coherent theory of literacy there must be a sophisticated account of the relation between spoken and written language, and a realization that this relation differs for different writing systems and for different societies and cultures. The relationship between the English spelling system and units of spoken language is particularly complex, although it is also highly organized, since English spelling relates not only to sound units (pronunciation) but also to words, grammar and meaning. These characteristics raise problems for learners, but have advantages for fluent adult readers, and also make the system peculiarly resistant to change. The English writing system is therefore partly autonomous since it does not correspond directly to the organization of spoken language. We have to understand these relationships, since, if we do not, then we do not know what a learner learns when he learns to read.

In addition to its linguistic characteristics, any writing system is deeply embedded in attitudinal, cultural, economic and technological constraints, and these pressures are particularly powerful in the case of an international language like English (see Chapter 4). Reading and writing are therefore also sociolinguistic activities. People speak, listen, read and write in different social situations for different purposes. Written material is, for example, used extensively in institutional and bureaucratic situations, for forms, notices, questionnaires, reports, letters, and so on, where spoken language is never used. Many of these purposes to which written language is typically put are not evident to children, since they are simply totally outside their experience (Chapter 5).

If a coherent theory of literacy is to be developed, it will have to account for the place of written language, both in relation to the forms of spoken language, and also in relation to the communicative functions served by different types of language in different social settings in our culture. Many discussions of reading simply make no mention of language at all. *Ipso facto*, they make no mention of the communicative functions of written language. I do not see that a theory of literacy can avoid a discussion both of how written language works, and also of what it is used for.

I have to emphasize immediately, however, that the forms and functions of written language have been neglected by both linguistics and by sociology and anthropology, and that often only rudimentary, common-sense observations are available. For important reasons in the history of linguistics, in the 1930s and 1940s the dominant school of American structuralist linguistics regarded written language as merely a pale reflection of spoken language, and did not study it in any detail. These reasons do not concern us directly here, but briefly they were a concern with the American Indian languages which were largely un-written, and a theoretical concern with phonology, rather than with syntax and semantics. The techniques developed in phonology were subsequently very influential, however, in orthography-making for exotic languages (see Chapter 4).

Within contemporary Chomskyan linguistics, from the late 1950s onwards, the dominant interest has been in language *per se*, and hence no attention is paid at all to distinctions between written and spoken language. Even within sociolinguistics, for which a central aim is to study language variation, the communicative functions of written language within different language communities has hardly been touched on. For example, this topic is not dealt with in what are arguably the two most important collections of papers in the last decade, by Hymes (1974) and Labov (1972a). Labov does discuss the English spelling system and its relation to standard and non-standard dialects of English (see 6.5), but he does not discuss the place of writing within the communicative networks of societies. In fact, writing, written language, literacy, etc. are not indexed at all in the following recent introductions to sociolinguistics and major collections of papers: Trudgill (1974b), Pride and Holmes (1972), Bell (1977), Edwards (1976), Dittmar (1976), Labov (1972a), Ardener (1971), Gumperz and Hymes (1972). Giglioli (1972) is an exception and contains important work by Goody and Watt. Another exception is Hertzler (1965), which contains a chapter on the sociology of writing: I have the informal impression that this book is not widely known in Britain. Similarly, in current standard introductions to theoretical linguistics, the usual approach is to state the views in favour of regarding spoken language as primary and written language as secondary, and then not to discuss the relationship further.

16

This approach is taken, for example, by Lyons (1968), a standard textbook. Apart from isolated examples, it is predominantly within European linguistics that some interest in written language has been maintained (e.g., Vachek, 1973; Haas, 1970).

Similarly, within sociology and anthropology, writing has been discussed only in isolated places. This is despite the fact that the presence of a writing system in a society has often been taken as a criterion of a particular stage of cultural development which serves conveniently to distinguish a 'civilization' from its antecedents. Only occasionally has this distinction been further explored (e.g., Goody and Watt, 1962; Goody, 1968, 1977).

What I propose to develop, then, is a *functional* approach to written language. (I take this expression from Vachek, 1973.) This will involve as its central question: What is the functional justification for the existence of a written language alongside the spoken language? (See Vachek, 1973, p. 15.) Why do societies and individuals often maintain two distinct means of communication? Why is their use typically restricted to more or less complementary situations? Why do users find it appropriate to use one medium rather than another in certain settings? What are the social factors which determine how written language should be used? What different classes of written communicative activities are regarded as distinct in the community? And, given that written communication is never the only means of communication in a language community, how does it relate to the other channels, including face-to-face conversation, telephone, radio, and so on? How is the ability to read and write distributed amongst the community? Several of these questions are suggested by Basso (1974) in his brief outline for an ethnography of writing. I take it that Basso's proposals for studying how the activity of writing is embedded in a society would be a necessary concomitant of Vachek's more abstract framework.

This approach therefore also involves the concept of *functional complementariness* (Vachek, 1973, p. 31). That is, written and spoken language are complementary to each other by being used, by and large, for different purposes in different situations. This view therefore allows us to make controlled value judgments about the appropriateness of written and spoken language for different functions. On the one hand, we can say that they are just different, and can take a non-prescriptive approach and demand that each be studied in its own right. On the other hand, written language clearly serves various functions which spoken language never could and is therefore superior from that point of view. Conversely, written language has clear disadvantages in other situations.

As well as investigating what communicative functions writing serves, we must also investigate what effect the tendency towards a

17

separation of communicative functions has on the forms, lexical and syntactic, of the two language varieties.

A comprehensive statement of the formal (linguistic) and functional (sociolinguistic) differences between written and spoken language is necessary if we are to be able to reach any conclusions about the place of literacy in a society and about what an individual has achieved when he has learned to read and write. This book will not be able to make such a comprehensive statement, but I hope it will at least be able to make clear some of the basic arguments, and state the requirements on such a theory.

Part of the Summary of Conclusions and Recommendations in the Bullock Report, *A Language for Life* (HMSO, 1975), is worth quoting here:

> ... we have been opposed from the outset to the idea that reading and the use of English can be improved in any simple way. The solution does not lie in a few neat administrative strokes, nor in the adoption of one set of teaching methods to the exclusion of another. Improvement will come about only from a thorough understanding of the many complexities, and from action on a broad front.

This policy statement corresponds closely with the view of the state of knowledge about literacy which this chapter has started to put forward: that what is required is a broad understanding of the sociolinguistics of literacy. I would therefore hope that this book might prove useful on the kinds of course on language in education, including reading, which the Report recommends (ch. 26, para. 15)

> should be part of every primary and secondary school teacher's initial training, whatever the teacher's subject or the age of the children with whom he or she will be working.

Part two

The relations between spoken and written language

Chapter 2

Spoken and written language: which is primary?

This chapter discusses some basic distinctions between spoken and written language. It will lead to a discussion in following chapters of the relation between spoken and written English, and how they differ in form and function: how the English writing system works and how it is related to spoken language, in particular how it is related to various dialects of English, including the social dialect known as standard English; and a discussion of the social pressures on the English writing system, and why it has remained as it is for so long, when it clearly no longer accurately represents pronunciation. There are several strong reasons for beginning with some fundamental distinctions of this type, and they will, it is hoped, become clear as the argument progresses. But here is one strong reason immediately.

Some people have maintained that writing is a secondary system, 'merely' a visual representation of spoken language. If this is true, then learning to read does not involve learning a new communication system, but merely transferring a language skill already acquired from one medium (speech) to another (writing): from sounds to visual symbols. If, on the other hand, writing is not merely speech written down, this conclusion may not follow. In fact, I think it is easy to show that the English writing system does not directly represent speech, but that it is more closely related to some varieties of spoken English than others. Some of the conventions of English spelling are more or less neutral between different English accents, but some of the conventions of written English are more closely related to standard English than to non-standard varieties of English.

Standard English is a geographical and social class dialect: a form of English used by a particular socio-economic group. (See 6.3 to 6.5.) Consider, then, the claim, which is frequently put forward, that children who speak a non-standard dialect of English (such as rural or urban dialects of British English, Jamaican Creole, or Black English

21

Vernacular in the USA) are likely to be retarded, because of this, in their acquisition of literacy. On the face of it, this is a plausible hypothesis: that there is a mismatch between the child's spoken language and the written language of books, and that this mismatch or interference between the two causes confusion. But it turns out that the hypothesis is rather vague, not clearly formulated as it stands, and depends on answers to prior questions, including: What is meant by standard and non-standard? And how do different varieties of English relate to the conventions of written English?

We have to know, then, what writing represents.

2.1 Confusion between spoken and written language

Confusion between written and spoken language is widespread. It is evident in commonly heard statements such as: What does this letter/ word *say*? *Doubt* has a *silent b*. What does it *say* in the papers? He drops *letters* off the ends of words like *huntin'* and *shootin'*. English is not a phonetic language. English is an alphabetic language.

These may seem like trivial examples: perhaps everyone knows what is really meant, even if the expression is careless. But they are potentially very confusing to a child who might reasonably try to interpret them literally. The evidence is, in fact, that many children are confused by such statements, and several studies (Reid, 1958; 1966; Mason, 1967; Downing, 1969; Vygotsky, 1962) have shown that most children, before they start to read and in the early stages, are extremely confused or vague about the relation of reading, writing and speaking. These studies discovered, by talking to five-year-old children, that reading was for them a mysterious activity about which they had only the vaguest expectations. Many children thought they could read when they could not; they had little idea of what the activity consisted of, or what its purpose might be; they were confused about the relationship between pictures, words, letters and numbers; they might think, for example, that written captions under pictures were merely a decorative border (Mackay *et al.*, 1970). Here might lie the main danger of confused statements found in many books about the relationships between speaking and reading. Reid (1966) found, for example, that many children would repeat phrases such as 'aitch for *horse*' with no idea what this might mean. This is not surprising when there is, in this case, no connection at all between the letter name (aitch), the pronunciation of the sound unit (phoneme) /h/, and the sound of the beginning of the word where /h/ might not be pronounced anyway. (See 2.6.)

More seriously, perhaps, much of the debate about whether English spelling is out of date, inefficient, arbitrary, irregular, illogical, misleading and so on, may rest on a confusion between a writing system and spoken language. Many such criticisms are heaped on English spelling (e.g., Pitman and St John, 1969, p. 40). Clearly, English spelling does not always accurately represent the sound of spoken words. But there is no *a priori* reason why it should. It might be more useful if it is not too closely tied to sounds, and it might systematically represent other units of language. This is a major topic and is fully discussed in Chapter 3.

Even in the statements of linguists, one finds confusions. Consider this recent statement:

> Writing is parasitic upon speech in that it is simply a way of recording the spoken language in an enduring, visual form.

I will not give the reference for this particular quote, since many similar statements could be found, and I am sure that, on brief reflection, the writer would admit that writing is not simply a way of recording speech, but that it has its own distinctive forms and functions. Nor is writing merely parasitic: for once a writing system exists, it takes on something of a life of its own, becomes partly independent of speech, and it is then often writing which influences speech, rather than the reverse.

We require, then, a systematic consideration of these questions.

2.2 The priority of spoken language?

It is only relatively recently that much attention has been paid to spoken language. Practical mechanical methods of recording speech have only been available since the beginning of the twentieth century. The first demonstration of Thomas Edison's phonograph was only just over a hundred years ago, in 1877. Ways of making disc records and producing copies from an original recording were invented years after that. Radio spread in the 1920s, and practical, portable tape-recorders did not become available till the 1940s. Before that time there was considerable practical difficulty in studying spoken language at all. Linguists could only study what they could hear and transfer to paper, that is, to some form of written representation. In England, some three hundred years of interest in phonetics did precede Henry Sweet (1845-1912), who is often regarded as the founder of scientific phonetics (Gimson, 1970; Abercrombie, 1948). But the difficulties of observing speech, and monitoring the movements of the vocal organs, with no mechanical recording aids are considerable. There was therefore an understandable bias towards studying written language and often towards literary language in particular. Samuel Johnson, for example, in the Preface to his Dictionary (1755), says that he has endeavoured to collect examples of language 'from the *writers* before the Restoration' whom he admires. He makes no claim to collect examples of everyday spoken English, regarding this, in fact, as unworthy of attention, and he dismisses the speech of the working and merchant classes as 'casual and mutable diction, … fugitive cant, which is always in a state of increase or decay … and therefore must be suffered to perish with other things unworthy of preservation'.

By the nineteenth century attitudes had taken an about-turn, and, especially in Germany where Romanticism was in full swing, linguists such as Grimm were recording the speech of illiterate peasants. The prevailing ideology within linguistics for the whole of the twentieth century has been that the spoken language is primary, that the written language is at best a pale reflection of the spoken, and that spoken language alone is the legitimate object of study of linguistics. There are strong reasons for this view, which will be summarized below, but also considerable limitations to it. It was in large part a reaction against the dominance given to written, especially literary, language in previous work. It was due also to the very flourishing phonetic research, especially in Britain in the late nineteenth and early twentieth centuries by Henry Sweet and Daniel Jones, which emphasized the phonetic and acoustic bases of speech. And it was due, in the USA, to the concern, particularly from the 1920s onwards, with largely unwritten American Indian languages. During this period of American structuralist linguistics the dictum was that language must always be studied without reference to writing. Famous statements are by Bloomfield:

Writing is not language, but merely a way of recording language by means of visible marks (1933, p. 21).

The art of writing is not part of language, but rather a comparatively modern invention for recording and broadcasting what is spoken (1942).

As I have emphasized, these statements were made to combat the denigration of spoken language at the expense of written, and usually literary, language. But it has to be admitted that, on a literal reading, the statements are simply untrue.

Linguists have put forward strong reasons for stating that speech has primacy over writing. These include: the universality of spoken language versus the recent development of writing systems and of widespread literacy; the apparent biological basis of speech; the more frequent use of speech than writing; and the resistance of spoken language to conscious manipulation of various kinds. We have to appreciate the force of these arguments. But we also have to appreciate that powerfully expressed aggressive and pejorative statements such as Bloomfield's have contributed to the virtual abandonment of writing as a central topic of linguistic study, and one which has been pursued in the main by isolated workers, outside mainstream linguistics. In addition, we have to appreciate that the traditional arguments are open to considerable modification, particularly in the face of the changing sociolinguistic situation in highly literate and urbanized societies.

2.3 The chronological priority of spoken language

Linguists have put forward the following reasons for arguing the primacy of spoken language.

1 *Spoken language came first in the history of the human race.* Although picture writing goes back much further, we have no evidence of a true writing system before 3500 BC (Diringer, 1962, p. 15). The first records we have are of a cuneiform script probably invented in Mesopotamia around 3500 BC, and some Egyptian hieroglyphic inscriptions appear also to date from about 3000 BC (Cottrell, 1971, pp. 8, 37). We know nothing about the origins of language, but there was speech long before writing, presumably as far back as the origins of the human race, say, a million years ago. It is difficult to conceive of a human society without speech, and spoken language is arguably a defining characteristic of humans. One might define man as a tool user, or as *homo sapiens*, but one might also propose *homo loquens* as his defining feature. In comparison, then, writing is a very recent historical event.

2 *Spoken language comes first for individuals.* Even in language communities with a tradition of literacy, almost all children first learn to talk and only later, if at all, do they learn to read and write. A Unesco estimate for the 1960s is that 50 per cent of the world's children of school age do not attend school at all (Malmquist, 1968). In addition, spoken language is learned spontaneously, without necessarily any explicit teaching by parents or others, and is learned often despite apparently crippling obstacles such as severe parental neglect and low IQ. Conversely reading and writing are almost always explicitly taught, and may not be learned in spite of prolonged and systematic teaching.

Exceptions to this order of acquisition occur with relatively rare cases of deaf children who may first learn language through another medium, written or tactile. In a famous account, Helen Keller (1903), who became deaf, dumb and blind through illness in early childhood, describes how she first learned language through her teacher signing into her hands. In general, however, the experience of the individual parallels the history of the race.

The fact that this is not quite always the case, however, means that we have to distinguish carefully between what normally happens and what is necessarily the case. For example, Holt (1967) and Kohl (1973) both argue that children can learn to read without explicit instruction from adults. And Torrey (1969) provides a case study of a five-year-old Negro boy who discovered how to read with no instruction from adults or other children.

3 *Speech is biologically based.* If this proposition is true, it would explain (1) and (2). It is true, first, in the sense that babies spontaneously babble and then later imitate the sounds of the adult language they hear around them. Even totally deaf babies babble initially and then only later fall silent. So vocal activity of some kind appears to be instinctive, and therefore is presumably produced in response to an innate biological drive, which does not initially depend on imitation.

It is also true in the sense that the human vocal tract has become anatomically adapted to facilitate speech. It used to be asserted that humans had no special vocal organs and that speech is a secondary function of the organs of eating, swallowing, chewing and breathing. But it is now known that the human vocal organs have evolved in ways which facilitate speech but which are dysfunctional for other reasons. It is clear that in order for *language* to evolve, man must have undergone modifications in the central nervous system. But Liebermann (1972) has also shown that in order for *speech* to develop, humans must have undergone modifications in the size and shape of the vocal tract. He has compared the vocal tracts in different monkeys and apes, certain fossil men, new-born human infants and adult humans. And he has shown that monkeys and apes cannot produce even crude approximations to most human speech sounds, due to their restricted tongue movements and other features in the shape of the vocal organs. (This is why, incidentally, recent attempts to teach language to chimpanzees have been attempts to teach them sign language or the ability to manipulate coloured shapes. Earlier attempts to teach chimpanzees speech had failed, but this could have been because the chimps were unable to produce the speech sounds, not because they lacked the language ability.) In order for speech to develop in humans, however, various other advantages have probably been lost. For example, the swallowing mechanism has been greatly weakened in adult humans, so that, although it is more or less impossible for a new-born human infant or an ape to choke to death on food, this is quite possible for adult humans. It seems, then, that humans have become anatomically adapted for speech at the expense of other, more basic requirements.

4 *Spoken language is highly resistant to conscious control.* Probably because spoken language is learned in early childhood without any special training, and partly in response to innate tendencies, the patterns of pronunciation, grammar, and so on, of one's native spoken language

are highly resistant to later change. For example, it is extremely difficult to acquire a high-prestige accent if desired late in life. In general,
non-standard forms of spoken language are extremely persistent over
long periods of time. In Britain, standard English (see 6.3) has had a
strong centralizing influence on all forms of written English, but local
regional accents and spoken dialects have by no means died out, even
under pressure from the standard language used by the mass media. It is
impossible to change the way people speak by, say, deliberate government decree, but writing systems are relatively open to such control by
government and education systems. Recent examples where writing
systems have been radically changed or replaced by institutional language
planning include Turkey, Indonesia and China, where governments have
replaced one system of writing with another. Until 1928 Turkish was
written in Arabic script, but Kemal Ataturk, the Turkish dictator,
abolished the use of Arabic script and replaced it with the Roman
alphabet. (See 4.7.) Similarly, Malay used to be written in a script
adapted from Arabic, but is now also written in Roman script. In
China, various reforms have been carried out on the writing system and
reform is still going on. The traditional logographic system has been
streamlined and many signs have been abolished or simplified, and a
Romanized orthography has now been introduced alongside the reformed
script; but none of this directly affects how people speak.

5   *Spoken language comes first for individual societies.* Even today
not all languages have written forms, by any means. There are hundreds
of languages, all over the world, with no writing systems, but all communities have spoken languages of great structural complexity. One can
therefore have spoken languages without written forms, but not vice
versa. The existence of 'dead' languages such as Latin, Greek, Sanskrit,
Egyptian or Ugaritic is, of course, not a counter-example to this claim,
since these written forms were based on spoken languages which have
now died out or changed so radically that they have developed into
different languages, as Latin developed into French, Spanish, Italian
and the other Romance languages. Spoken language is therefore a
universal, but written language is not.

6   *Literacy as a widespread phenomenon is a very recent historical
event.* Even for those languages with writing systems, it is only recently
that a large number of people in some countries have been able to read
and write. An estimate for England in 1850 is 30 to 50 per cent illiteracy.
Some countries were literate many centuries ago: in Athens in 500 BC it
is probable that a majority of the citizens could read the laws which
were posted round the city and on which Greek democracy depended
(Cipolla, 1969, p. 38; Goody and Watt, 1962). But Greece is an exception, and an estimate of world literacy today is that more than 40 per
cent of the world's adult population is unable to read or write, and

that 65 per cent fall below the level of functional literacy (Malmquist, 1969).

7 *We speak much more than we read or write*. One estimate is that an average person utters in about two months more words than are in the whole of Shakespeare (Halliday *et al.*, 1964, p. 3). There are no details of how this estimate was made, but it seems plausible! In contrast, most people read much less than this, and many people read very little at all. Also, most people, even in a highly literate country like Britain, write negligible amounts, apart from personal letters, and occasional form-filling. As a result, few people have or need comparable command of spoken and written language.

This point is true, but it requires some immediate modification in the light of the cultural changes which take place in highly literate societies, where many people, especially in cities, probably often read as many words in a day as they speak or hear. There is no doubt that some people use written material more than spoken at least some of the time. I certainly do some days: if I am working at home, and not teaching, I may speak hardly a word all day, but spend the time reading and/ or writing and possibly listening to the radio. An adequate sociolinguistic account will take into consideration the changing communicative behaviour which comes about because of written language, and the existence of groups of professionals, including teachers, civil servants and many others, whose existence depends on written language.

8 *Spoken language is used in a much wider range of functions than written language*. This final argument is sometimes stated in support of the primacy of spoken language, although it appears rather weaker than the others. It is true that spoken language is used in a wide range of functions from casual, spontaneous conversation to formal speeches and so on; whereas written language tends to serve rather specialized functions at the formal end of the scale, uses like personal letters being quantitatively small in comparison with the major institutional uses of written and especially printed language. But this formulation risks missing the more interesting point that the functions of spoken and written language do not overlap all that much. It is sometimes possible to choose whether to send someone a written note or to use the telephone. But more often there is no choice possible between spoken and written channels. Since the functions of written language are not entirely obvious, especially to young children learning to read, we shall devote a detailed discussion to this topic later (see Chapter 5).

The arguments that I have summarized amount to a demonstration that spoken language is chronologically prior to written language, (a) for the human race as a whole, (b) for all individual languages and societies, and (c) for almost all individuals: and in the cases of (b) and (c), many have access only to spoken language. This primacy probably has a biological basis. These statements about the chronological priority of spoken language are quite distinct, however, from questions of logical or social primacy. And the demonstrable universality of spoken language does not in any way diminish the functional importance of written language.

The claim that spoken language is primary and written language is merely a secondary representation of it is, in a way, a strange one for linguists to have insisted on so strongly. At the same time as linguists were insisting on the primacy of spoken language (that is, particularly in the USA from the 1920s onwards), there was also great insistence on the principle that one language system (say, English or an American Indian language) should not be forced into the descriptive categories suitable for another language (say, Latin or Greek), as pre-twentieth century linguists had often done. It was argued, on the contrary, that each linguistic system had to be described in its own terms, or in its own right. But precisely the same point can be made about the description of written language. Earlier grammarians had, it is true, attempted to describe spoken language in terms of written. But now many linguists simply reversed the equation, declaring spoken language to be basic, and denying the partly autonomous existence and organization of written language, which was, in effect, dismissed as a secondary, derived and, by implication, inferior system. Only a few voices (e.g., Bolinger, 1946) were to be heard arguing that this view was clearly an extreme over-reaction.

2.4   The social priority of written language

Some of the points in the previous section also require further comment in the light of changing social functions of written language in many countries.

It is true that many societies do not have writing systems at all, and that writing emerged relatively late in those societies where it is used. Writing is not therefore a universal, as spoken language is. This does not mean that written language is unimportant (cf. Vachek, 1973, p. 34). Although the number of languages with no written forms is still large, it is diminishing. And the number of language communities with no access to some form of written communication is rapidly dwindling, due to massive literacy programmes. In India, for example, the level of illiteracy is very high and many of the local village dialects have no written forms. But the local language communities nevertheless have access to the written medium in, say, the national language Hindi-Urdu; although this may, admittedly, be virtually a foreign language to speakers of some local dialects. The point is that an adequate sociolinguistic account must take into consideration such changing sociocultural facts.

In addition, language communities generally themselves believe in the importance of having a writing system, since this greatly increases the functional range of their language. It can be used for more purposes than spoken language, including the easy recording and transmission of messages (see Chapter 5). We must therefore recognize that speech and writing are different, without one being superior to the other; but also recognize that a language which has both written and spoken forms is a more powerful instrument of communication than a language with only spoken forms.

It is clear, then, that we have to distinguish between social and chronological priorities, in order to recognize that once a written language has developed in a community, it characteristically takes on something of a life of its own, and characteristically is regarded by its users as important and often superior as a form of language.

In literate communities, there are some fairly obvious ways in which written language has social priority over spoken language (see Householder, 1971). In general, it is written forms which have social prestige: hence Samuel Johnson's preference for literary forms, cited above. And it is written, often literary, forms which are explicitly studied in our education system. Spoken language is rarely studied at all, to the extent that people are generally very hazy about the actual characteristics of spoken language (see Chapter 6). In law, it is usually written forms which have precedence and weight. Decisions may be required in writing and signatures may be required on written documents, whilst verbal agreements may turn out not to be binding. ('I'd like that in writing, please.') The law does not care how I pronounce my name, but it objects if I change the spelling, without giving notice. Writing is thus public and official in a way that speech is not.

In fact, in a literate society, the written language takes on a life of its own, develops along partly independent lines, is used for different purposes, and is believed by many people to be superior in various ways. The linguist points out that written language is not superior, just different, and in any case is, in certain senses, a secondary system. But the sociolinguist and educationalist has to recognize that in education it is often people's beliefs, perceptions, attitudes and prejudices which are crucial, however false they may be on objective grounds.

We can gain quite precise evidence about whether spoken or written language has social primacy by deciding whether writing influences speech or vice versa. For example, does spelling influence pronunciation or is it the other way round? It is clear that individuals often do mis-spell words, sometimes under the influence of pronunciation, and examples can be seen on many signs in shop windows. But such alterations rarely, if ever, influence the spelling system permanently. However, it is common for pronunciations to be altered to bring them into line with the spelling. Well-known examples are:

often now frequently pronounced /ɒftən/ where it used to be /ɒfən/
forehead now frequently pronounced /fɔ·hɛd/ where it used to be /fɒrɪd/
Wednesday now frequently pronounced /wɛdnzdɪ/ where it used to be /wɛnzdɪ/
diphtheria now frequently pronounced /dɪfθɪ·rɪə/ where it used to be /dɪpθɪ·rɪə/

Many other examples could be cited. (Barber, 1964, pp. 66ff. gives further data for English; and Haugen, 1972, p. 274, has documented the growing influence of spelling pronunciations on cultivated speech in Danish.) Spelling pronunciations do not only affect isolated words, but can affect a whole subsystem of a language, and an example will be discussed in 2.6 below.

Conversely, there are nowadays only very rare cases where pronunciation has affected spelling. De Camp (1972) gives the following example for Jamaican Creole. In Creole /θ/ and /t/ fall together as /t/, so that *three* and *tree* are pronounced identically as /tri/. The /t/ form of words which have /θ/ in standard English are however, socially stigmatized, and schoolteachers often harangue pupils to restore the /θ/. The problem for a Creole speaker is to know in which words to restore /θ/. As a result, the restoring is often over-generalized to words which do not have /θ/ in standard English. Thus *filter* can be pronounced /fɪlθər/. This form is supported by a folk etymology: a *filther* is something which removes *filth*, in a cigarette or a car. And the spelling *filther* is seen in print, for example in newspaper advertisements.

The prevalence of spelling pronunciations depends, of course, on a population who are highly literate, and therefore on social and educational factors. The first legal requirements of literacy in Britain date from the Education Acts of 1870 and 1872, and spelling pronunciations have therefore become much more common in the twentieth century than previously. Spelling pronunciations depend also on a strongly enforced institutional standard of spellings. Such a standard developed in Britain after about 1650 (see 3.1): before that time variant spellings of individual words were common, and spellings were therefore sensitive to pronunciation.

One might argue that a speaker who produces spelling pronunciations (that is, who allows written forms to influence spoken forms) has misunderstood the relation between spoken and written language. On the other hand, one cannot ignore the fact that spelling pronunciations do occur, and are therefore sociolinguistic facts which have to be taken into account. One might therefore argue, on the contrary, that it is the linguist who believes that spelling pronunciations should not occur who has misunderstood the relation between spoken and written language. It is the linguist's job to describe what speakers do, and not the speakers' job to conform to linguists' expectations. After the spread of writing, varieties of the spoken language can no longer be described in isolation from writing, for the written language will act back upon the spoken, via spelling pronunciations, grammatical changes and so on, and will possibly slow down the rate at which spoken language changes (Zengler, 1962). The sociolinguist has to take account of the practically universal belief, amongst those communities with writing systems in regular use, that it is the written language which is 'real' and the spoken language which is a corrupt form.

We are here in the paradoxical world of self-fulfilling prophecies, where thinking makes it so. The linguistically naive native speaker may believe that written language is primary and spoken language secondary. The linguist points out that spoken language is primary, and in some ways he is right. But the native speaker is also right: for if he believes that written language is primary, then not only does the written language have more prestige (this follows immediately), but also written language then comes to have demonstrable effects on spoken language. What people think is important, is important. Certainly, the importance of folklore and beliefs cannot be ignored in any kind of applied sociolinguistics, whether language teaching, acquisition of literacy, spelling reform, or similar activity. (See 3.11.)

2.5 The logical relation between speech and writing

The claim that spoken language is logically prior to written language often involves some version of the 'symbols of symbols' view. That is, that spoken words are symbols of things or thoughts, and that written words are symbols of spoken words. However, although this type of argument appears to be concerned with logical relationships, it is, in fact, another disguised version of the argument for the chronological primacy of spoken language. It is true that in all true writing systems, the units of written language are relatable to units of the spoken language. In ideal systems, the units represented are phonemes (in alphabetic systems), syllables (in syllabaries) or morphemes or words (in morphemic or logographic systems). (See 3.2.) In fact, all writing systems which have evolved naturally are mixed systems, although some come rather close to one of these types. But this is a description of how systems were invented or developed. It is not a statement which covers the complexities of what happens when a system is in use.

To show that spoken language is logically prior to written language, we would have to show that it is necessarily prior, for example, in language learning. But spoken language is clearly not necessarily prior here. If it was, then deaf-mutes, with no spoken language, could not learn to read and write and therefore acquire language through the written medium. We do not wish to put too much weight on such pathological cases, but we do not have to. Once a highly literate community exists, it is quite common to learn foreign languages only through writing. It is quite common nowadays for someone to have reading knowledge of a foreign language which they cannot speak themselves and cannot understand if it is spoken. This is almost necessarily the case where it is a dead language such as Latin which is studied. The language may be studied primarily in order to have access to the literature or other writings.

This in itself may involve distorting the function of the material and lead to odd paradoxes, since what is now only read may have been intended originally as oral literature. We have a great deal of literature from Middle English (*c.* 1100 to *c.* 1450), originally composed in a period when most popular literature was not written down at all but recited orally, and if written down then still intended primarily for oral recitation. This was partly because relatively few people could read, and also because books were prohibitively expensive. People were therefore mainly read to by a class of professional reciters, and this tradition lasted up until the sixteenth century when books became cheap enough to be bought other than by the very rich. One reason why so much of Middle English literature is in verse and not prose is that rhyming verse is easier to learn by heart (Clark, 1957, pp. 135–46).

There are several other ways in which we can show that writing is not merely a representation of speech. We can show that (a) the spoken language makes distinctions that written language does not; (b) conversely, the written language makes distinctions that the spoken language does not; and (c) spoken and written language differ in grammar, vocabulary, and so on. The first two points can be demonstrated very rapidly:

(a) There are many cases where pronunciation disambiguates a spelling: for example, *read* can be /rɪ·d/ or /rɛd/. Cases of one spelling with two or more pronunciations are homographs.

(b) Conversely, there are many cases where traditional English spelling disambiguates a single pronunciation, for example, /rɪ·d/ can be *read, reed, Reed, Reid*. Note also, in this case, that English spelling distinguishes proper names by an initial capital letter. There is no comparable way of distinguishing word classes in this way in the spoken language (see Chapter 3). Similarly, compare the way in which the spelling distinguishes *find* and *fined*, not just indicating that two different words are involved, but marking one as the past participle of a verb (see 3.5). Cases of one pronunciation with two or more spellings are homophones, and these are much more common in English than homographs.

Such examples could be multiplied, but it is clear already that the written and spoken languages have different possibilities of contrast and ambiguity, and that we have to recognize written and spoken language as systems which are partly independent, although they clearly share a large central core. We shall develop these arguments in much more detail when we consider the precise relationship between the English spelling system and spoken English (in Chapter 3), and between the formal features of written and spoken English (in Chapter 6).

We already have enough data, however, to make a preliminary statement about the logical relationship between spoken and written language. In general, the argument has so far been that writing does not represent speech in any straightforward way. That is, the following relationship is wrong:

1 spoken language: basic or primary system
   written language: secondary representation

Rather, both speech and writing are representations or realizations of language:

2 language: abstract system
   speech, writing: realizations of language in different media

But neither speech nor writing is a direct representation of the other. This diagram (2) is only a first approximation: it will have to be modified later when we discuss whether written and spoken English do realize the same underlying language system, or whether there are significantly different language systems involved.

An understanding of this relationship will be crucial for an understanding of what someone is doing when he reads something. A common-sense view of reading probably often goes as follows. When we read, we recognize visual units, usually words or letters, and we decode these units into the corresponding units of speech in sequential order. If, however, we can show that writing does not represent speech in any direct way, then this would immediately throw doubt on a symbol-to-sound decoding view of reading. And, in fact, it seems that, if not fundamentally wrong, then at least this view of reading is only the tip of the iceberg.

There is available an interesting set of historical evidence of the uses to which writing was mainly put in the first 1500 years or so after it was invented in or near Mesopotamia around 3500 BC. Although writing can be used to make a record of spoken language, the evidence is that the earliest uses of writing were not to represent speech at all. From the earliest known periods of written cultures, we have tens of thousands of documents and inscriptions. The main bulk of these are administrative and economic documents, and their form is mostly very different from speech. Their most characteristic form is one that is rarely found in spoken languages at all: they are lists (Goody, 1977, p. 80). In such records, connected literary texts are relatively rare, but there are a large number of extant cuneiform lists of business transactions, property, people, kings, and so on. It is possible, of course, to make long lists of items in spoken language, but this is rare. Such evidence is open to various kinds of sampling error, but indicates that from the very earliest times, writing was being put to distinctive uses and not merely being used to represent speech.

2.6   A case-study of /h/ and *h*

So far in this chapter, the argument has been rather general and discursive, with illustrative examples. It will be useful now to take one particular example in more detail to demonstrate the complexity of the changing relationship between written and spoken English. I will therefore conclude this part of the argument by discussing the stereotype of 'dropping one's aitches'. This will allow me to illustrate in some detail, on a particular example, the power of social attitudes to speech and writing and the detailed ways in which they can operate, popular confusions about the relationship between speech and writing, and the influence of spelling on pronunciation.

It is crucial to distinguish clearly between the letter *h* and the phoneme (sound unit) /h/, because they behave quite differently and it is their interaction which is of interest: in particular, in this case, the influence of the letter on the phoneme.

Letter and phonemes

A *phoneme* is a minimal distinctive sound unit in a particular language. Its distinctiveness is defined by its ability to distinguish word meanings. Conventionally, phonemes are distinguished by slashes, for example, /t/, /h/, /ð/. We know that these are phonemes of English, because by substituting them in the same context, we can get three words which differ in meaning, for example:

/tɛn/	ten
/hɛn/	hen
/ðɛn/	then

By carrying out such substitution tests systematically, and by finding minimal pairs distinguished in meaning by just one sound unit, the phonemes of a language can be isolated.

Allophones are sub-members of a phoneme, or positional variants of a phoneme. That is, phonemes are realized by different allophones according to the environment. Allophones are conventionally marked by square brackets, for example [p] and [pʰ] are allophones (unaspirated and aspirated) of the phoneme /p/, in English. We know that, although they are different sounds, they are not phonemes in English, because they do not contrast. Substituting one for the other in some context, say /s_in/, does not produce two different words with different meanings: one, the aspirated [pʰ] just sounds odd. In fact, [p] and [pʰ], and allophones in general, could not contrast in meaning, since they never do occur in the same context. After /s/ in English [p] occurs, and elsewhere [pʰ] occurs.

Note that these definitions are inevitably brief and approximate. They are intended as explanations, for readers unfamiliar with linguistic concepts, of terms used in the text. And they are therefore phrased so as to reflect only the specific concerns of this book. Linguists have, in fact, never entirely agreed on a satisfactory definition of the phoneme. Different definitions with different implications have been proposed, and it has been seriously proposed that phonemes are not a significant level of analysis. As it happens, I disagree with this latter view, but this debate is not directly relevant to the argument here, since with alphabetic writing we are dealing with the practical consequences of intuitive phonemic analyses, and not with the precise status of the phoneme as a unit of theoretical linguistics. The fact that alphabetic writing systems which have evolved naturally are based (however approximately in some cases) on intuitive phonemic analyses, does, however, lend weight to their status as psychologically distinctive linguistic units. Conversely, the English spelling system, like most alphabetic systems, pays no attention to sub-phonemic, allophonic variation.

The letter h *and the phoneme* /h/

Prescriptive writers on linguistic etiquette have been warning speakers against dropping their aitches since the late eighteenth century (Ekwall, 1965, p. 80). That is, it is considered wrong to say, for example, *an 'orse*, or *'is 'at*, rather than *a horse* and *his hat*. The implication is often that it indicates a careless pronunciation, a slovenly way of talking, and so on: in the same way, I suppose that it is careless to drop soapy plates. Dropping aitches is also widely believed to characterize working class speech, and it is socially stigmatized on those grounds. In fact, however, dropping aitches before unstressed syllables occurs in everyone's speech, from all social classes, in all but the most formal language. And it used to be a marker of upper-class speech to drop word-initial aitch in words like *hotel* and *hospital*. It is quite inadequate in general, however, to attempt an explanation of a linguistic feature on external grounds, such as the moral worth (e.g., careless) of the speaker, or purely according to the social class of the speaker. What is required is a linguistic explanation of why aitches are dropped, based on an understanding of the function of /h/ in spoken English.

The phoneme /h/ is, in fact, a peculiar consonant in spoken English, for it does not occur in many contexts. (Note that in all of this section we have to distinguish sharply between the phoneme /h/, and the letter *h*.) The phoneme /h/ occurs only in syllable-initial position, in three contexts:

(a) + hV   i.e. word-initially before a vowel, e.g., *high, hay*
(b) + hju·   i.e. word-initially before /ju·/, e.g., *Hugh, huge, hue*
(c) VhV   i.e. word-medially between vowels, e.g., *ahoy, behold*
(+ = word boundary; V = vowel; C = consonant.)

In context, (a), /h/ contrasts with other consonants, e.g., *high, die, buy, lie*; *hay, day, bay, lay*. In context (b), contrasts are also possible, although very few words are involved, e.g., *hue, due, cue*. In context (c), no contrasts with other consonants occur.

The /h/ phoneme does not occur at all in the other combinations of consonants and vowels in which many other phonemes occur. For example, /d/ also occurs in the following contexts which are impossible for /h/:

(d) + dCV   e.g., *drum*
(e) VCd +   e.g., *wild*
(f) VdC +   e.g., *addle*
(g) Vd +   e.g., *red*

Not all consonants can occur with /d/ in these contexts, but this is irrelevant to the point at issue, which is that /h/ cannot occur in any of these contexts.

All in all, then, /h/ is not a particularly useful consonant phoneme in English, in the sense that there are relatively few words that can be distinguished solely by its presence or absence. Possible minimal pairs do occur, including *ill, hill, am, ham*, and *Ed, head*, but since these pairs all contain items from different grammatical categories, it is difficult to find sentences which could be genuinely ambiguous due to the /h/ being dropped. A plausible confusion might be between *ate* and *hate* which are both verbs; for example, *I ate it* versus *I hate it*. But, in practice, there is a very remote possibility of real confusion over meaning when such items are used in conversation. In linguistic terms, then, /h/ has a very low functional load, and its marginal function in distinguishing word meanings might partly explain why it is often dropped.

As well as only occurring in a restricted set of phoneme sequences (only syllable-initially, not in consonant clusters, and so on), and therefore contrasting only rarely with other consonant phonemes, /h/ also stands out as not being integrated into the same sets of contrasts as other phonemes. Whereas other consonants fall into more or less tightly integrated pairs and triplets, along different articulatory dimensions, /h/ remains a peripheral item. (See Vachek, 1966.) This can be seen by diagramming all the consonant phonemes in English according to place and manner of articulation: Figure 1. (See Appendix B for a definition of these terms.)

	labial	dental/ alveolar	post-dental	palatal	velar	glottal
stops	p b	t d		tʃ dʒ	k g	
fricatives	f v	θ ð	s z	ʃ ʒ		h
nasals	m	n			ŋ	
approximants	w	l	r	j		

Figure 1

Phonetically, /h/ is something of an oddity as well. In Figure 1, it is represented as a glottal fricative, but phonetically it is rarely fricative. In its phonetic realization, there is rarely friction: it is simply an unvoiced version of the following vowel. Thus *hat* is phonemically /hat/ and phonetically [åat]. [å] indicates unvoiced [a], and the square brackets indicate phonetic, non-phonemic transcription.

The concept of functional load has been questioned, and it does not in itself provide a good predictor of which phonemes are likely to be retained or lost in a language. However, the point about /h/ in English is that not only is its functional load low, but in addition its distribution in phoneme sequences is unusual, it is not integrated into the phoneme system, and it is phonetically unusual! (See Bynon, 1977, pp. 86–8.) Given the peripheral status of /h/ in these different ways, one would predict, then, that it could easily be dropped in spoken language, and this is precisely what has happened in various non-standard accents. It is arguable that it has been retained in the standard language only due to pressure from above, and in particular due to the influence of the spelling system. Explicit condemnation of dropping aitches began at the end of the eighteenth century. In 1755 Samuel Johnson's Dictionary was published, and it codified what were by then standard spellings in use by printers. The standardization of the spelling system and the spread of literacy led to the view that if a letter is in the spelling, then it ought to be pronounced.

The /h/ phoneme has mostly occurred in word-initial position throughout the history of English, and its history is closely associated with the stress patterns of English words. At the end of the eighteenth century /h/ was normally present at the onset of stressed syllables which would otherwise begin with a vowel, and absent before unstressed syllables. In present day Cockney /h/ is still most likely to occur at the onset of heavily stressed syllables, although its use is not confined to this position. Sivertsen (1960, p. 141) gives examples such as:

| *no, I ain't* | /naw aj 'hejnt/ |
| *time to get up* | /taim tə gɛt 'həp/. |

But *h* and /h/ have a confused history in English, especially due to borrowings into English from French. Word-initially, in the context +hV, /h/ was lost in many dialects. In native Anglo-Saxon (Old English) words, most, if not all, regional dialects of southern England lost /h/ in the Middle English period (post-1100). Thus, from Middle English onwards, we find forms like *he, his, her* with no *h*. But the surprising thing is that no native Old English word has lost its /h/ for good: /h/ has always been reintroduced, probably due largely to spelling pronunciations. French never had words beginning with /h/, since this had already been lost in Latin. But scribes in the Old French period were strongly influenced by the classical Latin spellings, and often reintroduced educated spellings. Many French words beginning with *h*, but not /h/, were borrowed into English. In the majority of cases, however, spelling pronunciations have reintroduced /h/ in these words also. Examples are: *horrible, hospital, host*. This process of reintroducing

/h/ under the influence of spelling is still continuing. For example, Johnson (1755) gave no /h/ in *herb, humble, humour*. And fifty years ago *herb, hospital, humour*, and *history* were still common without the /h/: hence the written forms still seen with *an*: *an history, an hotel, an hospital*, although these words now have word-initial /h/ in most people's speech.

Given the marginal status of the /h/ phoneme in English with its low functional load, and given the complex relationship between the spelling and the pronunciation (/h/ appears first to have been lost, then reintroduced), it is not surprising that some speakers are confused about its use, and often both omit it where it occurs in standard English, and insert it where it does not so occur! Further data on /h/ is given by Ekwall (1965), Gimson (1970), Sivertsen (1960), Strang (1970), Trudgill (1974a), Vachek (1964, 1966), and Wyld (1927).

Another example of a pronunciation change under the influence of spelling is the change from /n/ to /ŋ/ in unstressed syllables, in words like *hunting*. This extension is quite recent, and has spread outwards from the middle classes, leaving working-class and upper-class speakers with /hʌntɪn/ or /hʌntən/. The /n/ form was common in upper-class speech until the 1930s (Strang, 1970, p. 80). The spread of /ŋ/ is similar to that of /h/ in that it spread out from the newly literate middle class, but spread least amongst the working class, who were less affected by literacy, and only later amongst the upper class, who were more confident in their speech and habits.

A word of caution is also in order, however, for it is easy to overgeneralize the effect of literacy on pronunciation. One cannot assume that spelling is everywhere dominant. For example, there appears to be no tendency in Anglo-English to pronounce an initial fricative in words such as *why, when, where*. As with /h/, there are only a few minimal pairs involved, such as: *witch, which*; *wye, why*; *watt, what*. But, if anything, the use of a fricative to give /hwɒt/ is declining, despite the spellings (Strang, 1970, p. 45).

There are many factors at work in linguistic change, and particular changes usually have multiple causes. The point is that the written language is an increasingly important factor.

2.7 Conclusions

We have to distinguish carefully between: (a) *Chronological primacy*: spoken language is clearly prior here, and this is generally what linguists mean when they attribute primacy to spoken language. (b) *Social primacy*: here things are much less clear cut. Spoken language has primacy in some ways, but in present-day literate communities it is characteristically written forms of language which have social prestige, and from a sociolinguistic and educational point of view, we cannot ignore people's attitudes and beliefs about language. (c) *Logical primacy*: it is true that a writing system represents units of the spoken language, and that anything which is written down can be read aloud, but written language does not directly represent spoken language. It is evident from several facts that the two systems are at least partly autonomous: there are distinctions maintained in one, but not in the other; they typically change over time at different rates; and spoken language does not necessarily precede written language in the individual child, although it generally does.

The debate still continues between those who believe that written language is essentially dependent on spoken language and those who believe that written language is essentially distinct in nature. (For example, see Hall, 1975, reviewing Vachek, 1973.) One has to admit that both sides have a point, but also that writing can take many different forms and bear many different relations to spoken language. If we look at things from a sociolinguistic point of view, with regard to the functions which written language serves in the community, we see that the relationship is not a constant, but changes as scribal traditions, machine printing (see 4.5), and an education system develop. This changing relationship is evident at many different levels. For example, the spelling system for English has remained fairly constant over the past four hundred years or so, whilst pronunciation has changed quite considerably in this time. This means that the spelling system has changed from being predominantly phonemic, with fairly consistent phoneme-grapheme correspondences, to a system which has many devices for representing syntactic and lexical information (see Chapter 3). Whereas in the Middle Ages and later reading aloud was the norm, silent reading is now much more common. Readers are nowadays therefore required much less often to translate written material into spoken, and this might partly explain why the writing system now tolerates a much less consistent sound-letter relationship than previously. At any rate, we have to allow that in highly literate communities, at least for some people, the link between spoken and written language is markedly weakened, and written forms may lose something of their secondary character and gain more of an independent, primary character.

Another example of the different relations which may hold between spoken and written forms comes from comparing more and less conservative spellings in English. It is well known that family and place names are often very conservative in their spellings and that there is often a large discrepancy between spellings and pronunciation. Notorious examples are *Cholmondley* and *Beauchamp*. Names are often conservative in spelling, because of their importance in legal documents. A

41

different trend is that names often have particular local significance, and different pronunciations can develop which are not under the normal pressures of communication over a wider area. Nevertheless, many different spellings do occur for names in old documents, and spelling pronunciations are becoming more common even with names. However, names provide a good example of different relations arising between written and spoken forms, in this case different relations with proper names versus anything else.

Strang (1970, p. 13) sums up the main point as follows:

'... writing, having once started as a durable record of speech, can take many forms, bear many relations to speech, and finally, can take wing as an independent factor in (language) structure and history.'

Chapter 3

Some principles of English spelling

There is a growing consensus amongst linguists and others that the English spelling system is now fairly well understood. As with any subject of study at all, there are residual problems concerning the most economic overall description, but it is fair to say that in studies done over the past ten to fifteen years the main problems have been identified and that the main principles of English spelling are now clear. The essential argument is that English spelling is not only phonemic; that is, it is not merely a system which relates sound units to letters. It is, rather, morphophonemic, relating orthographic units not only to phonemes, but also to morphemes, and therefore to grammatical and semantic units. (See 3.3 for a definition of *morpheme*.) Broadly comparable studies of English spelling, arguing that it is a morphophonemic system, have been published by Albrow (1972), Venesky (1970), C. Chomsky (1970) and others. More generally, linguists involved in devising writing systems for exotic languages have proposed that such systems ought also to be morphophonemic and not purely phonemic (Pike, 1947; Nida, 1975).

There are obvious differences between the theories underlying these studies and others, but they do not need to concern us directly here. In particular, Noam Chomsky has, in several places, taken up an extreme view that the phoneme is not a significant linguistic unit. He therefore cannot use the concept of phoneme to account for English spelling (see Chomsky and Halle, 1968). However, there is general agreement that English spelling is more abstract in its principles than a grapheme-phoneme correspondence system, and this is the point I shall develop in this chapter.

This book is primarily about sociolinguistic and sociological aspects of reading and writing, but before we can develop the argument much further, we need a clearer understanding of just what is learned when someone learns to read and write English: that is, we need an understanding of the English spelling and writing system. This must be the single most important theoretical problem underlying the practical problem of teaching initial literacy in English. How is the writing system related to spoken English? In the last chapter, I questioned various views about the relation between spoken and written language, and concluded, contrary to frequent but inaccurate statements, that reading cannot merely be decoding visual symbols into sounds, for the simple reason that writing does not merely represent speech. In order to give this argument a more precise basis, we now have to examine the English spelling system, and see in detail why written English is not merely 'spoken language written down', in the sense of sound units coded into letter shapes.

However, even in discussing the formal and structural character-istics of English spelling, there are several reasons why we cannot ignore wider functional and sociolinguistic issues.

3.1 A functional view of English spelling

Numerous proposals have been made for reforming English spelling over the past four hundred years. But not one has ever been successful, and, if anything, any serious proposal for reform is now a more remote possibility than ever (see 4.1). This might be put down to the con-servatism of British traditions: that is, one could propose an extrinsic explanation in terms of the moral calibre of its users. But a more acceptable explanation is that the present system, despite obvious anomalies, has some considerable advantages in the ways it represents English. One could propose instead an intrinsic explanation, based on the ways in which the writing system represents units of language. We will therefore take a functional view of the spelling system: given that there are features of English spelling that appear 'odd', 'unmotivated' or 'irregular' at first sight, is it possible nevertheless to discover what positive function they might serve and why they have been preserved, sometimes over centuries, although the spoken language has changed considerably in this time?

In addition, we shall not be able to avoid purely social issues, for spelling is regarded by many people as a social skill, and a good speller has high social prestige (see Scragg, 1974, ch. 6). Bad spellers have been publicly ridiculed in Britain since the sixteenth century. Before that time, spelling was changeable, even in printed books, but by about 1650 printers had begun to use a stable spelling system which is very similar to our present-day conventions. By 1700 stabilization was com-plete, and the norms set by printers were recorded in Johnson's Diction-ary of 1755. The concept of a 'spelling mistake' is largely an invention of the period after 1770 (Strang, 1970, p. 107). Although spelling conventions had been established in printed materials before then, there were still divergences in spellings in handwritten papers, but dictionaries like Johnson's provided a norm for personal usage. By the end of the eighteenth century, spelling was big business: in the USA, sixty-five million copies of Noah Webster's *The American Spelling Book* were sold in the hundred years after it was published in 1783. In our society, spelling is often regarded as a sign of full literacy and a good education. In specific ways, which I will suggest below (3.6), a full competence in English spelling may in fact depend on a knowledge of learned substrata of words likely to be learned only through reading. But although a good speller is likely to be well educated, it does not follow that a bad speller is not.

We shall also have to consider the important sociolinguistic question of whom the present English spelling system suits best. The overall argument will be that the system we have is a fairly good one for fluent adult readers. It is, however, not an optimal system either for children learning to read, or for foreign learners of English. On the one hand, it is arguable that a writing system ought to suit its native users. On the other hand, English now serves as an international language, often in the written medium, and this would have to be borne in mind, if reform were ever seriously contemplated. (This fact has been one purpose of spelling reformers such as Wijk and Follick.) Any writing system, used as widely and for such diverse purposes as English, will have to compromise between the needs of learners, native and foreign, and fluent adult users.

Another implication of taking a functional approach is that it offers a synchronic explanation, that is, an explanation of how the system works at one particular point in time, such as the present. It is always possible to offer a diachronic or historical explanation of linguistic facts. One could account for the present state of the spelling system by pointing to the varying forces at work on it in the past: changes in pronunciation which have made the spelling out of date; the influence of French, which was the written vernacular in England after 1066; and of Latin, which was the main language of education until at least the sixteenth century; the etymological spellings, accurate and false, based on Latin during the Renaissance, and so on.

A major historical factor in letter-sound correspondences is that English spelling had been largely fixed before the so-called Great Vowel Shift took place around the fifteenth century. This sound change involved chains of alternations in the vowel phoneme system, primarily:

/a/ → /e/ → /i/ → /ai/
and /ɔ / → /o/ → /u/ → /au/.

But such historical facts would not explain why so many of the features of spelling introduced for these diverse reasons remain in the system today, despite continual attempts to erase them. We will not therefore dismiss features of spelling as 'out of date', although historical facts will occasionally be mentioned; but will enquire instead whether such facts have any positive functional justification in present-day written English.

One example of the limitation or even irrelevance of a diachronic view of English spelling occurs with words where there is a divergence in spellings over the suffix *-ise* or *-ize*. Such a divergence is itself rare, since there are very few exceptions to the norm of one-word-one-spelling. Etymologically, these affixes indicate whether a word has come into English direct from Greek (*-ize*) or indirectly from Greek via French (*-ise*). But often the source cannot be identified even by experts, and such etymologies are quite unknown and therefore irrelevant to most readers and writers (Strang, 1970, p. 27). The synchronic facts are that the form *-ize* is gaining favour where there is a choice, and this form is being recommended on the style sheets of the major publishing houses, and therefore becoming more and more common in print.

It will not be possible to give anything like a complete account of how English spelling works, but only to indicate some of its major underlying principles.

3.2   Writing systems

We require some very brief definitions of a writing system and of different kinds of writing system, since an important point about English is that it has a mixed system, basically alphabetic, but not consistently so.

In a true writing system, the symbols represent linguistic units: these may be words or morphemes, or they may be phonological units, such as syllables or phonemes. The writing system relates these symbols to units of language, not to concepts or ideas. A pictographic system is not therefore a true writing system in this definition, since here the symbols do relate to ideas, and then only imprecisely. Therefore, given a sequence of pictograms, there are various ways to interpret them. But given a series of symbols in a true writing system, and in a particular language, there is only one possible reading. For example, given the orthographic sequence, *The man hit the woman* (1), it would not be a correct reading to say. 'The chap bashed the lady' (2), since there is a strict determinism between the sets of orthographic symbols and some level of units in the language, in this case words. This illustrates again a distinction between reading and comprehension (see 1.2). If I see (1) and say (2), this proves at least comprehension; but (2) is not a correct reading of (1).

We can distinguish between two broad types of writing system. In a logographic system, symbols represent morphemes or words. There are various pure logograms in use in English, including: £, &, 827. (See Edgerton, 1941.) Thus, for example, when we read *827*, we have to go directly from the symbols to the words; there is nothing in the written symbols which gives any information about the pronunciation. Also various words in written English are distinguished by differences in spelling. For example, *ruff* and *rough* clearly give some indication about pronunciation, and are not therefore purely logographic, but the differences in spelling serve to keep semantically unrelated words visually distinct. English spelling is therefore partly lexical. It gives some information about word meanings directly, as well as giving information about pronunciation. The most consistently logographic writing system is traditional Chinese writing. (But cf. French, 1976, for further details and necessary qualifications on this; namely, that modern Chinese writing is morpheme-based and not word-based.)

Alternatively, a writing system can be phonological, and can use symbols to indicate the pronunciation of sound units, either syllables or phonemes. In a syllabary, there is ideally one symbol for each syllable. Japanese uses two syllabaries, alongside other writing systems, with less than fifty symbols. The phonological structure of Japanese is ideal for such a system, since the syllable structure is very simple. Syllables in Japanese have the structure: (C)V(N), that is, a vowel preceded optionally by a consonant and followed optionally by a nasal, /m/, /n/ or /ŋ/, depending on the following sound. No other possibilities exist, and therefore Japanese has a very small number of possible syllable types. A syllabary would on the other hand be very uneconomical in English, which allows so many other possibilities of syllable-type that a syllabary would require hundreds of signs. In modern English there are no syllabic signs in normal use. The spelling of *barbecue* as *Bar-B-Q* is about as near as we get, with *B* as a sign for the syllable /bi/ and *Q* for /kju/. In Middle English & was used as a syllabic sign for the syllable /ɛt/, since *et* meant *and* in Latin.

In an alphabetic system, there is, ideally, one letter (or pair or triplet of letters) for each phoneme. Some systems, such as Finnish, Swahili, Spanish and Serbo-Croat, approach this ideal fairly closely. But in most alphabetic systems, such as English, this principle is compromised in various ways, and English is best regarded as having a mixed system. The most commonly used systems in the world are based on the Roman alphabet. Other alphabetic systems include Cyrillic, used for Russian and other languages in the USSR, and the Greek alphabet. A variation on alphabetic writing is to indicate only consonants and to leave out almost all vowels, or to mark vowels optionally: such systems include Hebrew and Arabic. Alternatively some scholars have regarded Arabic

47

and Hebrew as syllabaries, rather than alphabetic with minimal vowel indications.

The main possibilities for writing systems are therefore:

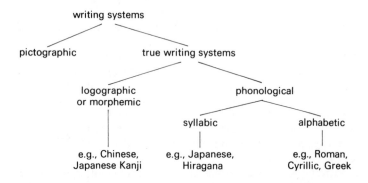

There are two interesting facts about alphabetic writing systems: most writing systems in the world today are alphabetic, but none are purely phonemic.

The historical progression of writing systems, well documented by Gelb (1963), Diringer (1962) and others, has been from pictographic to logographic to syllabic to alphabetic systems. And this progress is still continuing: witness the present concern of the Chinese government to introduce a Romanized orthography alongside a simplified traditional system. One would predict on grounds of economy in the number of basic symbols that a phonemic system would be preferred. In any language, the number of phonemes will be fairly small. Outside limits are from twenty or less (e.g., for Hawaian and Maori) to sixty or more (e.g., for some Caucasian languages such as Abkhazian), with most languages in the thirty to fifty range. English has around forty-four phonemes: different accents differ slightly in the number of their phonemes (6.4). The number of syllables in a language can be quite low, or can be in the hundreds. In any language, the number of morphemes or words in common use will number in the thousands.

(Strictly, if economy means the raw number of basic units, then a distinctive feature system, as developed by Jakobson and others within linguistic theory, would be more economical than a phoneme system. But no advance in this direction has ever been made in the three thousand years or so that alphabetic systems have been invented. The practical objection for a writing system is that several rows of information would have to be read simultaneously. For example, *p* would somehow have to be represented as plosive, unvoiced and bilabial. Neither is it clear what the psychological salience of such features is. In comparison, phonemes and syllables have high salience.)

Although some writing systems approach a one-to-one phoneme-grapheme relationship quite closely, none maintain it consistently, excepting only some systems which have been invented explicitly by theoretical linguistics (e.g., Yakut: see Vachek, 1973). But all alphabetic systems which have evolved naturally are mixed systems which involve compromises between phoneme-grapheme correspondence and the correspondence of graphemes to higher morphological and syntactic levels. There must be powerful reasons why the end point of the development of writing systems in the five or six thousand years or so since true writing was invented, and over the many languages to which it has been applied, is alphabetic systems with an admixture of morphological and/or syntactic information.

3.3   Words, morphemes and morphological alternation

Since English spelling relates not only to phonemes (see 2.6) but also to other linguistic levels, we require definitions of these. We need to go into the distinctions only far enough to discuss a fairly narrow range of phenomena in written and spoken English, however, and this can be done quite rapidly.

In written English, words are separated by spaces: these units are orthographic words. This is a convention used in writing English, but it is not used in all languages. For example, in classical written Latin there was often no space left between words, but only between major grammatical units. And modern written Chinese, in the traditional logographic writing system, leaves spaces between morphemes (see below) but does not indicate word boundaries. In spoken English, there are usually no pauses between words in connected speech, and words therefore have to be defined on other criteria, including positional mobility within sentences, indivisibility and stress. Since words are intuitively recognizable to anyone who has already learned to read English, their further definition need not directly concern us here. (But see 6.2.)

However, words are not the minimal meaningful units of language. For example, *mean-ing-ful* can be further divided as indicated by this hyphenation. *Mean* can occur on its own as a free morpheme; *-ing* also occurs as a morpheme in *eat-ing* and *act-ing*; and *-ful* occurs as a morpheme in *wonder-ful*, and with a spelling change as a free morpheme *full*. But these units cannot be further divided into meaningful units. A *morpheme* is, therefore, the minimal meaningful unit of a language.

In spoken English, many morphemes occur in different forms, depending on their sound context. That is, there is morphological or morphophonemic alternation. Alternants of morphemes are called allomorphs. A simple example of such alternation occurs with different alternants of the plural morpheme, which is most often represented in written English by *-s*. For example:

house-s	is pronounced	/hauzɪz/
cat -s	is pronounced	/kæts/
dog -s	is pronounced	/dɒgz/

In spoken language, the plural morpheme has three main alternants or allomorphs: /ɪz/, /s/ and /z/. These alternants do not occur at random. On the contrary, they are totally predictable:

/ɪz/ occurs after a preceding affricate or sibilant, e.g. /s,z,ʃ,ʒ,tʃ,dʒ/
/s/ occurs after other preceding unvoiced sounds, e.g., /t, p, k/
/z/ occurs after other preceding voiced sounds, e.g., /d, b, g, r, l/

The same rules of alternation also account for the allomorphs of the genitive *-s* (e.g., *Bess's, Jack's, Bill's*), for the third person singular of regular verbs (e.g., *hisses, kicks, kills*) and for contractions (e.g., *John's* where this is equivalent to *John is*).

Note that the assimilation of voiced and voiceless segments is not simply a general phonological one for English. Thus we have both

cease /si·s/ and *seize* /si·z/

with both /s/ and /z/ after the same voiced sound. There /s/ and /z/ are not predictable on phonological grounds alone. In an example such as

seas /si·z/

we can however predict that the final segment is /z/, given both the phonological context and also the morpheme structure: noun plus plural. The rule therefore takes into account both phonological and morphological context, and is therefore a morphophonemic rule.

Morphemes are, therefore, abstract units, and can be regarded as a class or family of allomorphs or positional variants. Allomorphs are, in turn, realized by phonemes. An understanding of English spelling depends on an understanding of the concepts of phoneme, morpheme and allormorph. The main points, developed in the rest of this chapter, are that English spelling relates to (1) phonemes and morphemes, but ignores (2) predictable morphophonemic alternation. It should be clear that principle (2) will often conflict with a systematic correspondence between letters and phonemes, as it does in the example of plurals discussed above.

This very brief statement of these points here may provide a reference section for the much fuller illustrative sections which now follow.

3.4   The unfortunate example of *ghoti*

George Bernard Shaw once proposed, presumably ironically, that *fish* might be spelled *ghoti*: *gh* as in enough, *o* as in women, and *ti* as in *nation*. If anyone has ever taken this suggestion seriously, however, then they have betrayed a severe misunderstanding of how English spelling works. *Ghoti* is not a plausible spelling for *fish*, and an analysis of why it is not will provide an informal introduction to a discussion of some basic principles underlying the English spelling system.

1   It is only possible to pronounce *gh* as /f/ at the end of morphemes, as in *enough, tough, cough, coughing, toughness*, and so on, or after vowels as in *draught*. In world-initial position it is always pronounced /g/. This illustrates an important characteristic of English spelling: that the same orthographic symbol can correspond to different pronunciations according to its position of occurrence within words. Expressed slightly differently, the rules for converting orthographic symbols into sounds are context-dependent. The rule here must involve such statements as:

Within syllables,	gh = /g/ in the context _V
e.g.,	*ghost, ghoul, ghetto, aghast.*
	gh = /f/ in the context V_
e.g.,	*enough, tough.*
Where V = vowel	

The rule is, of course, more complex than this, because of the small set of words such as *though, through, plough, taught*, and *bough*, where *gh* = zero; but the rule as stated already eliminates Shaw's spurious spelling.

Word-initial *gh* has, however, an odd history in English, contributing to its strange behaviour, which is not, it must be admitted, like that of any other orthographic symbol in English. It was introduced into English by Caxton in the fifteenth century. Caxton, who introduced printing into England, was born here, but spent most of his life in Holland. As a result, he was not up to date with the English spelling conventions of his time and seems to have been confused between English and Dutch spelling rules. In addition he employed many foreign compositors who were no more familiar with English spelling conventions than he was himself. He was therefore responsible for introducing the Dutch convention of *gh* into words which had previously been spelled as, for example, *gost*. He even introduced it into words such as *gherle* (*girl*), *ghoos* (*goose*) and others, in which it has now been dropped. Almost the only words in which it has been retained are ones with distinctly pejorative connotations: *ghost, ghoul, ghetto, ghastly*. We now have a small set of words which are marked as semantically negatively loaded by their spelling: this is not a general principle in English spelling. (*Ghana* and *gherkin* do not come out of this very well! Scragg, 1974, pp. 66-7 gives further data on this.) We can account for the *h* in *ghetto* by pointing out the historical fact that the word was borrowed from Italian, where it has this spelling, in the seventeenth century. But users of English today are unlikely to have this diachronic information. The synchronic fact is that words beginning with *gh* now often have a pejorative meaning.

2   The *o* in *women* is quite a different story, although very simple. It is used in order to distinguish the vowel in handwriting. If *i* was used, the *wim* would risk being an indecipherable series of up-and-down strokes. Compare *monk* (not *munk), and *wonder* (not *wunder). (An asterisk is conventionally used in linguistics to mark forms which are ungrammatical or otherwise not well-formed.) The problem was particularly acute in Middle English handwriting, where the letters *i, u, n, m* and *w* tended to be made simply by one, two or three upright strokes with no connecting horizontal strokes, and sometimes without a dot on the *i*. So any word with a sequence of two or three of these letters became illegible. Spelling of this period was also much influenced by French conventions, where *o* sometimes represented the same sound as *u*: hence spellings such as *son*, which are not necessary given the clarity of modern machine printing, or even modern handwriting styles (Clark, 1957, p. 120). We shall see in more detail later (4.5) the influence of such technological considerations on writing conventions.

For similar reasons, *ii is avoided. The only exception is *skiing*, whch is based on a foreign borrowing (see 3.8). Writing is a visual system, and some of its design features fulfil the function of keeping words visually distinct. This circumstance means that, due to a chance occurrence of letters in sequence, *women* and various other words have idiosyncratic spellings. Because the alphabet evolved naturally, as opposed to being deliberately designed, some of its visual features are not of the best. Compare, for example, the needlessly confusing alternations in *p, b, q, d*, and so on.

Again, although these facts have explanations, we cannot talk of an entirely systematic feature of English spelling. Although *monk* has *o*, *nun* has *u*, for example.

3   The *ti* in *nation* is different again. Here, *tion* has to be read as a single orthographic unit and *ti* cannot be read as a separate unit. As a unit, *tion* has a consistent pronunciation: /ʃən/ or /ʃn/. Also, it occurs in a consistent position, at the end of morphemes, and has a consistent grammatical and semantic function, to signal abstract nouns. That is, the spelling is related to the grammar: the suffix *tion* not only gives the pronunciation, but also gives direct grammatical information. But it gives both kinds of information only when interpreted as a whole in context.

This principle is quite a general one in English (see Haas, 1970, pp. 77ff.). It requires that certain word-final letter-sequences be recognized as noun or adjective markers. Compare:

-ion: *nation, pension, suspicion*
-ian: *patrician, musician*
-ience: *patience, conscience*
-ure: *fissure*
-ious: *officious, luscious*
-ial: *partial, special*
-ient: *efficient*, etc.

Then, any preceding
c, sc, ss, t is read as $/\int/$.
And any preceding
s   is read as $/ʒ/$ after a vowel, e.g., *decision, pleasure*
             and as $/\int/$ elsewhere,   e.g., *mansion*.

This second rule is an automatic phonological one for English.

These are rules for reading. The rules for writing are different; for, as we have seen before, reading and writing are not symmetrical. The problem for the writer is when to write, say, $/\int n/$ as *-tion, -cion*, and so on. One general principle here is that English tends to preserve the same letters in semantically related words. Hence: *nation, native; suspicion, suspect; partial, part*; etc. In order to know how to write these words, we therefore have to know about related words in the language. These relations will generally at least tell us which consonant letters to use.

I have so far shown that *fish* could not be spelled *ghoti*. Haas (1970, p. 57n.) has also shown that it could only be spelled *fish*! **ffish* is excluded as this is not a possible word-initial letter sequence. **phish* is implausible on lexical grounds: it is not a learned word based on a Greek borrowing, such as *philosophy* or *philately*. **fysh, *physh* and so on are excluded as *y* does not occur before *sh* or after initial *f*, except in proper names. No other possibility occurs in this position.

The reader should also be able to see, for reasons partly given, that *ghoti* could also only be read as $/gəutɩ/$. In reading it in this way, one would have to assume that it was a foreign word, since only foreign borrowings end in *i*, for example, *ski, Vinci* (see 3.8).

It should also be clear, without going into details, that *fish* can only be read as $/fɩ\int/$. For example, the word final *sh* must be read as a unit, since the phoneme $/h/$ never occurs word-finally in English (see 2.6).

We have shown then that

ghoti can only be read as $/gəutɩ/$
fish can only be read as $/fɩ\int/$
$/fɩ\int/$ can only be spelled as *fish*.

But: /gəʊtɪ/ could be spelled as *goaty, goatie, ghoty* and in other ways in accordance with English spelling rules. The problems of readers and writers are not symmetrical.

This initial analysis of *ghoti* tells us several important things about English spelling:

1   English spelling is clearly basically alphabetic and phonemic, and sets of words such as *pen, pin, pan, pun, ten, tin, tan*, etc. are perfectly regular, in the sense that pronunciation is predictable from the spelling alone, and, conversely, spelling is predictable from pronunciation.

2   No English word is ever spelled in such a way that it gives no information about pronunciation. Even orthographic units such as *gh* are quite restricted in their possible pronunciations, and may be quite unambiguous in certain contexts.

3   Some features of English spelling are idiosyncratic and have to be explained by one-off, idosyncratic accounts, sometimes historical.

4   More interestingly, there are features of English spelling which appear irregular only when one attempts to relate letters to sounds. But this irregularity is due only to trying to force everything into one system: regular letter-sound correspondences. But spellings also rely on (a) the position of occurrence of letters in words, e.g., initial versus final, and (b) relations between orthographic symbols and higher levels of language: morphemes, word-classes and grammar. That is, English spelling is not only phonemic but also *morphophonemic*, since the symbols give lexical and syntactic information, and are therefore not always good predictors of pronunciation. It is true that in isolation almost every English orthographic symbol can represent more than one phoneme, and that almost every phoneme can be represented by more than one orthographic symbol, but reading does not consist of pronouncing isolated letters, but relies on lexical, syntactic and semantic context.

5   English spelling presents different problems for writers and readers. (This is true of any writing system.)

A further example should make it clearer why English spelling has to be regarded as a morphophonemic system which gives information not only about pronunciation of words but also about grammatical and semantic relationships between words.

3.5   *-ed* as a past tense marker

We will take *-ed* in word-final position (e.g., *walked, showed, drifted*), and compare: how *-ed* relates to sounds, how *-ed* relates to grammar and meaning, and what other orthographic symbols relate to the same

<u>sounds.</u> Multiple correspondences are involved, and we will deal only with the following:

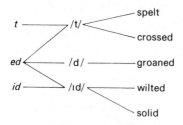

This set of correspondences is fairly complex, but nevertheless clear enough for further introductory discussion, and several interesting principles are involved.

In word-final position, *-ed* is an almost unambiguous marker of the morpheme *past*. That is, we know from the spelling that *walked*, *wanted* and *showed* are past tense. The symbol *-ed* is therefore a direct indication of a grammatical-semantic category, in this case a grammatical morpheme. It gives some indication of the pronunciation, but does not specify the pronunciation exactly, since we have:

walked /t/, *wanted* /ɪd/, *showed* /d/.

To a native speaker of English, however, this additional information would be redundant and does not require to be stated in the writing system, since the alternation is automatic and depends simply on the preceding sound. The main rule is:

-ed is pronounced as /ɪd/ after /t, d/ e.g., *wanted, boarded*
/d/ after a voiced sound other than /d/
e.g., *leaned, sewed*
/t/ elsewhere, i.e. after an unvoiced sound
other than /t/ e.g., *kicked, pipped*

This example provides us with several more principles which underlie English spelling. (Similar points could be made on the basis of *-s* as a plural marker on nouns: cf. *cats, dogs, horses*.)

1 Other things being equal, one symbol is used to give visual identity to different units, primarily morphemes, which mean the same. Units which look the same, mean the same. Thus the past tense morpheme is spelled *-ed* no matter how it is pronounced.

2 That is, the system ignores predictable morphophonemic variation: the variation in the pronunciation of morphemes in different sound contexts, but the same morphological context. One of the most

general principles underlying English spelling is that phonetic variation is not indicated where it is predictable by rule.

3   Conversely, we might add here, units which look different are generally unrelated in meaning. Thus *ruff* and *rough* look different although they are pronounced the same.

4   The spelling system is a visual system and is designed as such. Since writing is designed to be seen, it is reasonable that it should maintain visual distinctions and identities at the expense of letter-sound correspondences. Thus there are many more homophones (words which sound alike but differ in meaning) in spoken English, than there are homographs (words which look alike but differ in meaning) in written English. For example, homophones such as *bough/bow, seen/scene* are quite common. But homographs such as *read, lead* are much rarer.

5   It follows that the written language pays more attention to disambiguating word meanings than the spoken language does.

6   It follows from 2 that English spelling is well designed for a native speaker of the language who knows its automatic phonological and morphological rules. But it is not good for a foreigner who needs a higher level of redundancy and help in pronouncing words.

In summary so far, English spelling is a predominantly visual system which assumes that its users have native competence in the phonology and morphology of the language. In order to read English, one has to know the language.

A further complication in our example is that we have sets of words which rhyme, that is which sound the same in their final syllable, but which are spelled differently: compare *wanted, sculpted*, etc. versus *solid, fetid, putrid, acid*, etc. We see here that while *-ed* marks a grammatical morpheme, *-id* does not mark a morpheme at all. Thus again, grammatical relations override letter-sound correspondences.

Word-final *-ed* is not an entirely unambiguous marker of a past tense however. Compare *misled*. A common joke is that this is misread as /mɪzld/. In English writing, word boundaries are marked by spaces, but morpheme boundaries are generally not marked at all. So a problem for readers is to know where to put them. For example, nothing indicates that the word structure differs in *finger* and *singer*. One simply has to know that *sing* is a word, but **fing* happens not to be one. Similarly, one has to decide whether to read *misled* as *mis-led* or as *misl-ed*, assuming a verb 'to misle'. Compare the problems of finding the correct morpheme boundary in *bedraggled, bedridden, rediscover*. Fluent readers do occasionally have problems with this. For example, I recently came across the word *homerun* and tried for several seconds to read it as *homer-un*, until I saw the correct morpheme structure.

It is only relatively rarely, then, that morpheme boundaries can be inferred unambiguously from the spelling alone. (It is equally true, of course, that morpheme boundaries are not generally marked in spoken English.) There are cases where it is possible, however. For example, /kw/ has two possible spellings, *kw* and *qu*. We know that *qu* always has to be read as a single orthographic symbol and therefore always occurs within a single morpheme. Conversely, *kw* is a sequence of two symbols and always occurs across morpheme boundaries: e.g., *breakwater*. But such cases are not systematic, and many pairs of letters can occur equally within morphemes or across boundaries: compare *th* in *think* and *pithead*.

How do we know then that *-ed* is most likely to be a morpheme, but that *-id* is not? One clue is the *e* which is a marker of grammatical suffixes. Compare its use in:

-er : *smaller*
-est: *smallest*
-en : various suffixes: *wooden, soften, flatten, oxen*
-ess: *poetess*

Again, this clue is not entirely unambiguous (compare *water, sudden, impress* where it does not mark a suffix), but it helps. We have then another general principle: that letters do not only signal sounds, but may have other functions also such as signalling, albeit ambiguously, grammatical suffixes and giving clues as to morpheme structure. The letter *e* is unique in the functions of this type which it serves (see Albrow, 1972, pp. 29ff.).

Finally, there is a small set of words which can take either *-ed* or *-t* as a past tense marker, and in some cases there are also alternative pronunciations of the morpheme in speech. The main examples are:

(a) *burned/t, learned/t, spoiled/t*, which have no other change of spelling.

(b) *spelled/spelt, spilled/spilt, smelled/smelt*, which lose an *l* in the spelling.

(c) *leaned/leant, leaped/leapt, dreamed/dreamt*, which obey the general principle that related words look alike by retaining the same spelling in the stem despite a change in pronunciation from /i·/ to /ɛ/.

(d) *kneeled/knelt, creeped/crept, weeped/wept*, which change the spelling to reflect a change in pronunciation.

The use of written forms of these verbs does not necessarily correspond to people's use of the spoken alternatives, and people also differ in their use of the spoken forms. In so far as intuitive evidence is reliable, my impression is that I never use the *t*-spellings in writing, but do use the /t/ forms in speech. So I would always write *He's burned it* (1), but could say either (2) /bə·nd/ or (3) /bə·nt/. I could therefore read (1) as either (2) or (3). It appears that both graphic forms are used in both Britain and the USA, but with differing frequency.

57

In Britain the preferred form in print appears to be -*t* (Quirk, 1970).

We therefore have to alter our correspondences slightly to allow:

$$
\begin{array}{c}
-t \\
-ed
\end{array}
\begin{array}{c}
\diagdown \diagup \\
\diagup \diagdown
\end{array}
\begin{array}{c}
/t/ \\
/d/
\end{array}
$$

but noting that the crossover pattern is permissible only in the small set of verbs which have both forms. Thus both *spelled* and *spelt* can be both /spɛld/ and /spɛlt/. For verbs outside this class, alternative forms are not possible. Thus *called* can only be read /kɔ·ld/ and not */kɔ·lt/.

Other verbs only take -*t*. An example is *slept*, but not **sleeped*. Similar examples are *sent, went, bent, lent*, etc. If English spelling was consistently morphological, then we might expect forms such as *sleeped*, which could be read as /slɛpt/. But we do not have such forms in the wrting system because /slɛpt/ is not predictable. The spelling, as we have seen, ignores morphophonemic alternations which are predictable from phonological context. *Sleep* is an irregular verb, but the spelling is quite regular since it tells the reader how to pronounce an irregular form.

It is therefore verbs of the *spelt, knelt* class which are exceptional. First, they break the principle of only having one spelling for each word. Second, they break the principle of the visual identity of morphemes. Such spellings were in fact introduced in the sixteenth and seventeenth centuries during a period of interest in 'phonetic' spellings (Strang, 1970, p. 108) and are thus a small example of the dangers of spelling reform which attempts to revise the system in the interests of more consistent sound-letter correspondences, but does not appreciate the deeper levels of organization in the system.

There is no reason why such morphological spellings as *sleeped* could not serve. For example, the verb-ending -*eth*, as in *giveth*, remained common in writing after it had been replaced by /z, s, ɪz/ in speech. But *giveth* could be read as *gives*, that is /gɪvz/ (Strang, 1970, p. 110). Expectations about the relationship between written and spoken language have not always been as they are now.

We started with the apparent case of one-to-many correspondences between graphic forms and phonemes, but we have now seen that, although the situation is complex, it is certainly not random. In order to explain the facts we have had to relate the spellings to grammatical morphemes and therefore to word structure and meanings. We have shown also that the type of multiple correspondence diagram which we started from in this section is rather unreal. One often sees in books on spelling and reading diagrams of the type:

letters   sounds

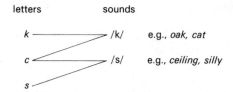

e.g., *oak, cat*

e.g., *ceiling, silly*

Such diagrams are misleading, since the rules are not context-free. For example, in this case, *c* cannot correspond to /s/ in word-initial position before *a*. As Haas (1970, p. 57) points out, such diagrams have the same air of unreality as decontextualized lists of translations of words in, say, English and French. We might have:

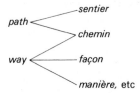

But the translations cannot simply be chosen freely within this framework: they depend on the surrounding context. This type of context-free presentation of spelling correspondences is sometimes taken to tedious lengths, as when Pitman and St John (1969, p. 46) claim to show that there are 596,580 possible spellings of *scissors*: there aren't!

There is real complexity in the system, but it arises rather from the variety of types of contextual constraint which we have to specify. For example, as rules for pronunciation only we have:

1 *o* = /i/   in *women*
2 *gh* = /g/ in word-initial position
3 *ti* = /ʃ/   before *-on, -ous*, etc. in morpheme-final position in nouns and adjectives
4 *ed* = /ɪd/ in word-final position in verbs, after a preceding *d* or *t*, where *-ed* represents the morpheme *past*

So in specifying letter-to-phoneme correspondence rules (reading to pronunciation) the contexts are: (a) idiosyncratic, (b) word position, (c) following letters, plus position in morpheme, plus word category, and (d) preceding letters or sounds, plus word category, plus position in word. But 'complex and context-dependent' is not the same thing as 'irregular', and no competent reader could possibly be assumed to be operating on the basis of unordered multiple correspondences between letters and phonemes.

59

3.6 Spelling and learnèd words

We have noted that a basic principle of English spelling is that it tends to maintain visual identity between morphemes which are related in meaning even if they differ in pronunciation. However, this principle is only fully accessible to someone with an extensive vocabulary of learned words and is therefore not apparent to young children learning to read. Many of the crucial examples for this principle come from words which are quite unlikely to be in a young child's vocabulary, and are for that matter unlikely to be in many adults' vocabularies or to occur frequently in everyday conversation. Some of the most striking examples are with non-native, especially Latinate words. Consider the following pairs, in which the justification of the underlined letter in the first item is only apparent when compared with the second word.

medicine	*medical*
paradigm	*paradigmatic*
existence	*existential*
righteous	*right*
sign	*signal*

A further principle of English spelling is that one form of a word tends to be spelled phonemically. Thus *sign-* in *signal* and *paradigm-* in *paradigmatic* are phonemic spellings. But once the spelling is fixed for these forms, it remains constant, making *sign* and *paradigm* morphologically regular but phonemically irregular.

This principle immediately suggests a teaching technique to cope with this type of spelling error. Suppose a student mis-spells *medicine* as, say, **medsine*. He can be shown the set *medic, medic-al, medic-ate, medic-ine*, either as a simple mnemonic, or in order to explain the underlying principle. (See Keen, 1978, pp. 42ff., who suggests this technique.)

There are hundreds of such sets of words, where in order to know how to spell one word, one has also to know other related words in the language. But the fact that the principle is most evident in this stratum of erudite, often Latinate words, including a network of affixes, suggests that this may be to formulate the principle back-to-front. For, in our literate society, probably a large number of such relatively learned words are acquired through reading. It may be, therefore, that such a principle is essentially opaque to a non-literate speaker, because it is precisely through reading that such words are often learned in any quantity. Obviously there is a paradox involved in this statement: somehow one has to break into the circle. In any case, it is a precise example of why children learning to read must be considered to be distinctly different in their linguistic competence from adults (see 1.1 and Haas, 1970, pp. 69).

I have recently collected many spelling mistakes from my university students' work, and it is clear from many of these that they have never acquired this principle. For example, a student would never write *grammer*, if he had noted the relevance for spelling of the correspondence between *grammar* and *grammatical*. Only *a* is possible in the second syllable of *grammatical* since this vowel is stressed. The same letter is therefore used in *grammar*. The mistakes generally result from confusion over the alternation between stressed and unstressed vowels. Further comparable examples are:

*cognotive cf. cognitive, cognition
*existance cf. existence, existential
*presidence cf. precedence, precede

Written material is a source of new words for the individual reader and also a channel whereby new loan words are introduced into English from other languages. If there is confusion about how a word is pronounced, then this may be evidence that the word has been introduced into the language via written material. An example is *apartheid*, which is pronounced as both /əpɑ·tɛɪt/ and /əpɑ·taɪt/ (Strang, 1970, p. 33).

It is true that children have tacit knowledge of complex phonological and syntactic systems in their language from a very early age. But there are areas of linguistic organization that require some time for children to grasp, and there is evidence that one of these areas is morphology and morphophonemics. The language underlying English spelling is quite clearly the adult language and the system is maintained by adults competent in that language (Ives and Ives, 1973, p. 245).

3.7 Regularity in spelling

What we are pointing to here are general principles underlying the spelling system. It does not follow that these general principles are never broken. For example, the general principle that words which look different are unrelated in meaning is violated by pairs such as:

beast   bestial
absorb   absorption
crux   crucial
pronounce   pronunciation
repeat   repetition

A mis-spelling such as *pronounciation*, which my students often make, shows that in this case they have followed the general principle correctly.

The important point is that there are many fewer such exceptions if the general principles are appreciated. English spelling is not 'regular' in any superficial way, but is more highly organized than is often realised. However, due to the number of different principles involved, 'irregularities' can arise when a more general principle is contradicted by a less general one.

An exception to the general principle of the orthographic stability of morphemes occurs with examples of *in-, im-* and *ir-* as a negative prefix in words such as: *indecisive, indeterminate, inclement, inchoate*, compared with *impossible, imbalance, immoral, irregular, irreversible*. On the one hand, these forms are regular for this set of words. We have the following spelling-pronunciation correspondences:

	spellings			phonemes
negative				
prefix =	*im-*	before *b, p, m*	=	/ɪm/
	ir-	before *r*	=	/ɪr/
	in-	elsewhere	=	/ɪŋ/ before velar sounds /g, k, n/
			=	/ɪn/ elsewhere

On the other hand, this specific rule contradicts the more general rule which states that morpheme variants are not indicated in the spellings if they are predictable from the phonological context. The /n/ versus /m/ alternation is predictable, for example. If the spelling remained consistent with the more general principle, we would write ?*inpossible* and ?*inmoral* and allow the automatic morphophonemic rules of assimilation to take care of the pronunciations. One meaning of 'exception' is that a specific rule contravenes a more general rule.

Note that these comments apply only to cases where *in-* and its variants represent a negative prefix. The same forms can also represent a different prefix meaning 'in' or 'into'. Arguably there are two such further prefixes. Compare:

1	*imbibe*	2	*inborn*
	imprison, impress		*input*
	immigrate		*inmate, inmost*
	irradiate, irruption		*inroads*

There are historical reasons for such variations in the spellings, but these are not known to the majority of speakers of the language and therefore do not concern us directly here. Synchronically, these two sets appear to be distinguished in that for (1) only one syllable in the word receives a main stress, whereas for (2) both syllables are stressed.

Such examples therefore raise the problem of what is meant by 'regularity' or 'irregularity' (see Venezky, 1970). It is often asserted that the spelling of one word is regular, whereas the spelling of another is not. But spellings can only be regular or irregular relative to a particular system. A problem with English spelling is that it demonstrably does not work according to one single system. A spelling can therefore be regular relative to one system, but irregular relative to another.

3.8 Spelling and foreign words

Another major characteristic of English spelling is that words of different linguistic origins are spelled differently. That is, there are different spelling rules for words of Germanic and Romance origin, and miscellaneous foreign borrowings and proper names form a third class or set of classes. There is, in this sense also, no single spelling system: English spelling is polysystemic. (Albrow, 1972, develops this argument in detail.)

Often, isolated words are marked as foreign borrowings, or as being oddities such as trade names, by their spellings. For example, two rules of English spelling are that words may not end in the letters *u* or *v*. To prevent this, *e* is often added as a dummy letter, thus:

argue, (but *argument*), *clue*
love, dove, relative, seductive

Similarly, words may not end in *i*, which is replaced in word-final position by *ie* or *y*. Therefore, the few words which do end in these letters are marked as foreign or as artificial creations:

guru, flu, Bantu, Peru, gnu
spiv, Derv (the trade name)
timpani, ski, pi, Vinci, khaki

Other words which are recognizably foreign because they break the rules for native English spelling are: *llama, bureau.*

In general, there are constraints simply on which sequences of letters may occur in different word-positions. Some sequences of letters do not occur because the corresponding phoneme sequences do not occur in English. Thus there are phonotactic constraints in English which prevent words such as */fnak/ or */viʃtʃ/. But there are also graphotactic constraints on letter sequences as such.

One function of breaking such constraints is to mark the etymology or historical origin of words. For example, *llama* is thus marked as a borrowing from Spanish. This provides a diachronic explanation of the spellings. But such spellings also have a synchronic function, in that they are often international. If the spelling of such words was altered to bring them into line with their English pronunciations and spelling patterns, this function could be destroyed. It is well known that English has borrowed words omnivorously from other languages for hundreds of years. But many English words are also being borrowed into other languages, often from American English. Words which are at present current in French and other languages include *parking, shopping, weekend.* Examples from further afield are not hard to find. For example, Alisjahbana (1971), in an article on literacy in Indonesia and Malaysia, suggests that internationally used Greco-Latin terms should be accepted in Indonesian/Malay, and he points to the problem of spellings. Indonesian/Malay is effectively one single language, but has different spelling conventions, such as:

Indonesian: *museum, stasion*
Malay: *muzium, steshen*

In this discussion, I am referring to words which are recognizably foreign or international to the average reader, and which therefore have a genuine synchronic function in the spelling system. Some spellings would identify loan words only to an expert, but the mere fact of many false etymologies in English spelling demonstrates how limited the relevance of such facts can be for many speakers. For example, the *s* in *island* was introduced on the false assumption that the word was cognate with the French *isle*. But in fact, *island* derives from Old English *iegland* which had no *s*.

On the one hand, one might want to argue that more 'irregular' spellings in English are due to foreign borrowings than to any other cause (Venezky, 1970, p. 121). On the other hand, since such spellings often fulfil the function of marking such words *as* foreign, this is not from this point of view a mere 'irregularity'. The importance of such factors is developed as follows by Strang (1970). She points out (p. 17) that English is probably spoken by 350 to 400 million people as a native language in Britain, the USA, Canada, Australia, New Zealand and South Africa. It is impossible to estimate accurately the number of people who speak English as a near-native language in those countries where it has official status or is used in education, including India and many parts of Africa; or the number who speak it as a foreign language. But such speakers of English as a foreign language must also run into hundreds of millions. The English speech community is of unprecedented size in its history, and so therefore is the bulk of written English. She quotes (p. 73) an estimate that three-quarters of the world's mail is in English. She points out further (p. 28) that, especially in the fields of science and technology, some words are so current internationally that it becomes rather meaningless to enquire into their etymology. She gives the example of *complex*, a word borrowed from Latin, which has been current in English since the seventeenth century. But its psycho-analytic sense was established by Jung, writing in German in 1907. So, in this meaning, it is a borrowing from German. The word *ski* was originally borrowed from Norwegian as /ʃiˑ/, and occurs with the spelling *she-running* in English in the 1850s. But then a general European spelling pronunciation arose as /skiˑ/, and the earlier pronunciation and spelling were displaced.

In the case of words with extensive international status, one can even call into question whether the words or their spellings are English. And in a period when technical vocabulary is growing on an un-precedented scale, the boundary between English and non-English is blurred. Strang (1970, pp. 28, 30, 120-1) argues that the concept of 'English' vocabulary has become less clear cut over the past 400 years, and that many words now belong to the whole of the civilized world. Such points about the relationship between writing systems in different communities will be developed in Chapter 4.

An easy way to gain an idea of the extent of the phenomenon to which Strang is referring is to look at any contemporary book in a foreign language, particularly on an academic or technical subject. For example, all the following words, recognizable to an English speaker, occur on the first page of a recent book in German on linguistics (Schmidt, 1976, p. 1). Note, however, that less than half a dozen of the words are concerned exclusively with linguistics:

> *politisch, publiziert, Thema, Disziplin, intensiv, kritisch, Texttheorie, zitiert, Diskussion, Interesse, Prozess, Kommunikation, konzentriert, intern, Struktur, konkret, sozial, isoliert, funktional, Produktion, Linguistik, analytisch, Philosophie, Fakt, strukturalistisch, generativ, Grammatik, Charakter*

Most of these words would also be recognizable to speakers of other European languages. Several of the words cited occur more than once on the same page, or occur also in different forms (e.g., *Theorie, theore-tisch*). Further, such words become even more recognizable once certain common affixes are known, including *-iert* (e.g., *publiziert, konzentriert, zitiert, isoliert*) which marks recent foreign borrowings (*published, concentrated, cited, isolated*).

Such international functions of English spelling are of central importance when English is considered in its role as a world language. They are, however, completely beyond the needs, experience or interests of young children learning to read. (See Chapter 5.)

3.9 Incompatible demands on a spelling system

We have seen in some detail now that English spelling is not based on one single principle, for example, that of consistent sound-letter correspondences. On the contrary, it is a mixed system. It is quite inadequate to dismiss it as 'irregular' or 'out of date'. However, it is equally clearly not a single integrated system, but based on several different organizing principles which are often inevitably in conflict. The complexity of the system arises from different sub-sets of rules, which tend to be fairly consistent in themselves, but which are not obviously related. In other words, the system is based on several general principles, which are in themselves fairly straightforward, and which have to be carefully considered by anyone involved with the teaching of reading or with spelling reform; but the realization and integration of these principles is not always consistent. Presumably the extreme claim by Chomsky and Halle (1968) that English spelling is 'near optimal' has to be interpreted in this light. The system is based on near optimal principles, but the working out of these principles is not always consistent or well integrated.

I am not therefore arguing that the present system is optimal or even near optimal. For practical reasons, which I will discuss in Chapter 4, I do not think that any reform at all is likely in the foreseeable future. But by taking a functional view, I have tried to show some advantages in the organization of the system as it stands. I have tried to illustrate that, far from being optimal, the English spelling system represents, on the contrary, a fairly good compromise solution to several incompatible demands. Given the role of English as a world language, as well as the native language of millions of adults and children, the writing system has to serve fluent adult users, young learners, and foreign users of every degree of competence, as well as serving the different needs of readers and writers. As it stands, English spelling is biased clearly in favour of native adult users, but no single system could possibly be optimal for all these groups.

3.10 Some implications for teaching reading

There is no room here to discuss the precise implications of this view of English spelling for actual teaching strategies in the classroom. It is not evident, in any case, that any recommendations about teaching practice can be shown to follow directly from any particular theoretical view of spelling. It is possible, however, to mention two important general implications for teachers of reading.

First, consider, for example, the following rules of English spelling. The first two were discussed above; Albrow (1972) discusses the second two.

1   No word, except foreign borrowings, ends in *-i, -u* or *-v*.

2   Predictable morphophonemic variation in spoken language is ignored by the spelling system.

3   Word-initially in grammatical words (i.e. articles, pronouns, conjunctions) *th* is pronounced /ð/. Examples are *the, this, that, then, though*. Word-initially in lexical words (i.e. nouns, verbs, adjectives, adverbs) *th* is pronounced /θ/. Examples are *thin, thick, thought*.

4   Only grammatical words (i.e. pronouns, conjunctions, auxiliary verbs, prepositions, articles) may have less than three letters. Examples of grammatical words with one or two letters are: *I, a, me, we, be, am, of*. The only relatively common lexical word with less than three letters is *ox*. Other exceptions are artificial creations or foreign: *id, em* (a printing term), and so on. (Incidentally, the American spelling *ax* breaks this rule and is not a good revision, for this reason. The letter *x* is unique in the English alphabet, in that it is the only single letter which can represent a two-phoneme string, /ks/.)

Such a list of rules could be extended, but the point is already made. Individually, such rules are quite clear cut. But they operate at rather different levels of abstraction: relating variously to constraints on letter sequences, word classes and morphophonemics. In addition, such individual rules are not obviously related to each other. This provides a major teaching problem, for although it is important for the teacher to understand such characteristics of the spelling system, it is not at all obvious just what ought to be explained to the pupil.

It has been argued that it takes children, on average, one or two years longer to learn to read English than it takes them to learn to read other European languages which use varieties of the Roman alphabet. Such comparisons are always difficult and approximate, but let us assume that the estimate is meaningful. Let us assume also that the major reason lies in the spelling system, rather than in the multitude of cultural factors, including parental attitudes, differences in the educational systems, and so on. It has then been further argued that the reason is that English spelling is 'antiquated', 'irregular' and so on, and that children are confused by 'illogical' features of the system. It has been argued, for example by Pitman and St John (1969, pp. 53-4), that the system of English spelling can frustrate the child's logic and permanently damage his faith and ability to reason things out.

Although we have clearly rejected this superficial formulation, it might be that children are confused by the number of different subsystems operating. But even this need not necessarily follow. The reason for confusion may be that children simply do not have things explained to them correctly. They may be taught that letters correspond to sounds, which is true only some of the time. Or they may be taught that words have to be read as wholes, which is again only partly true. On common-sense grounds alone, it would seem only sensible not to mislead children. One reason why some children have problems in reading may be that they are told that English spelling works in one way, when in fact it works in several different other ways. Beyond these general comments, there are important pedagogical problems which we cannot discuss here. For example, should all the complexities be explained? And in what order? Or should children be started on a deliberately simplified writing system which does operate according to a single basic principle? (ITA is an attempt, although not entirely systematic, along those lines.)

A second, more positive, implication is as follows. We have seen in some detail that it is impossible to read a passage of English intelligibly if one does not understand quite a lot about how the language works. English spelling is designed for native speakers of English, and it is impossible to read English correctly without, for example, making decisions about stress-placement, allomorphic alternations, morpheme boundaries, and so on. Conversely, an adult who can read English could learn in an afternoon to read any passage of Spanish so that his pronunciation would at least be understandable to a Spaniard, although the reader might not understand a word of what he was reading. This is because Spanish has a fairly consistently phonemic spelling system.

Suppose we accept then that it does take children, on average, longer to learn to read in English. At the end of this time, they have learned, generally unconsciously, a lot about the morphology and syntactic organization of English, as well as learning to read. Since they have to learn this anyway, it would be helpful to explain to them explicitly as much of this as is appropriate. This might help their reading, and in any case it would teach them a lot about how English works as a language.

3.11 Attitudes to spelling mistakes

It might be appropriate to add here a brief note on attitudes to spelling mistakes. To illustrate such attitudes, I take more or less at random two items from a national and a local newspaper. The *Guardian* of 30 January 1978 reported on the comments made by the Chief Examiners of the GCE Board about purported declining standards of English amongst teenagers. The article reported that spelling and pronunciation mistakes were reaching 'epidemic proportions'. Whether or not the original remarks by the examiners were accurately reported is irrelevant here. What is important is that it was felt worthy of report in the national press that many teenagers write *thank you* as one word (a spelling 'mistake' that I have to admit I often make myself in personal letters). The *Derby Trader* of 29 March 1978 published an article entitled 'The disgrace in our skools'. The author complained about an example of a spelling mistake (*properley*) made by a teacher, and writes:

> Teachers should be licensed — and hauled in front of the bench every time they make a spelling mistake. Endorsement should be automatic upon conviction.... My wife and I are over 50.... Our elder son and daughter are aged 23 and 20.... The younger has gone to Oxford.... One cannot spell for toffee.

Readers must often have come across items and been involved in discussions about purported declining standards in spelling.

There is a powerful convention that words in English should have one fixed spelling. But it is simply a convention, which has developed over only the last two hundred years, but did not hold before that. When we complain that students 'can't spell these days' we should be clear what we are objecting to. Unless the errors are particularly gross, there are rarely any problems of communication. Given the following sentence, there is no ambiguity about what it means: *Their are several seperate reasons why grammer is important.* But it breaks strong social conventions.

Let me be explicit that I am not saying that spelling is not important. Spelling is clearly important, because people attach so much importance to it. What people think is important. (See 2.4.)

Children require an explanation of the genuine linguistic principles which underlie English spelling, of the strong social conventions attached to spelling, and also an explanation that linguistic and social rules are, in principle, quite distinct. It is only fair to warn pupils that if they write a letter to a prospective employer which contains spelling mistakes, they will probably not get the job. Written language is heavily standardized and conventionalized, and learning these conventions is part of acquiring literacy. However, pupils also deserve an explanation of why standard spelling is regarded as a key to the good life, when this equation is not self-evident.

Chapter 4

Spelling and society

The last chapter illustrated some principles underlying the English spelling system, and although it concentrated primarily on the internal, linguistic relations between orthographic symbols, phonemes and morphemes, it was impossible even there to exclude all references to the social uses of the writing system. But in order to account further for the form of the writing system, we must now look more directly at the conflicting pressures placed on it by the societies which use it.

4.1 Why has English spelling never been reformed?

We shall approach the question again from the point of view of possible reform. Why is it that the spelling system has remained unchanged in spite of some four hundred years of reform and continuing complaints about some obvious inconsistencies in it?

It is likely that English spelling used to be based on much closer grapheme-phoneme correspondences than it is now. We do not have direct information on the phonology of early English, since we have to make inferences about the sound system on the basis of written forms. But the spelling conventions were fixed in their major characteristics around five hundred years ago, and apart from minor details, the spelling has hardly changed since around 1650. Since this time, the pronunciation of English has changed considerably. In fact, to confound the issue, major changes in pronunciation were occurring between 1400 and 1600, at precisely the same time as the spelling conventions were becoming codified. In addition, the alphabet we use was not originally designed for English at all, but for a foreign language spoken around two thousand years ago: a system designed for a Semitic language was adapted by the Greeks, and further adapted by the Romans. We use a variety of this Roman alphabet. (Gelb, 1963 and Diringer, 1962 give standard accounts of this development.)

However, to say that we are using a borrowed alphabet, with not enough letters for the phonemes of English, and that the relationship between spoken and written English has changed as pronunciation has made the spelling out of date, is only to propose a historical or diachronic explanation for why the spelling is like it is. It does not explain why the system is not reformed.

The last chapter proposed that English spelling is rather more strongly motivated on strictly synchronic and linguistic grounds than is often realized; but it is clearly not ideal. From the point of view of strictly linguistic criteria, there would not be too much difficulty in producing a better, more consistent system than we have at present, although we have already seen that any system would involve compromises between phonemic and morphological regularity, between readers and writers, and between other linguistic and psycholinguistic demands. There are no serious problems; and several systems have already been published which are more consistent on certain linguistic grounds than traditional orthography. Examples are Regularized English (Wijk, 1959), Anglic (Zachrison, 1930), the Initial Teaching Alphabet (Pitman and St John, 1969), New Spelling (see MacCarthy, 1969), and other suggestions (e.g., by Joos, 1960). I emphasize that we might disagree over the direction of the linguistic compromises even within these systems, which have, after all, made different decisions about several problems. My personal view is that Wijk and Pitman have made wrong decisions over morphophonemic correspondences, that Joos pays too much attention to regional accent differences, and so on. Nevertheless, one broad type of aim, which would gain a large consensus amongst linguists, would be a basically phonemic system, with bi-directional phoneme-grapheme correspondences as far as possible, but compromising this requirement where necessary, to maintain stable orthographic forms for morphemes. This ideal is proposed, for example, by Haugen (1966: p. 514), Nida (1975: p. 229), and Garvin (1954).

The major reasons why spelling has never been reformed must, therefore, be sought in sociolinguistic, social and technological factors. The first principle of applied sociolinguistics must be: it does not matter how elegant, rigorous, or systematic your linguistic analysis is, if the native speakers do not like it, then it is a waste of time. Or, more briefly: if it does not work in practice, then it is bad theory. There are many cases on record of linguists producing elegant and consistent writing systems for languages (including English) only to have them remain unused because the potential users rejected them for various reasons. (See 4.3, 4.4.)

The English writing system, even more than most, is embedded in a

71

powerful social and technological network with enormously complex inter-relations, and therefore enormous inertia against change. The network includes: the attitudes of its millions of users; educational systems and libraries; the publishing trades with the demands of machine printing; international communications and the role of English as a world language; and the relation between English and other languages and writing systems. Any change in the system would have enormous attitudinal, institutional, technological, and therefore economic repercussions, and it would be a brave government which would bring in such changes in a (the?) principle medium of modern world communication.

In explaining why English spelling is not reformed, simple conservatism and the inertia of habits and tradition undoubtedly have a part to play. People invest considerable effort in learning to read and write a complex morphophonemic system such as English spelling, and are unwilling to abandon it. And the first comment often made about proposed reformed spellings is a quasi-esthetic one that 'they don't look right' or that 'they look illiterate'. There are, furthermore, social functions (which I would not want to defend) in writing systems which are difficult to learn. They may be just what a leisured class has the leisure to acquire, providing for a small social group a mark of education, as well as all the incidental pleasures of a system which allows its educated users to discover analogies with foreign and classical languages, and snippets of linguistic history (see Haas, 1969, p. 5). Whatever linguists and educationalists may say, someone who can spell well is often regarded as well-educated, hence the frequency of spelling bees on radio and television quiz programmes (such as *Brain of Britain*). The most extreme example of this kind of linguistic conservatism and elitism is probably the Chinese traditional writing system, which was said to take twenty years for full mastery.

However, to attribute linguistic conservatism to the moral conservatism of speakers and readers is to propose a relatively superficial and circular explanation, and we have to look beyond psychological explanations to the social functions of writing systems.

4.2   Checklist of criteria for writing systems

We can set out a checklist of the types of conflicting criteria which any writing system has to meet, proceeding very roughly via partly overlapping categories from internal linguistic criteria to external social and cultural pressures.

1   *Linguistic* (as discussed in Chapter 3): Is the system economic,

consistent, unambiguous in terms of the number of its symbols, its phonemic and morphological representations, etc?

2   *Psycholinguistic*: Does the system respect the psycholinguistic processes of reading and writing? (This is not discussed in any detail in this book.)

3   *Educational*: Is the system easy and quick for native and/or foreign learners? (See 3.6, 3.10.)

4   *Sociolinguistic*: (a) *Internal*: Does the system relate in appropriate ways to different social and regional language varieties (See 6.3, 6.4, 6.5.) (b) *External*: Does the system relate in appropriate ways to other writing systems and languages in use in culturally important language communities? or to other systems already in use in the community? (See 4.3, 4.4, 4.7, 4.8.)

5   *Cultural*: Are the attitudes of the users favourable? e.g. do they find it aesthetically satisfactory? (See 4.5, 4.6.)

6   *Technological*: Is the system suited to the requirements of modern machine printing, information storage, etc? (See 4.5.)

These categories clearly overlap, but such a checklist shows immediately that the development or reform of a writing system is a sociolinguistic problem in language and culture (see Garvin, 1954). It is also clear immediately that these criteria will often conflict. A writing system may, for example, be pedagogically ideal for young children because it represents the language in a consistent way; and yet it may, by using a different system from that in use in the wider language community, cut its users off from cultural and economic opportunities. Alternatively, an orthography may be linguistically consistent, having one-to-one phoneme-grapheme correspondences; and yet may be economically impractical because it uses many special symbols which printers do not normally have and which they are unwilling to have specially made for a small book-reading public in a minority language.

In order to gain some distance from the question and also to get some comparative data, it is useful to consider the problems which linguists face when they have to devise writing systems for previously unwritten languages or languages with no satisfactory and standardized writing system. We will then see that entirely comparable problems explain why there has always been such resistance to any reform of English spelling. Useful summary articles of the social and linguistic problems characteristically encountered in setting up writing systems for pre-literate communities are Berry (1958), Sjoberg (1966) and Fishman (1971). This chapter will draw on these articles as well as many other more specific studies.

4.3 A case-study of Ponapean

Garvin (1954) gives a now classic case-study of his work in setting up a revised spelling system for Ponapean in Micronesia. The speech community comprised about five thousand seven hundred people, most of the adults and adolescents being already partially literate.

A major problem was that Ponapean has two main dialect divisions which differ in their phoneme inventories. Any spelling system which consistently represented one accent would be rejected by the speakers of the other variety. A further problem was that there were already at least five other spelling systems in degrees of use and disuse, due to a changeable history of colonization by the USA, Germany, Spain and Japan, with their various attendant administrations, missions and education systems. As Garvin says (1954, p. 129):

> The problem of devising an acceptable spelling system, which initially might have appeared purely, or at least primarily, a linguistic matter, upon closer inspection thus turned out to be a language and culture problem par excellence. At each step linguistic judgment had to be tempered by the consideration of cultural attitudes, traditions, and even prejudices.

It was not therefore possible to devise a spelling system which would represent the phonology of both dialects consistently. Garvin could not select one variety to be represented consistently by the spelling, since the system would not then have served the whole island. Solutions were found which violated one-to-one grapheme-phoneme correspondences, but which were a compromise between the accents and were therefore accepted by the native speakers. All the time Garvin worked with a commission of native speakers representing the different dialect regions. This proved essential for gauging the possible attitudes to the proposals, as well as for making detailed judgments at all levels. Also Garvin had to take into account the native speakers' knowledge of other spelling systems, and their consciousness of such relationships. Often, for example, the native speakers were willing to accept a particular solution to some problem when it was explained to them that this solution was used in German or French or some other socially prestigious writing system.

It should be clear even from this very brief summary that comparable problems would face any revision of English spelling:

1   There is no single standard English accent. There are both different standard accents, including RP (Received Pronunciation), and an educated Scottish standard, and different American standards, and also a wide range of regional and social variation in accent beyond those. (See 6.4.) The choices are (a) to select one accent for consistent phonemic

representation, thus favouring speakers of this accent and causing problems for everyone else; or (b) to compromise on a consistent phonemic representation so that a wider range of accents is accommodated, although inconsistently at the phonemic level. The present English spelling system is a type (b) solution which therefore has powerful social functions.

2   Readers of English have deeply ingrained and semi-automatic habits in using the present system, and any new system would have to take account of these. It would be totally unrealistic, for example, to replace the present system by another suddenly: they would at least have to be used side-by-side for years. In addition, readers of English are highly sensitive to the relations between English spelling and the systems used by other world languages (see below).

4.4   A case-study of Haitian Creole

A case where severe conflicts have arisen between a linguistically consistent orthography and cultural demands is Haiti (Berry, 1958; Burns, 1953; Ferguson, 1959; Hall, 1972; Valdmann, 1968, 1973). One orthography which was set up was impeccable on purely linguistic grounds, but was rejected by its users and had to be replaced by a less consistent but culturally more appropriate system. Haiti provides a well-documented example of the various factors which have to be taken into account in devising a writing system: not only the phonemic analysis of the language but also people's reasons for acquiring literacy, the dialect situation, and the relation of local and world languages.

Haiti is in the Caribbean, about seventy miles from Cuba. The present population is probably between five and six million. When it was owned by France in the eighteenth century it was the richest colony in the West Indies. In 1804 a slave revolt defeated Napoleon and formed the first free Black state. From 1957 to 1971 the president was Francois Duvalier (Papa Doc); under his reign of terror, foreign aid dried up, and Haiti is now regarded as the poorest country in the western world. Duvalier's son is now president for life.

The official language is French, which has a local standard very close to Parisian French, but this is spoken by only 10 per cent of the population. The 90 per cent majority, who are mostly illiterate, are monolingual in Haitian Creole, a French-based Creole, which is mutually unintelligible with standard French. There is great variation in the Creole however, from rural varieties (known as *gros créole* or *créole natif-natale*) to a high prestige variety spoken in the capital, Port-au-Prince, which has an emerging unified standard form. A small literate social elite are diglossic (Ferguson, 1959) in French and the Port-au-Prince variety of Creole. That is, they are bidialectal, tending to use French in formal settings and Creole in informal settings. The functional relation between French and Creole is changing, however, and there is a growing tendency to use Creole more frequently, even in formal public settings, and a growing consensus that Creole is the national language. Nevertheless, French is the dominant cultural language, and literacy in Creole is regarded only as a bridge to French.

The first attempt at an orthography for Creole was by McConnell, an Irish priest, in 1941. This was a consistently phonemic system, based on the International Phonetic Alphabet (IPA), although it was marginally amended by Laubach in 1943 to bring it slightly closer to French conventions. A literacy campaign was started with the McConnell–Laubach system, and a newspaper was published in Creole, but the impetus was lost by the end of the 1940s. For the most part the McConnell–Laubauch system deliberately rejected French spelling and devised an orthography which took account of the phonological structure of Creole as a language in its own right, drawing on IPA to provide symbols for one-to-one phoneme-grapheme correspondences. On linguistic grounds it was an ideal system, but it ignored various cultural demands which the speakers made of a writing system; crucially it ignored the reasons why people wanted to become literate in Creole. Political arguments were quickly put forward against the system: it was pointed out that it needlessly exaggerated the differences between Creole and French orthography, that it used foreign, non-French symbols, (that the inventors were themselves foreign!), that it did not provide a bridge to literacy in French, and that it therefore restricted the economic mobility of Creole speakers.

It might be thought on *a priori* grounds that speakers of a language would welcome an orthography tailor-made for their language, and which treats their language as a variety in its own right with its own patterns and regularities, and does not impose the system from another language upon it. But speakers' attitudes to their language are not always evident to outsiders. It often happens with minority languages that their own speakers devalue them in relation to a neighbouring national language. This fact has been noted with speakers of Creoles, French Canadians, and speakers of non-standard dialects of English (Lambert, 1967; Hall, 1972). In addition, McConnell and Laubach misunderstood the dialect situation and designed the orthography to suit *gros créole*, a low-prestige variety regarded as a country bumpkin language by the natives. The system confused, then, the functions of a phonemic transcription with a writing system (see 6.2), and ignored the functions of literacy in Creole for its users.

Subsequently, the Faublas–Pressoir system was developed for Creole, and is now adopted by official and religious organizations. It introduced French spelling conventions where this did not disturb bi-directional phoneme-grapheme correspondences. And it was based on the high-prestige Port-au-Prince variety.

4.5 The requirements of typography and machine printing

Pressures on writing systems can therefore be nationalistic and atti-tudinal, economic and commercial. In the next sections we will look at these technological and cultural restraints.

Advanced literacy depends on a large volume of available material which is clearly printed: handwritten manuscripts are not only slow and expensive to produce, but also much more difficult to read fast than printed matter. Havelock (1976, pp. 68ff.) points out how much our whole concept of literacy depends on the technology which allows books to be produced in bulk and in forms which are easy to read and consult. It is often stated (e.g., by Goody and Watt, 1962/3) that the Greek democracy of the fifth century BC was literate. But Havelock points out that there must have been fairly severe restrictions on their literacy, due to the character of the materials available to them. Writing was done on stone, baked clay, wax tablets, parchment or papyrus. Widespread literacy cannot be based on inscriptions, since there are not enough of them; and rolls of parchment are awkward to consult. He argues that rapid reading, and hence full literacy in the sense in which we understand the term, would have been difficult to achieve due to such material constrictions, and that, without large volumes of materials to practice on, reading was probably constricted, deliberate and careful. A major factor in the development of effective and full-scale literacy is therefore the development of machine printing.

The English alphabet is remarkable amongst other Roman alphabets in use for European languages in that it uses (a) no diacritics: compare French é, à, etc.; German à, ü, etc.; and similarly for other languages. I am discounting the dot on the *i* since users do not regard it as a dia-critic, but as an integral part of the letter, and since it occurs in all other European alphabets. It uses (b) no letters of unusual shapes; com-pare German β, Danish ø, etc. and (c) no ligatures: compare French œ, Danish æ, etc. (Vachek, 1973, pp. 49–50). Such items may on occasion be used in English for foreign words, but none have to be. This has the disadvantage of making a large number of digraphs (e.g., *ie, sh, ea,* etc.) necessary, many of them ambiguous. But it has enormous practical and aesthetic advantages.

Esthetic and impressionistic considerations are not negligible. Quite apart from the question of type-design and letter shapes, a page of English looks distinctively different from pages of printing in most other European languages. The overall impression is largely due to the complete absence of accents and diacritics, which gives words a clearer outline, more distinctive overall shape and probably higher legibility. These characteristics immediatey touch also on purely practical concerns. Accents and diacritics are time-consuming to write and type; writers tend to miss them out, leading to ambiguities; and printers, in the past at least, did not like them because they are easily broken on metal founts and wear out quickly. The lack of diacritics and unusual letter shapes also has the crucial practical advantage that English can be typed or printed anywhere in the world that has a standard Roman typewriter keyboard or a basic stock of Roman characters. Such factors are of major importance, given the function of written language in the modern world and the role of English as an international language.

The typewriter is now a major factor in the use of any writing system, and English as it stands at present is easy for typists compared with other Roman alphabets. For example, German requires upper case letters word-initially in all nouns. This might appear to be a useful morphological device, but it breaks the flow and is time-consuming for typists. In any case, the fact that this device is not used in other European languages presumably means that it provides redundant information for readers. Similarly, any system with accents or diacritics requires either extra keys with whole signs (e.g., for French ç, é, è, etc.), or dummy keys for signs (such as ˆ, ¨) which do not move the carriage forward, or some system which requires the typist to back-space. If we followed a system which required extra letters to cope with the forty-two or so phonemes of English, then this would immediately make all typewriter keyboards obsolete and would require less compact machines to accommodate the dozen or more extra characters. A typewriter is, of course, hopelessly unwieldy for a morphemic writing system like Chinese, and this must have been a major consideration in the decision of the government to introduce a Roman orthography alongside a simplified system of characters.

A machine which moves the carriage forward by the same amount after each letter also puts constraints on the writing system. In English it means only that thin letters (like *i*) look rather isolated, whilst fat letters (like *m*) appear squashed. On the other hand, different letter widths and outlines of letters can increase legibility. The printed Cyrillic alphabet contrasts strongly with Roman on such characteristics: all the letters are more or less the same width; and there is only one ascender and only one clear descender, plus two rather ill-defined descenders. As a result, no words have particularly distinctive overall shapes. Hebrew is similar to Cyrillic in these respects.

It turns out, then, that questions of visual appeal, legibility and the requirements of machine printing are closely related problems. Some scripts are definitely handicapped for modern use since esthetic factors conflict with the needs of machine printing. For example, Arabic has a script with a long tradition of calligraphy. The Koran has been believed to be the actual words of God, and there has therefore been a great concern with the written word and with copying and preserving it. It is the most widely used script in the world after the Roman alphabet, and because of the wide spread of Islam (see 4.8), it has been used in the past for Slav languages, Spanish, Persian, Urdu, Turkish, Berber, Swahili, Malay and Sudanese, although in many cases it has now been replaced in these languages by Roman scripts. It has several characteristics which make it awkward for machine printing. The script has seventeen outline characters, to which dots can be added above and below, giving twenty-eight characters. Certain characters must be joined to the neighbouring letters, whilst others can be joined only to the following letters. Letter forms differ according to the position of the character in the word: lone or word-final letters terminate in a bold stroke, but initial and medial letters are much abbreviated. Printing has to try and simulate these characteristics, which are really only suitable for hand-writing. Because printing cannot easily allow letter shapes to overlap, yet the writing requires some letters to be joined and so on, letter shapes have to be distorted, and a lot of wasted white space is left on the printed page.

Chinese and Japanese writing systems are similarly well known for their long traditions of calligraphy, and have features which are not easy to transfer to printing. Given the relatively few letters in the Roman alphabet, for example, it is possible to design many new type-faces: an estimate is that between eight and ten thousand typefaces have been designed since Gutenberg. But Japanese has around one thousand eight hundred and fifty Kanji characters (logograms) in daily use, plus two syllabaries of forty-eight characters each, which are normally used in a mixed writing system in most printed material, with Kanji and syllabic characters alongside each other in the same sentence. As a result of this enormous number of characters to redesign, Japanese has had only two typefaces to choose from up until the 1960s, when a third was introduced.

Evans (1977) discusses the series of different typefaces which have been used for printing the *Sunday Times*, on the occasion of the recent introduction of a newly designed typeface for the newspaper. He lists the main factors requiring consideration as being: legibility, involving especially letter-width and the comparative size of letters with and without ascenders and descenders; economy of space; and the particular requirements of very rapid printing on thin newsprint.

A major consideration in machine printing and later storage of printed books and articles is simply the amount of space which words occupy. This also affects the amount of print a fluent reader can scan in single eye-movements. It is significant that the few changes in English spelling which are trickling into use via printed material are in the direction of shorter spellings which economize on space. Scragg (1974, pp. 85ff.) cites such examples as the tendency to abandon digraphs such as *ae, oe* in words like *encyclopedia, medieval, fetid, hemorrhage*, although this process is not complete and two spellings are still seen for these words. Other random examples include *hiccough* to *hiccup*; *curtsey* to *curtsy*; and *focussed* to *focused*. Scragg estimates that 'brevity is the keynote of present developments in spelling'. In a pre-printing age, this was not necessarily the case. Scragg also notes (1974, p. 52) that throughout the Middle Ages etymological spellings such as the longer Latinate *pauvre* for *povre* were particularly favoured in legal language, since lawyers' clerks were paid for their writing by the inch!

One example of a shorter spelling becoming 'official' was reported by Ezard in The *Guardian* of 21 August 1978. The article concerns the publication of the thirty-eighth edition of *Hart's Rules for Compositors and Readers* at the University Press, Oxford. Different newspapers and printing houses have their own style-sheets and official style of spelling, but Hart's is widely accepted as a general standard. Among other changes, the thirty-eighth edition adopts the American spelling *gram* as a metric measure, instead of *gramme*. This brings the spelling into line with *telegram*. But in Britain, *program* is still used only for *computer program*, retaining *programme* for other uses.

Shortness is not everything however, and may be overriden on other grounds. Forms such as *thru, tho* and *nite* have never shown any sign of catching on in Britain, except in very restricted contexts such as advertising. Economic arguments are of no use if the users' attitudes are against the change. Some American spellings 'look illiterate' because they break the rules of English spelling. For example, *thru* breaks the rule that no words, except foreign borrowings, end in *u* (3.8). *Ax* breaks the rule that only grammatical words, including prepositions, pronouns and conjunctions, can have less than three letters (3.10). *Ox* is the only other relatively common word to break this rule.

The savings of space and time for writers and printers were the major reasons why George Bernard Shaw advocated spelling reform (MacCarthy, 1969; Shaw, 1962). He pointed out the wastage involved in writing redundant letters, in learning their use, and so on. The alphabet which was eventually designed in accordance with Shaw's wishes, as expressed in his will, uses simple letter shapes, the simplest for the most frequent, does not have redundant letters to the extent that English spelling has at present, and in all takes up considerably less space on the page than traditional orthography. It consists, however, of a totally non-Roman alphabet, since Shaw argued that there were not enough Roman letters for English phonemes, and that modified spellings looked simply 'illiterate'. These points are valid, as is his economic argument. But to propose a totally non-Roman alphabet is to ignore so many other factors as to condemn Shavian to the oblivion in which it now lies. These factors include the present readers' semi-automatic familiarity with the Roman alphabet, the amount of retraining necessary for teachers, printers, and so on, the need to translate printed material into a new alphabet, and the relations between English spelling and other European and world languages.

4.6   The power of edited print

There are reasons other than purely technological why printed matter has a powerful braking effect on changes in spelling. Joos (1960) has pointed out one of the major mechanisms which prevent new spellings from ever becoming current in printed matter. Suppose an author initially writes some form such as *nite* or *thru* in his manuscript. An author's manuscript does not pass directly to a printer. It is most likely retyped by a secretary, then checked by at least one editor and most probably by several people, and finally set up in type. Typists are taught to play safe, and to 'spell things out in full'. Editors have the reputation of their publishing houses and authors to protect. The copy-setter is working to house rules explicitly laid out in such manuals of usage as *Hart's Rules for Compositors*. As Joos points out, only a fanatic would try to get a novel spelling through this filter, whose power derives from the fact that nobody likes to appear uneducated. (Precisely the same pressures serve to standardize the punctuation, vocabulary, grammar and style of printed material.) Joos's arguments are in the context of a review of a projected reformed spelling for English (Wijk, 1959), and although he has many good things to say about the scheme on purely linguistic grounds, his view is that 'it is written as though for another world' and has no hope whatsoever of implementation.

A powerful brake on any change in the present writing system is therefore the circularity in the process which determines how forms are defined as correct. Authors, editors and compositors all consult standard dictionaries when in doubt about spellings. But standard dictionaries are themselves compiled from the spellings which appear in what is regarded as the best printed material. The author, editor or compositor consults the dictionary, which is compiled from printed matter, and therefore continues to spell as previous printed matter has done before. Samuel Johnson compiled his Dictionary of 1755 almost entirely from what he regarded as the best practice of the time and this process has not changed in its essentials.

In fact, dictionaries are amongst our most stable and conservative institutions. Quirk (1977) discusses the reasons for this lack of innovation in dictionary making, where procedures have changed only marginally since the eighteenth century. The first reason is financial: new dictionaries are very expensive to produce. Webster's Third International Dictionary of 1961 represented an investment of three-and-a-half million dollars. Dictionary makers cannot risk innovations which might mean losing customers to rivals, hence their policy of selling a dictionary to every home, and promoting them as a dependable institution, not unlike the Bible. Second, the dictionary maker's recourse to printed material is understandable, since it means that the evidence for words is citable and verifiable, and many words in spoken language may have a short life. On the other hand, print is only an infinitesimal fraction of all the language used, and if a word is only recognized as being in the language when it is attested in print, then dictionaries will always be out of date. Third, Quirk simply points out that lexicological theory has advanced little over the past two hundred years or so. There is no coherent theory, for example, of how new words come to be established in a language, or conversely how words drop out and become obsolete.

4.7 The wider writing community: cultural, political and economic

The cultural affinity between languages and nations can often be a major factor in the choice of a script, and affects both major world languages and minority languages.

A clear-cut case of a conflict between linguistic factors and the relations between languages in the wider cultural community occurs with Eskimo (Sjoberg, 1966, p. 265). The phonological structure of Eskimo is particularly well suited to a syllabic writing system, and a syllabary is still used amongst the eastern Eskimo in Canada, although various Roman orthographies are also used alongside it. The syllabary was introduced to the Eskimos in 1878, and is deeply entrenched. Since 1953 it has been used alongside a Roman orthography in a Canadian government-sponsored periodical. In addition, many linguists would argue that a syllabary is preferable for those languages with a suitable phonological structure, and a syllabary is therefore possibly easier to learn. However, although a syllabary is arguably efficient on linguistic and pedagogical grounds, and is widely used and accepted by the Eskimo, it is clearly at odds with the broader socio-cultural needs of the Eskimos' place in Canadian society. Children might find the Roman alphabet not ideally suited to their language. But the use of a Roman alphabet would facilitate their learning to read and write English (or French) and ultimately make it easier for them to find jobs in Canada or the USA. Thus the short-term educational needs of the individual are in conflict with the longer-term economic and cultural needs of the individual and of the social group. This type of conflict is always most clear cut when it is between the language system of a small ethnic group and an international language such as English.

We require, then, the concept of a writing community (Berry, 1958, p. 741) to which a language belongs; that is, the community comprising the neighbouring trade, official and cultural languages with which it is important to be in contact. In the case of major national and international languages, the choice of script can directly symbolize political and cultural affinities. Well-known cases involve the USSR, Turkey, China and Germany.

Soviet Union

The interpretation of Soviet policy which is given by several Western commentators (Goody, 1968, p. 23; Goodman, 1960; Steinberg, 1961, p. 289) is as follows. Lenin favoured Roman script, and described Romanization as 'The great revolution of the East'. In the early 1920s he set up a commission to investigate the possibility of a revised Roman alphabet for Russian. After the revolution of 1917 efforts were made for about ten years to introduce Roman alphabets for non-Russian languages spoken in the USSR. By 1933 it was reported that seventy-two previously unwritten languages had been given alphabets, sixty-four Roman-based, and that many scripts (e.g., Arabic) had been Romanized. But after 1930 all these new orthographies were replaced by Cyrillic equivalents. Intensified nationalism under Stalin put an end to the policy of Romanization and introduced undisguised Russification. Roman alphabets were converted to Cyrillic with the expressed aim of broadening the influence of Russian culture in the USSR and accelerating the learning of the Russian language. Certainly, the use of Roman alphabets often meant that pupils were using different writing systems for their native languages and for Russian. At the end of the 1930s almost all nationalities in the USSR adopted the Cyrillic alphabet which gives easier transition to the national language. (Comrie and Stone, 1978, especially ch. 8, give further details about spelling reforms in Russian itself.)

A Soviet account of language planning policy in the USSR is given by Isayev (1977), and his interpretation differs from that stated briefly above. He provides first a great deal of information on the extremely complex language situation in the USSR, based on the 1970 census. About one hundred and thirty languages are spoken in the USSR, from at least five or six genetically unrelated language families. (Not all the genetic relations are yet understood.) Eighty-five per cent of the population speak an Indo-European language, that is, one of the group of languages to which Russian itself belongs (along with English, French, German, Latin, etc.). Russian is the native language of over 50 per cent of the population, and around 75 per cent speak Russian or one of the closely related East Slavic languages, Byelorussian or Ukrainian. But large numbers of speakers speak quite unrelated languages: for example, there are twenty-five million speakers of some twenty-five closely related Turkic languages alone. (The total population of the USSR is around two hundred and fifty million.)

In 1917, four different scripts were in use, their using being related to different religions. Cyrillic and Roman alphabets were used by some Christian peoples. Jews in East Europe and Central Asia used Hebrew script. An ancient writing system was used by members of the Lamaist faith. And Arabic script was used by sixteen Moslem ethnic groups in the USSR, in Central Asia and the Caucasus, for three genetically unrelated groups of languages: Indo-European (e.g., Tadjik), Turkic (e.g., Azerbaijan, Uzbek), and Iberian-Caucasic (e.g., Chechen). The Arabic script is complex in ways described elsewhere (4.5), and was primarily used by the Moslem clergy: literacy was therefore low, between 4 and 25 per cent in different areas.

Isayev (p. 242) then asks why a transition to Cyrillic was not carried out immediately. His answer is that during the first years of Soviet power, this could have been interpreted as a return to the policy of Russification of Tsarist Russia. The language policy under the Tsars was based on the inequality of languages and nations, so that, for example, Russian speakers were administrators in non-Russian speaking areas, and national languages were not allowed to be used in publishing and education. The fundamental principle of Soviet policy, on the contrary, is the fundamental equality of all peoples and languages. The Romanization of scripts began, not as a central Soviet initiative, but as a local initiative in those areas where Arabic scripts were in use, primarily in the Caucasus and Central Asia. According to Isayev, the movement towards Romanization was initiated by Azerbaijan scholars in the 1920s, and later followed by all the other ethnic groups in Central Asia by the early 1930s. A certain period was then needed for people to realize the need for a transition to Cyrillic script, and it is Soviet policy that any such unification must be voluntary. By the late 1930s interest in studying Russian was growing amongst all the people of the USSR and the value of the Cyrillic system was becoming evident. The present policy is the intensive development of bilingualism, with the voluntary study of Russian alongside the native language, so that Russian can serve as a common medium of communication. Russian is the obvious choice for such a lingua franca, since it is already the native language of

55 to 60 per cent of the population, and has relatively little dialect variation.

In his account, then, Isayev neither mentions Lenin's plans for a Roman script for Russian itself, nor does he mention at all Stalin and the increased nationalism in the 1930s. However the facts are interpreted, it is clear that the Russian situation is particularly complex, and that any policy decisions are open to political interpretations. The pubisher's introduction to Isayev's book (p. 5) discusses the opportunities which exist 'for false representations by bourgeois critics of the principles applied by the Soviet government in its language policy as well as of its concrete achievements'.

China

China is another country where the choice of a script has major political implications, and where a Roman orthography has so far failed to gain widespread adoption in practice. (The main Western authority is De Francis, and the discussion here is based mainly on De Francis, 1967, and Fishman, 1971.) Various Roman orthographies have been proposed for Chinese, beginning in the 1890s, with major proposals in 1913 (National Phonetic Symbols), 1928 (National Language Romanization) and in the 1930s (Latinxua). In 1958, the National People's Congress adopted pinyin. This has not been officially dropped, but it is only in inconsistent use for miscellaneous purposes alongside other writing systems, and is only in third place in government language planning, behind the development of a national standard language and the simplification of the traditional characters.

Chinese is generally regarded as 'a language', but this is on political grounds. Linguistically, Chinese comprises many dialects, in eight major dialect groups, and languages in different groups are not mutually intelligible, and sometimes only as closely related as, for example English and Dutch, or Italian and Spanish. (The total population of the People's Republic is over eight hundred million.) A major language planning problem, involving a colossal teaching task, is therefore the aim of developing the Pekin dialect (Mandarin) as the national language. An area of particular political sensitivity has been the suggestion that an alphabetic script would threaten national unity. The argument is that the dialects are not mutually intelligible in speech, and therefore not mutually intelligible in a phonemic script, whereas the traditional writing system, not being phonological, provides a bridge between different dialects and peoples. Precisely how accurate this statement is on linguistic grounds is beside the point: it is widely believed, and the belief has had to be taken into account in language policy.

85

The policy of the present Communist government, since 1949, has been to simplify the traditional characters, and this policy is well on the way to success, although there is still considerable inconsistency and confusion in use. A phonetic alphabet policy was also instituted by the new government in 1949, but has proceeded much more slowly. Pinyin was adopted, but is repeatedly said not to be intended to replace traditional characters, at least at present. It has merely various auxiliary roles, including: an aid to teaching the standard Pekin dialect, in China and abroad; transliterating foreign names and technical vocabulary; and indexing. It is in use by the Chinese navy and fishing fleet, but only inconsistently by the railway system. In school, children acquire initial literacy in pinyin, but then transfer to characters, and often forget pinyin.

Turkey

Another well-known case is Turkey. When Kemal Ataturk (1881–1938) became President of the newly formed Republic of Turkey in 1923, he saw his major task as being to modernize the country and destroy the influence of the old Ottoman Empire. One of his first acts was to abandon the Arabic script in which Turkish was then written, and the use of a Roman alphabet was made obligatory in November 1928. This was clearly part of the programme of modernization and Westernization, and a major part of a wider programme of linguistic reform (including the elimination of Persian and Arabic words in Turkish) and literacy training. (Other symbolic measures in the Westernization included the obligatory use of surnames in Western style, and the forbidding of the fez!)

It is arguable that Ataturk lost a few opportunities when he introduced a Roman alphabet. For example, the Turkish alphabet now uses one non-Roman letter: ı as well as *i*. It also uses various diacritics: ö, ü, ş, ğ, ç. And some phoneme-grapheme correspondences, although consistent, do not fit in well with other widely used European conventions: for example,

$$ç = /t\int/ \qquad c = /d_3/$$
$$ş = /\int/$$

On the basis of these three pairs, one would predict

$$s = /_3/,$$

but *s* is used in English for /s/, and *j* is used for /_3/.

Germany

Within Europe, an interesting case is Germany (Steinberg, 1961, pp.

228–9). Up until the 1940s, the standard typeface in use in Germany
was Fraktur (Gothic). By modern standards this is a highly ornate typeface, and not totally legible to readers of standard west European types,
since it uses several characters rather different from the letters in the
standard Roman alphabet, for example:

s = f   S = ᠖   ss = ᠊   k = ᛗ

Gothic script was abandoned in England in the seventeenth century;
and the Scandinavian countries began to use Roman typefaces in the
eighteenth century alongside Gothic. By the twentieth century Fraktur
was a peculiar German provincialism. The first within Germany to
object strongly to Fraktur were those who were highly conscious of
Germany's relations with a wider non-German reading public, such as
scientists and economists. It was eventually Hitler who decreed in 1941
that Fraktur should be replaced by what we know as standard Roman
typefaces. The Nazis had been in two minds about the decision, initially
regarding Fraktur as essentially German and Nordic, but then realizing
the advantages of a typeface similar to those used in the rest of western
Europe.

It is easy to see the adoption of the Roman alphabet by Turkey in
the 1920s and by Germany in the 1940s as major steps towards the
cultural unity of Europe, and conversely to see the Soviet Union's
refusal to abandon Cyrillic as symbolic of a deep division between East
and West. It is clear also, therefore, that English orthography represents
linguistic and cultural unity in various ways. First, the use of a Roman
alphabet relates English to most other European languages and further
to many other languages in the world. Other major writing systems in
the world reflect, although not directly, major political groupings.
Second, the highly codified forms of English spelling provide an almost
totally fixed set of conventions for printed material in Britain, the
USA, Australia, New Zealand, and large parts of Commonwealth Africa
and Asia.

When there is a problem of setting up a new or revised orthography
for a pre-literate or semi-literate community, it follows that the orthographies already used by the dominant world languages in the same area
will be major factors. It is important, for example, that orthographies
for native languages in South America take account of Spanish orthographic patterns, since Spanish is the culturally dominant language in
much of the area; and that orthographies in French Africa take account
of French. A major problem in developing orthographies in sub-Saharan
Africa has been to maintain unitary and intelligible alphabets for all the
major languages in one country and/or neighbouring countries (Tucker,
1971). Apart from various non-Roman orthographies and French-based
orthographies in some of the French colonies, there are at present two

main solutions. One is the 'Africa alphabet', which was strongly influenced by the International Phonetic Association (established in 1886), and developed by the International African Institute (established in 1926). To maintain a general principle where possible of one letter per phoneme, the Africa alphabet uses various IPA symbols, including: ŋ, ʃ, ʋ (bilabial [v]), ʒ, ɖ (retroflex), ɓ (implosive [b]), and so on. It is prevalent in Ghana, Sierra Leone, Northern Nigeria, Uganda, parts of the Congo and parts of South Africa. The other solution is the 'Swahili' or English-based system, using only Roman letters, and it is used mainly in Central and East Africa.

It is not only in newly literate societies that orthographies are designed or redesigned to reflect cultural sympathies; the widescale adoption of etymological spellings in English in the sixteenth century symbolized the closeness to actual or supposed Latin models. Well-known examples are the insertion of *b* in words such as *debt* and *doubt* in order to mirror more closely the spellings of cognate words in Latin.

To complete the picture, we ought to note that there are also many cases on record of writing systems being altered to reflect cultural antipathies and to symbolize the separateness of language communities. For example, Lithuanian abandoned the digraphs *sz* and *cz*, replacing them with *s* and *c*, the changes being motivated by a wish to have Lithuanian look different from Polish. Similarly, in the 1840s Czech abandoned the graphemes *w* and *au*, replacing them with *v* and *ou*, this change being motivated by a desire to appear different from German (Vachek, 1973, p. 48).

It is significant, then, that the four major writing systems in the world today (major in the sense of being most widely used) — Roman, Cyrillic, Arabic and Chinese — correspond rather closely to major political economic groupings. Perhaps Japanese should be added as a fifth major system. And other less widely used systems, such as the Hebrew writing system used in Israel, can also be easily seen as symbolizing cultural values and unity.

Australia

We will look briefly at one final case where there are complex relations between indigenous languages and the language of the wider political and economic community: Australia. The facts about language and education in Australia are not widely known, and it is therefore worth while attempting to summarize some of the main facts, if only very briefly. The language situation in Australia is extremely interesting to linguists, and involves many practical educational problems, but it is only within the last few years that the Australian government has begun to develop any educational programmes which attempt to tackle the educational problems faced by many Aboriginal children.

The first British settlement was established in Sydney in 1788. At that time there were probably around three hundred thousand Aborigines spread over the entire continent, speaking about six hundred languages. Today, the number of Aborigines is around forty-seven thousand and only about two hundred languages remain (Ruhlen, 1975, p. 99). The British brought the English language which now exists in three main forms: standard English, very close to British and American standard English; non-standard Aboriginal English (Sharpe, 1977; Gardiner, 1977); and various contact varieties of English-based pidgins or creoles (Sharpe and Sandefur, 1977). In addition, there are a large number of immigrants speaking other languages, in the past often German and Italian, but nowadays increasingly the languages spoken by immigrants speaking non-European languages. There are seven hundred thousand children in Australian schools whose first language is not English (Grassby, 1976). The total population of Australia is only something over thirteen million.

Most, if not all, the Aboriginal languages are thought to be genetically related to each other, but no relationship has been proved with any other languages in, for example, neighbouring New Zealand, Papua New Guinea, Indonesia or elsewhere. Counts of the number of languages are inevitably approximate, particularly as they involve sometimes arbitrary decisions about the distinction between languages and dialects. There are twenty-eight main sub-branches of Australian Aboriginal languages, but their distribution is extremely uneven over the continent. Twenty-seven of the branches, with mainly just a few member languages each, are spoken in the relatively concentrated area of Arhnem land in the north; whilst the remaining branch, Pama-Nyungan, with about one hundred and seventy languages, covers the rest of the continent. Some languages have only a few speakers left and are most likely to become extinct within the next few years. Many tribal languages have somewhere between fifty and five hundred speakers: it seems that many languages in Australia have survived with what seems to us very small speech communities. There are probably about a hundred viable languages left. The numerically strongest language is Mabuiag, with around seven thousand speakers on the western Torres Stait Islands; and the Western Desert language, spoken over much of Western Australia, has around four thousand speakers (Ruhlen, 1975, p. 99).

The Australian languages never developed written forms, and this, combined with the relatively small number of natives speaking individual languages, with the wholesale slaughter of Aborigines in some notorious cases by white settlers, and with the imposition of English as the sole official language in the country, meant the inevitable loss of hundreds of languages. Until the 1960s the language policy of the Australian government was one of outright hostility, aiming to suppress and eradicate Aboriginal languages. All administrative dealings with Aborigines were in English or pidgin English, and the government policy on education was that English should be used from the start. The first time that government blessing was given to the study of native languages was a course in Pitjantjatjara (the main dialect of the Western Desert Language) for government welfare officers and others in 1967 (Wurm, 1971).

Australian languages have many exotic grammatical and lexical features. Particularly relevant to literacy problems are their phonological systems, which also seem exotic to speakers of western European languages. First, the phoneme systems are quite surprisingly uniform across the whole continent: this obviously simplifies the problem of creating orthographies for them. Second, they have the following characteristics.

Dyirbal (Dixon, 1972, p. 37) has the smallest number of phonemes in any Australian language, but is nevertheless characteristic and can serve as a brief example. The phoneme system is:

```
b  d  ɖ  g      i    u
m  n  ɲ  ŋ          a
   l
   r  ɻ
w     j
```

The following are characteristic features: there are no fricatives (only a few Australian languages have fricative phonemes); there is no voiced-voiceless distinction in the plosives (only a few languages have this distinction); there is a nasal corresponding to each plosive (some languages have six of each); there are two contrasting /r/ phonemes (some languages have three).

Clearly such phoneme systems are very different from English (see 2.6) and can therefore cause interference problems for Aboriginal speakers learning English. Orthography problems therefore do arise with creoles since there may be a continuum through from 'heavy' creole which is much influenced by the Aboriginal language, to varieties close to standard English: words therefore occur in different forms, for example in Roper Creole (Sharpe and Sandefur, 1977): *biya, spiya, spear; jiribala, thrribala, thribala, three.*

These are, very briefly indeed, some of the main linguistic facts. The problems facing teachers with Aboriginal children in the classroom are clearly bewildering, but training in Aboriginal linguistics is still uncommon in teacher-training (Brumby and Vaszolyi, 1977, p. x). In addition, it is only since 1972 that the government has publicly formulated any policy on language problems in Aboriginal education.

In 1972, the Prime Minister announced that the Australian government would launch a campaign to have Aboriginal children given primary education in Aboriginal languages. Australian education is organized within states, and the federal government is able to implement this policy only in the Northern Territory. There have been courses in English for Aboriginal children in the Northern Territory since the 1950s. South Australia was pursuing a policy of bilingual education before 1972; there are five South Australian schools which serve Aboriginal communities where Pitjantjatjara is the main language. And there has been a great deal of work by the Summer Institute of Linguistics (see 4.8) and by missionary groups, although the Australian branch of the SIL was established only in the early 1960s, and missions only seldom used native languages until government support began to be given in the late 1960s. In response to the Prime Minister's announcement, there were five schools with bilingual programmes in the Northern Territory by December 1973, and in seventeen schools and thirteen Aboriginal languages by 1976. There is now also a bilingual programme in Aboriginal Creole and standard English at Bamyili in the Northern Territory (Grassby, 1976; Kaldor, 1977; Scott and Coker, 1977; Ian Malcolm, personal communication).

4.8   The wider writing community: religious

Diringer (1962) proposes the general principle that alphabets have followed religion. That is, the movements of religious conversion have often introduced scripts into a vast geograhical area.

The Cyrillic alphabet, for example, was adopted by the Slavs who adopted the Greek Orthodox religion: Russians, White Russians, Bulgarians and Serbs. But in adopting Catholicism, other Slav peoples adopted a Roman alphabet: Slovenes, Czechs, Poles and others. Yugoslavia is an interesting case, since both Cyrillic and Roman alphabets are used for the same language. Cyrillic was adopted by the Serbs along with their adoption of the Eastern Orthodox Church. The Croats were influenced by the Western Roman Catholic Church and use a Roman alphabet. The two alphabets are exactly equivalent and each can be transliterated unambiguously into the other (Partridge, 1964).

A major example of Diringer's principle is the spread of the Arabic language and script into countries especially in the Iberian peninsula, the Balkans, the Near East, North Africa, India and South East Asia, with the spread of Islam and the Koran, and particularly as a result of the conquests of the seventh and eighth centuries AD. Arabic was originally restricted to the Arabian peninsula, but is now a world language, due to Islam. In contrast to Christianity (see below) the Islamic faith was never proselytized in translation: the Koran has to be read and chanted in Arabic, which is still believed by many Muslims to be the language of God (Ferguson, 1959). This in turn led to the development of highly cursive and elaborate scripts, since the scribes could not change the words, but could embellish them (see 4.5).

Other less widespread cases of alphabets following religion are also on record. Around AD 740 the Khazars, a people of Turkish stock living in Eastern Europe north of the Caucasus between the Black Sea and the Caspian, were converted to Judaism, under circumstances about which little is known (Koestler, 1976). By the tenth century, if not before, the Khazars were using the Hebrew alphabet, and from Khazaria the alphabet spread into neighbouring countries, including Crimea and Poland. The Hebrew alphabet is, of course, still used for some varieties of Yiddish and for modern Israeli Hebrew, and was formerly used for Ladino, a Spanish-Hebrew dialect spoken by Spanish Sephardic Jews until the fifteenth century.

In contrast to Islam, Christianity has always believed that missionary expansion should take place via linguistic multiformity. The fact that Christianity is essentially a missionary religion has meant the enormous spread of Roman alphabets into Africa, Asia and South America. It has often been due to Christian missionaries that many areas of the world have acquired writing systems. Even today, outside the Communist bloc, the majority of those involved in developing orthographies for unwritten languages, and in studying the languages in order to translate the Bible into them, are missionary linguists. Welmers (1971) estimates that in the 1950s and 1960s there were eight to ten thousand missionaries working in sub-Saharan Africa alone.

The extent of the influence of the Christian church on language-study and orthography making can be estimated from the figures in Table 1 which Nida (1975, pp. 206, 216, 175, 193) gives for Bible translations. For the 1971 figures, Nida estimates that the whole of the Bible or the New Testament is translated into languages used by 98 per cent of the world's population. On the estimate that there are around two thousand five hundred mutually unintelligible languages spoken in the world, this means that the remaining two per cent speak around one thousand languages. Nida claims that translators are at present working on at least half of these remaining languages. In order to carry out this enormous programme of Bible translation, Christian missionaries have been involved in the study of exotic languages and in the development of orthographies for unwritten language for hundreds of years. (Nida and Wonderly, 1963, give a very full summary of this work.)

TABLE 1

	before invention of printing	1806	1900	1962	1971
Number of languages with entire Bible translated				226	253
Number of additional languages with translation of New Testament	no figures given			281	330
Number of additional languages with at least one book translated				674	874
Total: i.e. number of languages with at least a substantial part translated	33	80	563	1181	1475

Some illustrative dates of translations (from Sarna *et al.*, 1974) are: third century BC, translation of the Hebrew Bible into Greek (Septuagint); fourth century AD, Ulfila's Gothic translation (see below); *c.* 1270, first partial Dutch translations; 1382, first completed English translation credited to John Wycliffe; fifteenth century, partial translation into seven Asian and four African languages; 1534, Martin Luther's German version, which was the basis of Swedish (1541), Danish (1550), and Icelandic (1584) versions; 1611, King James English version; 1613, complete Japanese New Testament; 1661, first American Indian translation for Massachusetts Indians; 1727, complete Tamil Bible; 1823, complete Chinese translation; 1829, New Testament in Tahitian and Javanese; 1835, New Testament in Hawaiian; 1862, Cree translation in syllabary invented by James Evans.

A famous early example is Bishop Ulfila's translation of most of the New Testament and parts of the Old Testament into Gothic in the fourth century, for the Visigoths of the lower Danube. For his translation he devised an alphabet based on Greek, with Roman and possibly Runic adaptations. This translation is almost the only record we have of Gothic, which is now extinct. The earliest, and many cases the only, records we have of many languages are partial Biblical translations and related religious works. Another early example is Old Church Slavonic, for which St Cyril allegedly devised an alphabet in the ninth century, based on Greek letters with some additions.

Ferguson (1967) provides an interesting case-study of St Stefan, a Russian Orthodox bishop of Perm in the fourteenth century. St Stefan (born *c.* 1335) was a native of the pagan region of Komi, who trained in the Russian Orthodox Church, then returned to Komi to preach the Gospel. Ferguson points out that he faced all the major problems of linguistic development in a non-literate society. He had first to choose a language to preach in. If he chose Russian, then texts would be immediately available without translation, further missionaries would require no special linguistic training, and so on. In fact, he chose to preach in Komi (a non-Slavonic, Finno-Ugric language), requiring him first to devise an alphabet, which he based on Greek and Church Slavonic, and then to translate material. He adopted the policy, in other words, followed by many missionaries after him, and in particular by the Summer Institute of Linguistics (see below), of using the local language. St Stefan was apparently very successful. He converted a pagan, non-literate society of several thousand people to Christianity, devising *en route* an orthography which was used for around three hundred years. Ferguson suggests that not all that much progress has been made on his competence of five hundred years ago!

Christian missionary work gradually gathered pace from the sixteenth century onwards. Before the twentieth century, the invention of a new orthography was necessarily a hit-and-miss affair, since missionaries' knowledge of linguistic studies was largely restricted to English, Latin, Greek and Hebrew. But from the beginning of the twentieth century, several major factors came together. These included:

1 The establishment of the International Phonetic Association in 1886 and the development of the International Phonetic Alphabet (IPA).

2 Practical work with IPA in foreign language teaching and orthography-making which led to the development of phoneme theory. A major theoretician in Britain was Daniel Jones, and he and his colleagues working in London were a major influence on missionary linguistics and the development of orthographies.

3 The development of structural linguistics, especially by Boas, Sapir and Bloomfield in the USA, and the development of techniques for recording and describing unwritten languages.

4 The establishment of the Summer Institute of Linguistics, which was the main way in which the work of the American structuralists was mediated for missionaries. The SIL was set up in 1935. It grew out of a linguistic mission to Mexico and was first organized to train Bible translators for Central and South America. But it later expanded into a much broader range of languages; now conducts training courses for missionary linguists in the USA, England,

Germany and Australia; has had several thousand people through its courses; and is now the largest group involved in developing orthographies for unwritten languages. It has been the base for several of the world's leading linguists, in particular Pike and Nida.

The SIL Publication Catalogue for 1976 lists over three hundred books and periodicals with studies of hundreds of languages including: native languages of Central and South America spoken in Bolivia, Guatemala, Mexico, Peru, Ecuador, Colombia and Honduras; Eskimo; languages of Papua New Guinea and the Philippines; Australian Aboriginal languages; Vietnamese languages; languages of India and Nepal; and West African languages. This is in addition to a large amount of important theoretical work on phonetics, phonology, morphology, syntax (especially tagmemic theory), semantics, discourse analysis, tone languages, translation theory, comparative linguistics, field work procedures, literacy and writing systems.

4.9   Conclusions

One of the most influential books in this area, written as a practical training manual for fieldworkers, was Pike's (1947) *Phonemics: A Technique for Reducing Languages to Writing*. Most of the book deals with analytic procedures for working out phonemic analyses of an unknown language, and this is clearly intended to be the basis of any orthography: 'A practical orthography should be phonemic' (p. 208). But Pike distinguishes carefully (p. 244) between (a) a technical orthography, with a one-to-one phoneme-letter correlation, (b) a practical orthography, which is modified in line with local traditions, facilities, and so on, and (c) a scientific orthography, whether technical or practical, designed to take account of all relevant linguistic and social pressures. And in a long concluding chapter on 'Practical alphabets', he discusses the frequent conflicts between phonemic goals and social goals.

Nida is probably the other most influential linguist concerned with orthography-making. He proposes (1963, in Nida, 1975, p. 229): (a) that an adequate orthography should be prepared primarily on phonemic lines, but with two important qualifications; (b) that an orthography resulting from a phonemic analysis should be adjusted, if required, to preserve a unique written form for morphemes; and (c) that an orthography resulting from a phonemic analysis must be adjusted as much as possible towards the orthography of the dominant language in the area, for example, to Spanish in much of Latin America, to Arabic in the Sudan, to French in West Africa, and so on.

The principle is, then, (a) a phonemic alphabet, compromised where necessary by (b) morphological considerations, and by (c) the writing systems of the wider writing community. Note that the recommendation is that a new writing system should be similar to systems for even unrelated languages which are culturally important to the users: a clear case of cultural pressures overriding purely linguistic considerations.

4.10 The ideal orthography

The ideal orthography would be designed by linguists, in collaboration with educators, publishers and politicians, and have the support of the mass of the people who are to use it. That is, it would embody systematic phonemic and morphological analyses, be easy to teach and to print, convey appropriate sociocultural implications, and be acceptable to its users. Since none of the many proposed reforms of English spelling has ever been implemented, it follows that they have all failed to meet one or more of these criteria. And since it is impossible to imagine a situation occurring in practice where all these criteria could be met, it follows that there is no ideal orthography.

Chapter 5

The functions of written language

In many developing countries, the aim of teaching reading is functional literacy (see 1.2), that is, the ability to read and write well enough to fulfil the duties of family, occupation and society. But literacy is a relative concept, and in Britain, the USA and many other countries, a literate individual is also expected to be able to read both for pleasure and intellectual stimulation: hence the overwhelming dominance of school English courses, at least until very recently, by literary works of fiction. This chapter discusses the intellectual functions of written language, as well as its administrative and bureaucratic functions.

It is clear that spoken language serves a very wide range of functions and that in important ways that were discussed in Chapter 2, it is prior to written language. But it is also clear that a language with a writing system can serve many additional functions (Vachek, 1973, p. 34; Goody, 1977). This chapter discusses the ways in which writing can lead to the increased functional capacity of a language. For much of the chapter, the argument will not be able to progress much further than common-sense discussion, since it is only recently that scholars have begun seriously to consider written language from a functional perspective. Traditionally the only kind of written language to be considered in schools and universities has been literary language, although this is now changing and increasing attention is being paid to non-literary varieties of written language. Often the functions of written language have not been considered, since the view has been that written (that is, literary) language has no function, in the sense that it is for pleasure, an end in itself.

I see no reason to take up here a position of extreme cultural relativism and to avoid making value judgments about the ways in which language can develop functionally. On the one hand, we have to recognize that all oral cultures are very complex in ways which have often been underestimated. This has been demonstrated by anthropologists (notably Lévi-Strauss, Lounsbury, Frake and Conklin) who have examined the complex systems of classification used by non-literate peoples. For example, complex folk-taxonomies might cover such areas of knowledge as botanical terminology, disease categories, kinship, ice and snow conditions, or whatever areas of the social world are of particular importance to the speakers. And, in the context of educational linguistics, it has been shown by Labov (1969a, 1972b), Kochman (1972) and others, that predominantly spoken cultures such as black American working-class culture are based on highly developed forms of verbal art quite unknown in white middle-class literate culture. On the other hand, a language which has both written and spoken forms has the potential of being used for more purposes than a language which has only spoken forms. We must neither underestimate the complexity of spoken language, nor overestimate its identity with written language.

Linguists are agreed in attacking the 'primitive language myth', but the argument that 'all languages are equal' or that 'there are no primitive languages' has to be stated as follows. In terms of their structural organization, especially their grammatical structure, all human languages, whether they have written varieties or not, are just very complex, and it does not make much sense to compare languages as wholes at this level. Nothing useful is known, in fact, about the evolution of grammatical systems, nor about the origins of spoken language. Further, languages do not appear to differ in their potential or functional development. That is, Eskimo or Yoruba, say, could be perfectly adequate media for use as international languages of science. There is nothing in their linguistic structure to prevent this (and the fact that they do not have adequate technical vocabularies is a matter which could in principle be dealt with if necessary), although such a development is unlikely, due to the social dominance and prestige of English and other world languages.

On the other hand, languages clearly do differ, as a matter of social and historical accident, in their functional development, and a language without a writing system is not as powerful an instrument of communication as a language with writing conventions.

5.1   Children's confusions over the purposes of written language

People read books and other material for a variety of purposes: to pass the time (e.g., escapist literature), to get information they require (e.g., recipes), to gain aesthetic experience (e.g., poetry), and so on. And they write for a variety of purposes: to transmit information to another person (e.g., personal letters), or to a bureaucracy (e.g., form filling); to aid their own memories (e.g., shopping lists); and so on. These purposes are often assumed to be self-evident, as they are to highly literate people. They are, however, not entirely natural functions of language, in so far as some of them are partly created by writing itself. Such functions are therefore likely to be unclear to children learning to read.

Further, in different societies writing can play a complete range of roles, from the overwhelming impact of printed material in most of Britain and the USA, to the almost totally peripheral use of Runic writing in early Germanic society, where writing was not in general use, but only used as a special or priestly system (Trager, 1974, p. 436). Goody (1968) provides a great deal of data on 'restricted literacy' in different countries, and points out that the vast majority of people who have been in contact with writing over the past two thousand years, have been influenced to some degree by literacy, but have remained on the margins of full literacy. I pointed out earlier (2.4) that although there are now few communities in the world which do not have access to a writing system, there are nevertheless millions of individuals whose contact with writing is marginal or non-existent. Similar points can also be made about the different roles which writing plays in different social groups within one country (see 5.7).

We have already (2.1) referred briefly to the evidence that children learning to read are often very vague and confused about the functions of written language. The work already cited by Vygotsky (1962), Reid (1958, 1966) and Downing (1969) has been confirmed by many other studies, and two points are probably now widely accepted: (a) young children often have difficulty in understanding the purposes of written language, since many of these purposes are completely beyond their needs and experience; (b) young children will have particular difficulty in learning to read if they grow up in a home or cultural background with no tradition of literacy and hence no appreciation of the purposes of written language.

It used to be widely believed, in addition, that young children take many years to understand the communicative processes involved in spoken language. If true, then this would explain (a). This argument is best known in Piaget's (1926) formulation. He argued that a great deal of the language of young children, up to about seven years, is ego-centric: that is, it does not have the function of communicating with others; and further that young children do not appreciate what is involved in communicating with others and cannot accommodate their language to their listeners. It is obvious from common-sense experience of talking to young children that they often fail to take account of what their listeners know. But it does seem now that the stereotype of young children as non-communicators has been exaggerated, and that from an early age children take account of their addressee in making conversation. It is only very recently that work has begun to appear which

directly studies children's conversational competence. (Major collections
of articles are by Ervin-Tripp and Mitchell-Kernan, 1977; and Ferguson
and Snow, 1977.) Much of this work now shows that young children
are much more competent conversationalists than has often been sus-
pected. For example, Keenan (1977) finds twins of two years nine
months systematically varying their language to follow appropriately
on the utterances of other speakers, both child and adult. Children of
five years, in contact with children who speak different languages, can
be seen teaching names and distinguishing information which requires
translation. And pre-schoolers already use identifying information such
as 'my aunt' rather than just a proper name: that is, they can choose an
appropriate term for the addressee. (Ervin-Tripp and Mitchell-Kernan,
1977, p. 10.)

As I have argued elsewhere in this book (1.1, 3.6), we must try
neither to underestimate nor to overestimate children's communicative
competence. There are clearly many functions of written language
which are quite beyond young children's experience, and this is the
topic of the rest of this chapter.

5.2   Different limitations and advantages

We have already, in Chapters 2 and 3, in different ways rejected as unhelpful statements such as 'writing is a pale reflection of speech, a mere
secondary system, parasitic upon the spoken language'. Such statements
carry the implication that writing ought to represent speech, has tried,
and failed in some way. But it seems more useful to explore the different functions which written and spoken language serve. If writing was
just 'speech written down', then it would not be very different from
speech and would not be as useful as it is. One easy way to demonstrate
that writing is not speech written down, is to compare a close transcript
of normal conversation with any piece of written language. Many of the
differences in form, particularly in grammar, between spoken and
written language are due to the different purposes they serve, and are
especially due to the rather restricted and specialized functions of most
written language. So we must discuss these. Some of them are obvious
enough once they have been pointed out, but they are not at all obvious
to young children.

Compared with gestures, for example, spoken language has several
distinct advantages. It can be used in the dark, or when speaker and
hearer are out of sight, or not looking at each other; when the hands are
occupied; and, in fact, when one is doing almost anything else simultaneously. It is even perfectly easy to talk while eating, although our
culture considers it rude to do so. On the other hand, spoken language

has some obvious limitations. It can only be heard over short distances; it is difficult to remember today what exactly was said yesterday, and is therefore very susceptible to errors in transmission. Only recently, since the invention of the telephone, radio and tape-recorder, has it been possible to record speech and transmit it over long distances or preserve it accurately for indefinite periods of time. And even tape-recorded speech has severe limitations as a record: it requires special machinery for playback, and it is difficult both to skim quickly and to index.

In a non-literate society, the total content of social traditions, conventions, laws and organization has to be held in the memory. And in every generation the memories of individuals will mediate this social heritage, modifying and restructuring it, inevitably forgetting some bits and adding others. Hence the various mnemonic devices found in oral cultures to help to preserve important social facts: formalized speech, ritual recital, and professional rememberers (Goody and Watt, 1962; Hertzler, 1965: p. 49). There is no doubt that members of a non-literate society are often capable of feats of memory which appear prodigious to us. Andrzejewski (1963), for example, documents the place of oral poetry in Somalia, where poetry is composed, recited and remembered entirely without the aid of writing. The poetry has a rigid alliterative and rhythmic framework, which doubtless helps the prodigious feats of memory, allowing poems hundreds of lines long to be composed in large quantitites, to spread over huge areas with great speed, and to be remembered for over a hundred years.

Similar characteristics can be found in much other material designed for oral transmission (see 2.5). Once a recording medium is available, however, such mnemonic devices no longer have to be built in; and in abolishing the need for memorization, writing simultaneously abolishes the need for techniques such as rhythm, repetition or alliteration, although such devices are still available for stylistic effect if desired. The medium of transmission can thus affect the form of the language used.

It is also interesting to note that the relationship between author, written language and reading public is not self-evident, and that different conventions have held at different periods. The concept of personal authorship, for example, had little meaning in the Middle Ages in Britain, and books were published with no author's name. Works were seen rather as a collective cultural enterprise. The whole notion of a definitive 'text' of a work was therefore very different, if it made any sense at all, and plagiarism could not be conceived of. At every stage, the changing sociolinguistic relations between written and spoken language have to be considered.

101

5.3 Recording and administrative functions

The social organization of non-literate societies can be extremely complex, but new possibilities are immediately available to societies with writing systems. The basic function of a written language, on which other functions logically depend, is what we could call the recording or storage function, and hence the transmission function. Writing provides a way of recording language which is at once accurate, permanent to all intents and purposes with no limitation on time, and transportable, with no limit on distance. Whilst spoken language is very limited in these respects, written language can provide an intact, durable record of any message: an external social memory, available to anyone who can decipher it. This means that accurate financial records can be kept, without which a complex commerce is impossible; that a complex legal system can develop, depending on accurate records of decisions and laws; and that large empires can be controlled from one central point by means of accurate messages sent out over any distance.

Obvious social and intellectual effects immediately follow, and I will mention only a few. Writing has clear administrative or bureaucratic functions, in so far as a complex state would be impossible without written records of commercial dealings, legal decisions, diplomatic treaties, and so on, and without means of conveying decisions over geographical space and time. Whilst such functions of storing information for later reference by readers may seem obvious to us as skilled readers, these functions of written material are not obvious to inexperienced readers. There are two kinds of evidence for this, historical and educational.

After the invention of printing by movable type, it took almost a hundred years before page numbering was regularly added in books for readers' benefit (McLuhan, 1960). Similarly, early manuscript books were often studied in detail by their readers and memorized. It took some considerable time, then, before even the reference information-storage potential of written language became fully appreciated by printers and readers. There are many other cases of value being placed on memorizing large quantities of text, often religious, even after written versions were available for consultation. Goody (1968, pp. 12ff.) documents such cases for India, where the emphasis on rote learning continued into the new universities established in the nineteenth century. There is always bound to be a time lag, of course, before the potentialities of a new medium are realized. Thus early type designs for English copied the complex ligatures which are convenient for scribes, but an encumbrance in machine printing. (Modern Arabic printing still has this problem, see 4.5.) And rote learning, when knowledge is available for permanent consultation, similarly misses the potential of the medium: in the same way that a schools programme on television is wasting the opportunities of the medium if it merely shows a teacher lecturing in front of a blackboard.

It is likely also that the permanence of written language is often not exploited by beginning readers. (See Lunzer and Gardner, 1978.) Spoken language, being impermanent, has to be listened to and interpreted linearly, and at the same speed and in the same sequence in which it is presented. But written language, being permanent, can be read faster or slower, re-read, skimmed, scanned for isolated words or phrases, read only in parts omitting large sections, read in an order other than that in which it is presented, and so on. In other words, many different strategies are possible reading written language, whereas in listening to spoken language the listener is almost entirely in lockstep with the speaker.

Since these different strategies are not applicable to listening, it is probable that they ought to be taught explicitly to readers, who otherwise may not learn to take full advantage of the permanence of text. It is well known that many children and inexperienced readers have only one reading speed, independent of the difficulty or interest of the material being read, or of the purpose of reading it. Even at the level of university studies it is clear that many students have not developed flexible enough reading strategies and do not take sufficient advantage of the fact that they have the initiative, with written material, to skim, skip forward to conclusions, to re-read difficult sections, to omit sections and return to them later, and so on; and that they often are even more lost when they have to deal with the information stored in a large library.

5.4 The intellectual functions of written language

The recording function of written language leads also to intellectual gains. Again, it is important not to underestimate the intellectual achievements of pre-literate societies, and it is no longer seen as adequate to consider the intellectual life of pre-literate societies as 'primitive'. Nevertheless, a writing system immediately offers distinct new possibilities. A society which has a writing system immediately has new intellectual resources which greatly facilitate thought in many areas. Accurate records can be kept of discoveries, inventions, theories and blind alleys, and each generation no longer has to begin from scratch or from what the previous generation can remember and pass on. An accumulation of recorded wisdom can immediately begin to be gathered. The fact that findings are recorded in unchanging form also makes them easier to study and consider critically, and this in turn leads to more discoveries.

103

Without writing, science and history are inconceivable, since at one stroke writing overcomes the limitations of human memory.

A most important discussion of the function of language, and of written language in particular, is Popper's theory of World Three. (See Popper, 1972, where the theory is developed in several chapters, and also Popper, 1974; Magee, 1973.) Popper uses the term World One to refer to the objective world of physical objects or material things. World Two refers to the subjective world of minds, mental states and consciousness. World Three refers to what Popper calls 'objective knowledge': that is, knowledge as it exists in books and libraries, and as it is taught in universities. World Three objects include statements, theories and hypotheses. The phrase 'objective knowledge' is not at all intended to imply that the knowledge is 'true'; but that it exists independently of the subjective experience of someone who knows it. It is autonomous knowledge or knowledge without a knower.

Popper's discussion has far-reaching implications for theories of knowledge, but only the following points concern us here. First, he points out that for a statement or theory to be objective, it has to be formulated in language. You might hold some belief or other, but it is only when you formulate this belief in words that I can discuss it, examine it critically, test it or refute it. World Three therefore depends on language, and, more precisely, it depends on the descriptive and argumentative functions of language: that is, on the ability of language to make descriptive statements which can be true or false, and the ability of language to make statements which are logically related, contradictory to other statements, and so on.

Second, if you formulate some statement orally, this does make it amenable to critical and rational discussion; and the critical and rational discussion of ideas does take place in conversations, seminars and lectures. But it becomes at least much more convenient to examine statements carefully, if they are written or printed (Popper, 1972, pp. 25, 84; 1974, p. 182).

Third, it is perfectly possible for statements and theories to exist in books and libraries, and yet not to be known by anyone. That is, ideas and statements can exist independently, formulated in language and recorded in writing: knowledge without a knower. The statements were, of course, originally written by someone, but this person may have died or forgotten them or never realized their implications even when they were first written. A book is a book even if never read (the fate of many books), and it contains autonomous World Three knowledge whether anyone reads it or not.

There are real examples of knowledge being formulated in written language, of the writers perishing, of the writings existing over a long period of time and finally being deciphered by someone else. One such

104

case is the decipherment of Egyptian hieroglyphics in the nineteenth century and the subsequent discovery of historical facts about the Egyptians from their writings. Clearly, the knowledge had continued to exist independently, formulated in the written language, although for a long time not known by any individual. All that was necessary was that it was capable of being understood. Only with the development of writing could such a World Three of objective knowledge accumulate. As Popper says (1972, p. 239): 'Instead of growing better memories and brains, we grow paper, pens, pencils, typewriters, dictaphones, the printing press and libraries.'

Goody and Watt (1962/3) suggest that it was the widespread diffusion of writing throughout the Greek world, and the consequent recording of what had previously been oral tradition, that led people to notice many inconsistencies in their records, and hence led to a much more conscious and critical attitude to accepted world views. In general they suggest that in non-literate societies inconsistencies in beliefs are less likely to be noticed or are more likely to be adjusted or forgotten, and that criticism is therefore less likely. This is precisely Popper's point, that one function of written language is to facilitate a critical attitude towards statements and theories. (See also Goody, 1977, ch. 3.)

There are several science fiction stories which play on these ideas in various ways. One (Piper, 1957) recounts the tale of archaeologists who discover books, journals and eventually a whole library written in the language of a race of Martians who have perished thousands of years before. The knowledge of their lost culture is there, in the books, if only the language can be deciphered. Another (Asimov, 1956) is about a brilliant but mad scientist who discovers the secret of travelling by mass-transportation through space and time. He has given no one the details of his discovery and has written them only in one copy of a paper. He dies of heart failure, an ex-colleague photographs the paper and destroys the original, hoping to pretend later that he has made the discovery himself. But he leaves the undeveloped film in sunlight where it is over-exposed and the contents destroyed. If a copy of the paper still existed, the knowledge would still exist, but the knowledge has been lost with its only written formulation. These two stories are linguistically and philosophically quite plausible, if unlikely on other grounds!

It might even be possible to relate particular intellectual developments quite closely to writing as a mode of communication. Mathematics, for example, was encouraged by written records and accounts needed by trade and commerce. Astronomy was stimulated by written records of dates and calendars. It might be that different concepts of time are related to the presence or absence of writing. A cyclic concept of time is primitive in so far as it does not require records, whereas a concept of

105

time as linear requires the ability to record sequences of events (Gough, 1968). It is arguable that the logical mode of thought embodied in syllogistic reasoning could only develop in practice once propositions could be written down, set one against the other, read and re-read, and contradictions and consequences noted (Goody and Watt, 1962). It is probably not a coincidence that syllogistic reasoning developed in Greece following on the widespread diffusion of an alphabetic culture, and that it also developed early in India and China which had non-alphabetic writing systems (Gough, 1968).

Major work on the intellectual functions of written language has been done by Goody (Goody and Watt, 1962; Goody, 1968; Goody, 1977). Goody (1977) attempts to explain the way in which modes of thought have changed over time and space by an examination of changes in the means of communication, especially in the development of writing, and argues that a change in the technology of communicative acts must have had great implications for intellectual development.

One example he discusses in detail is the effect of making lists. Such lists are very common in what remains of written material from the first fifteen hundred years or so of writing in the Near and Middle East from about 3500 BC. Various types of list, made for business, trading and other administrative purposes, and later obviously as teaching exercises, form the bulk of thousands of documents which have been found; connected literary texts are much rarer. He argues that such lists, of property, transactions, people, events or just words, have no direct oral equivalent. Speakers can, if required, list things, but do not commonly do so. First, then, they are not 'speech written down', but a distinct written form. Other forms of presenting information which are similarly restricted to a written form are tables and formulae. Second, he argues that the visual format of lists opens up cognitive and linguistic operations which are difficult if not impossible in spoken language. Lists of words or phrases are decontextualized in a way which is unusual in speech. And the layout of abstracted linguistic units makes a different kind of inspection of the units possible, setting units clearly one against another, thus raising problems of classification and ultimately of structural semantics; that is, of the relations between words in a language. Lists of kings and events are a necessary pre-requisite to constructing chronologies and therefore a pre-requisite to history. Finally, making lists may even have contributed to the development of the alphabet out of logographic and syllabic systems: many of the lists which have been found are clearly exercises for scribes, in which words are ordered according to initial symbols, thus bringing out the sound-symbol structure of the words.

In comparison with the bulk of writing and printing today, lists are clearly only a small part of the use of written language. But they appear to be characteristic of the earliest uses of writing, and to be the basis of intellectual operations which are unlikely to arise in spoken language.

In all such cases of the possible intellectual functions of writing we appear to be dealing with the facilitating effect of written material. For example, one thing which it is easier to analyse if it is written down is language itself, but it is possible to think about and analyse language without a writing system. In everyday conversation, people do routinely discuss language, even fine points of grammar and style. And, more importantly, there is evidence that the grammarians of ancient India developed elaborate analyses of Sanskrit before they had a writing system at all (Trager, 1974, p. 373).

The concept that there can be knowledge without a knower, existing independently in books, can also revolutionize the relationship between teacher and pupil, and this fact has not been missed by authorities at various times. The potential disruption which can be caused by easy access to books, and to the ideas in them, has frequently been realized by governments. Printing was first introduced into Britain by Caxton in 1476, and by 1520 unorthodox ideas were being circulated in books printed in English. An Act of Parliament of 1536 restricted access to the authorized English Great Bible on a social class basis: women and the lower classes of men were forbidden to read it (Lawson and Silver, 1973, pp. 84-5). Goody (1968) similarly documents cases where the guru–pupil relation is maintained steadfastly in spite of the availability of books: all knowledge is channelled through the teacher.

political consequence of literacy

Such effects of writing are clearly profound in their social and intellectual consequences, but any further discussion along these lines would take us beyond our immediate concerns here, which are to point out that writing is primarily responsible for the creation and maintenance of World Three, and hence for the development of a rational and critical attitude to knowledge.

Work on the relationship between language and thought has frequently been speculative and unsatisfactory. The best-known work by Whorf (1956) appears to be open to irremediable circularity. Whorf argues that the grammatical structure of a speaker's language influences thought; but it is difficult to see how evidence of this could be obtained, since evidence of what someone thinks can only be obtained via language. The consensus view amongst linguists at present is probably that Whorf's view is neither provable nor refutable, and is therefore rather uninteresting. Whorf is best known for his work on the Hopi Indians of North America, and for his argument that differences between their language and West European languages explain differences in their ways of thinking about concepts such as time, space and matter. But Whorf makes no attempt at all to relate such conceptual differences (assuming for the present that such differences genuinely exist) to cultural differences in general, or to the presence or absence of writing or of a long tradition of literacy. At the very least this could provide an alternative explanation of differences in cognitive style.

Further, it may be possible to investigate the cognitive effects of writing systems much more precisely and without circularity. First, we have historical evidence of the types of scientific progress which the invention of writing did actually spark off at different periods. Second, we have the possibility of comparative research, since some individuals and societies are not literate. As Goody (1977, p. 10) suggests, we may be able to study the 'technology of the intellect' and provide some actual mechanisms to explain cognitive development.

5.5   The specialization of written language

It is not surprising that many children are initially very vague and confused about such purposes of written language, when we realize that many of its functions are often so specialized and particular, and mostly quite beyond children's experience. Relatively few people, even adults, are regular consumers of World Three, and very few people actually contribute to it. But there are also more mundane reasons why the functions of writing may be quite beyond many children's experience.

Speech and writing are not in free variation. That is, it is not usually possible to choose either one or the other. There are occasions where I may consider whether to send someone a note rather than ringing them up or going to talk with them face-to-face, but the choice of a particular medium is likely to have particular implications. Further, the choice of medium is normally determined by the social function of the communication. In our society, there are conventions, usually quite clear cut, which determine whether messages are conveyed orally or in writing, and little choice is possible. Thus a committee meeting comprises face-to-face interaction, but the minutes must be recorded in writing: they cannot, for example, conventionally be recorded on audio-tape.

A difficulty for children is that many of the situations which conventionally require writing are of a fairly specialized and restricted kind. Either the function of the language is to make a record of some kind or the addressee is not available. The addressee may not be accessible either because he is geographically distant or because there is, in fact, no well-defined addressee. We must also distinguish therefore between personal correspondence to some particular individual who is physically distant (for example, a postcard to grandmother), and institutional writing addressed to some group of people, that is, all normal published books and therefore the vast bulk of written material.

Not only is the addressee unknown for institutional writing, but there is only indirect feedback, if any, and usually there is none. Communication is one-way. In reading, one at least has both the message and one's own reactions to it.

Major differences between spoken and written language are closely related to this rather tenuous relationship between most written language and social situation. Typically, speech takes place in a particular social situation; and typically, in everyday conversation, speech is only one component of communication, alongside facial expression, gesture, and reference to the physical surroundings. But a piece of writing typically has to stand on its own entirely, without any help from the situation, and therefore has to supply all the necessary contextual information explicitly. Mixed varieties, such as radio talks or discussions (5.6), are typically those which are closest to written language. Thus, normal language is usually heavily context-dependent, whereas written language usually has to be context-free as far as possible.

Although institutional writing is decontextualized in these ways, it nevertheless has some firm points of contact with social situations and social purposes, even if these are indirect and heavily conventionalized. Usually it is fairly clear who is sending what message to whom. That is, it is typical communicative behaviour; and one can at least talk meaningfully of a sender/addressor, a message, a receiver/addressee, and a purpose. Another link, although indirect, to social situations is that writers always write as incumbents of known social roles: academic, journalist, newspaper editor, lawyer, 'expert', and others. Widdowson (1975, pp. 47ff.) argues that literary works (poems, novels, stories, plays) are even further decontextualized to the extent that they are designed as self-contained wholes, formally and functionally. With reference to the linguistic form of literary works, he argues that it is a defining characteristic that the language is patterned over and above what is required by the language code itself. That is, the style of the language used has its own value, and the author may use stylistic features to convey his message. This point is particularly clear in poetry, but holds also for novels. With reference to function, he points out that literary works are independent of normal spoken or written interaction in that it is no longer useful to talk of an author sending a message to an addressee. There is a convention that an author does not have to accept the social responsibility for what he says in the first person (see Searle, 1975). As Widdowson puts it (p. 53): 'Love letters can involve the sender in action for breach of promise, but love poems do not count as binding in the same way.'

These points about the self-contained nature of literary communication may be clearer if we contrast various functions and formal characteristics of literature with the present book. First, I am responsible for the views expressed in this book, and these views are open to criticism in reviews. A literary work is not open to criticism of this type. Second, this book is not independent of other books and articles; on the contrary it makes constant reference to other work and therefore constant references to other written discourse. Third, a summary of the ideas in this book, as presented in Chapter 8, is essentially the same in kind as the book itself; whereas a summary of a poem or novel is no longer a poem or novel. Fourth, the style of the book is inessential, in the sense that all that is required is that it should be clear what is being said. The style has no value *per se* and is not deliberately patterned beyond what is required to write grammatical and meaningful English.

5.6   Written text as edited language

Relative to spoken language, written language is permanent and unable to rely on extra-linguistic context. These two factors have contradictory formal effects. Being permanent, written text can be more condensed, since, if the reader fails to understand something on first reading, he can read it again. But since the reader has only the text, with no other context to help him, things must be spelled out more explicitly.

Because of the functions it serves, the situations in which it is used, and its permanence, written text is generally highly edited. Whereas normal conversational language is composed spontaneously in real time, written language is often drafted then redrafted, often several times over, and often by several different people, for example, author and editor. Extreme cases such as legal language and civil service documents are not the product of any recognizable individual at all, but the product of combined composition by many people. On the one hand, such written language should be easier to understand than spoken, since it is more carefully organized, and can be re-read if necessary. On the other hand, it should be more difficult to understand, since it has to stand on its own without the support of context; and in addition, the editing is likely to make the text 'denser' and less redundant. Many important formal lexical and grammatical differences between written and spoken language result from these functional and situational constraints.

Compared with spoken text, written text is likely to be higher in information load in various ways. The written text is likely to be shorter and therefore less redundant, because containing fewer repetitions; and to contain relatively more lexical (content) words and fewer grammatical (structural) words. By lexical words is meant nouns, verbs, adjectives, adverbs; grammatical words means pronouns, prepositions, conjunctions, auxiliary verbs, articles. Lexical words comprise large classes containing up to thousands of items; there are thousands of nouns in English, for example, and the class is open-ended, as new nouns are regularly created or borrowed from other languages. Grammatical words, on the other hand, comprise small closed classes; for example, in English there are only a dozen or so conjunctions in common use; *and, but, so, however*, etc., and this number is not open to increase by borrowing from other languages. Since lexical words are less predictable (there are many more of them in the language), the information content of written language is correspondingly higher and less predictable. This informational 'density' can be overcome by a skilled reader, but it does require flexibility in reading techniques, including the use of skimming, back-tracking, re-reading and similar skills. I have emphasized elsewhere that reading is a linguistic activity which is highly dependent on the language skills which the beginner brings to the task. These are skills which are not relevant to understanding spoken language and which will therefore almost certainly require a great deal of explanation and practice.

It has been suggested in several places (Milroy, 1973; Cook-Gumperz, 1977; Lunzer and Harrison, 1979) that Bernstein's distinction between restricted and elaborated codes is related to distinctions between spoken and written language respectively, and therefore to the acquisition of literacy. The definition of the codes is complex, and their definition has changed quite fundamentally over Bernstein's many papers published from 1958 to 1973 (see Bernstein, 1971; Stubbs, 1976, ch. 3). However, the point which concerns us here is that restricted code has been defined consistently as implicit, particularistic and context-bound, because it relies on shared understandings between speakers and shared knowledge about contexts; whereas elaborated code is, conversely, explicit, universalistic and context-free, because it has to stand without such shared understandings. Thus restricted code is characteristically used within the family, where there is a high level of shared expectations; whereas schools are 'predicated upon elaborated code' since their major aim is to teach pupils to use explicit language. It should be clear that these distinctions are very much the same as those we have drawn between spoken and written language. Whereas spoken language can often rely on features of context in order to be understood, written text has to stand on its own and in that sense is context-free. We are clearly dealing with relative freedom from context, since all language is to some extent dependent on context for its interpretation. Cook-Gumperz (1977, p. 106), an ex-colleague of Bernstein's, suggests that teaching literacy to children involves teaching them to free language from its context in actions, and to use the linguistic channel alone. It is surprising that Bernstein himself never discusses the distinctions between spoken and written language at all.

I suggested above (5.4) what the Whorfian hypothesis about the relation between language and cognition might be more usefully reformulated in terms of the types of thinking which are facilitated by written language. Similarly, Bernstein's work may be pointing out an important distinction between forms and functions of language, but he may have located the distinction in the wrong place. Bernstein (1971, p. 195) himself cites Whorf as a major influence on his own work.

5.7 The relation between speaking and reading aloud

There are intermediate cases between spoken and written language. A lecturer may choose to speak entirely impromptu, or may speak from notes, or may actually read from a script, or deliver a talk without notes which has been rehearsed beforehand, or give a repetition of a previously delivered lecture. Some pieces of language are written down for no other reason than to be read aloud later. Examples are news broadcasts and speeches. In fact, all combinations of written and spoken are possible:

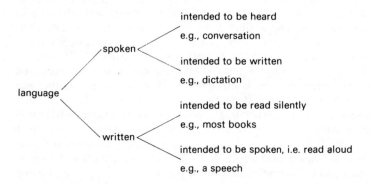

(Similar distinctions are made by Crystal and Davy, 1969, p. 70; and Bell, 1977.) We could further distinguish between spoken language, intended to be heard and spontaneously composed (e.g., conversation), spoken language intended to be heard but rehearsed and possibly based on a written original (e.g., reciting a poem from memory), and so on. But in general one set of social situations and communicative purposes requires spoken language, and a separate set, with only a small overlap, requires written language.

Confusion may be caused for children by two things: requiring them to read aloud written material, and the specialized situations in which written material is used.

In fact, very little is known about people's attitudes towards reading aloud. In modern European and American society, fewer and fewer people do regularly read aloud, apart from the occasional bedtime story or reading out instructions. But the evidence which is available suggests that reading aloud is viewed rather differently in different communities and consequently that the relation between written and spoken language is different in different communities (see 2.7). The different functional relationships which can hold between spoken and written language can be illustrated precisely from studies done in the USA, primarily in New York, and in Belfast.

In a large number of well-known studies, Labov (1966, 1972a and elsewhere) has investigated the stylistic variation from casual to formal language, within varieties of English in New York used by speakers from different social-class groups. The point which concerns us here is that he suggests that it is possible to view styles along a linear continuum, from casual to formal, which may cut across the spoken-written distinction. He collects speech data from different social-class groups, from working to middle class, in situations of increasing formality: (1) casual conversation, (2) careful speech in an interview, (3) reading a connected passage of text, (4) reading lists of isolated words, and (5) reading lists of minimal pairs, that is, words that might be pronounced identically (e.g., for New Yorkers: *guard* and *god*). Labov's argument is that as a speaker moves from situation (1) to (5), he is made to pay more and more attention to speech and that his speech becomes more and more formal. The finding is that each situation forces the speaker to move further in the same direction.

For example, it is more prestigious in New York to pronounce post-vocalic /r/ in words like *guard* and *beer* than to omit it. And one finds that speakers in all social classes produce more post-vocalic /r/ in situation (2) than (1), and so on. Also (ignoring some complications which do not affect the argument here) speakers higher up the social class scale produce more post-vocalic /r/ than speakers lower down. Speaking and reading styles are therefore found to be on a stylistic continuum, and the same norms hold for written and spoken language.

The validity of this continuum, which cuts across spoken and written styles, has been questioned in studies done in other places. Macaulay (1978), for example, questions whether reading style is a 'speech style' at all. The most extensive empirical data on the problem has probably been collected by Milroy and Milroy (1977) in a study of working-class speech in Belfast, Northern Ireland. Milroy and Milroy carried out the same type of procedures as Labov, but were led to propose a dual norm hypothesis, and to propose that reading is perceived as a quite different activity from conversation. They found that there was predictable stylistic shifting from casual to more formal conversation, but that for certain variables the same direction of shift was not maintained in word list styles where there was a shift back to a vernacular style of pronunciation. They propose that the written channel is evaluated quite differently in New York and Belfast.

First, the reading task often created considerably anxiety. Some informants said they would never read anything aloud normally, except possibly instructions on a can of food, and some simply refused to read connected texts, although they were quite happy to read word lists. Word lists tended to be read rapidly, with a characteristic rhythm and rise–fall intonation: *bág, bàd, rág, stàb*. They suggest that Labov's findings may depend on the activity of reading aloud fluently having some cultural value in the community. For their Belfast working-class informants, it seems that reading aloud is a speech event partly or wholly outside the norms which govern other speech events. It might even not be a recognized speech event at all: the informants do not normally read aloud, characteristically do it only with embarrassment, and may refuse outright. The view of speaking and reading as lying on a stylistic continuum may therefore only be applicable to confident and highly literate speakers. The Milroys point out further that a high percentage of their informants were in fact totally illiterate.

5.8 Implications for teaching reading and writing

The argument of this chapter has been that it is not surprising if children are often vague and confused about the functions of written language, because written language has complex and sophisticated intellectual and social functions which are inevitably beyond the needs, interests or understanding of young children.

The specialized functions, especially of institutional writing which is the largest proportion, may partly explain why it is often so difficult to teach pupils to write. It is rare for people to have to do much writing, and many people simply have no need to do any at all. A normal child could not exist for long without talking, but he simply has no natural need to write for some only partly defined group of readers of whose ideas, interests and attitudes he is unsure. The people who regularly do produce institutional writing are mostly professionals, doing it as part of their professional work, academics, civil servants, journalists, lawyers and authors, and each group has rather different, sometimes very well defined, conventions as firm guidelines. Consider, for example, the style sheets produced by publishers and professional academic organizations. Among the most firmly conventionalized styles are scientific papers and legal writing, although more stylistic latitude has been allowed in such areas recently. But the school pupil faced with a writing task often has no such guidelines.

It follows that a major task in teaching literacy must be to get children to understand the purposes and conventions of written language. A general principle in teaching any kind of communicative competence, spoken or written, is that the speaking, listening, writing or reading should have some genuine communicative purpose. It is clear from many studies of classroom language (e.g., Barnes, 1969; Sinclair and Coulthard, 1975; Stubbs, 1976) that much of the spoken language in classrooms has no genuine communicative function. The majority of questions which teachers ask in many classrooms are not genuine questions asked because the teacher wants to know something: they are test questions, asked by a teacher who wants to know if the pupil knows something. It follows that a lot of the spoken language which pupils produce is monosyllabic, since they are simply responding to pseudo-questions. If children are to be encouraged to produce complex spoken language, they must be placed in social situations where they can initiate conversational exchanges and not just respond, and where the language has genuine communicative functions.

With reading and writing, it is difficult to provide children with tasks which have genuine purposes, especially in the early stages. Requiring children to read aloud, for example, often has no genuine communicative function, although it is unavoidable as a teaching technique and check for the teacher. Similarly, it is difficult to provide a genuine audience for a child's writing, for the simple but awkward reason that genuine institutional writing has only an abstract audience which it is difficult if not impossible to simulate in the classroom. At any rate, the traditional classroom task of 'writing an essay' may in some ways be more difficult than the task performed by professional writers, since it may involve writing without clear stylistic conventions, with no genuine communicative function, and with no genuine audience in mind.

Chapter 6

Transcriptions, orthographies and accents

This chapter will discuss differences of form between spoken and written language. The differences are important and not always evident. Nevertheless, focusing on the differences may give an unduly exaggerated view. It is therefore worth while to begin by stating that, although written and spoken language are different in some respects, and are to some extent independent of each other, writing and speech are nevertheless primarily different realizations of the same underlying language system. As we saw in Chapter 2, the relationship takes this form:

6.1 Formal features of written and spoken language

As we have seen in various ways, the relations between speech and writing are not symmetrical. As an approximation, the following asymmetry is apparent: (a) anything that is written can be spoken, i.e. read aloud; (b) but not everything that is spoken can be written down. This is a useful generalization to make, if the following modifications are immediately added. (a) is true in so far as anything written can be read aloud; but much written text is not intended to be read aloud and it is difficult and unnatural to do so. An obvious example is written legal language. In addition, (a) is restricted largely to continuous written text. Some types of written material which depend heavily on layout, such as tables, diagrams and formulae, may lose almost all their point or comprehensibility if read aloud. As for (b), it is true that any spoken utterance can be transcribed, but a transcription is not the same as conventional writing. This is discussed in detail in the next section

116

(6.2). But the major reason for asserting (b) is that there are many features of spoken language such as rhythm, tempo, intonation, voice quality, and so on, for which there are simply no corresponding writing conventions. The same is true of all the features of spoken conversational language which are interactional and concern verbal and non-verbal feedback between speaker and listener, and therefore have no direct counterpart in written language, which is essentially one-directional. Examples of utterances which have no close functional equivalent in normal written language are: *hello!, you know, isn't it, pardon?*

It is useful to list some of those formal features available to either spoken or written English but not to both.

Speech (conversation): intonation, pitch, stress, rhythm, speed of utterance, pausing, silences, variation in loudness; other paralinguistic features, including aspiration, laughter, voice quality; timing, including simultaneous speech; co-occurrence with proxemic and kinesic signals; availability of physical context.

Writing (printed material): spacing between words; punctuation, including parentheses; typography, including style of typeface, italicization, underlining, upper and lower case; capitalization to indicate sentence beginnings and proper nouns; inverted commas, for example to indicate that a term is being used critically (*Chimpanzees' 'language' is* ...); graphics, including lines, shapes, borders, diagrams, tables; abbreviations; logograms, for example, *&*; layout, including paragraphing, spacing, margination, pagination, footnotes, headings and subheadings; permanence and therefore availability of the co-text.

For the purposes of such a list, I am assuming the paradigmatic examples of a published book versus an everyday conversation. As we have seen (5.7), mixed types such as scripted radio talks will have mixed formal characteristics. If we bear in mind such a list, we may have a clearer initial idea of which elements in the writing system have no counterpart in speech and therefore we may know better which characteristics of language can be assumed to be transferred from speech to reading and writing, and which need to be taught explicitly. Note in particular that different choices are available in the two systems. It is not the case, for example, that punctuation directly corresponds to features such as intonation, stress and pausing, although their functions overlap. In fact, none of the characteristics under *writing* have direct equivalents in spoken language, and therefore they probably all require formal teaching to some extent.

6.2 Words in transcriptions and orthographies

A theme which constantly comes up in the literature on reading and spelling is the question of whether English spelling ought to be more 'phonetic', by which is normally meant 'phonemic'. Chapter 3 showed in detail that English spelling does not relate only to phonemes, and it showed some advantages of a mixed morphophonemic system. Here we can approach the question from the other end and ask what is the nature of a phonemic transcription, and how does a transcription differ from an orthography in form and function?

Transcriptions are used by linguists to represent sound features of spoken utterances. Some of the major differences between a transcription of an utterance in English and its representation in the spelling system are that: (a) English spelling has only one form for words which have a range of pronunciations and therefore different possible transcriptions. (We shall be talking in this chapter about different pronunciations within the particular accents of individual speakers, as well as about differences between accents.) (b) The spelling corresponds most closely to the 'citation form'; that is, to the pronunciation of the word in isolation. (c) But some words, such as prepositions, are never naturally pronounced in isolation. One way of summarizing these three points in to say that a spelling represents most closely an ideal form of a spoken word.

Written English uses one single written form for each word in the language, apart from marginal exceptions, including the very few abbreviations permitted in informal writing, but not normally in formal printed material, such as *I'll, I'm, we'd, isn't, didn't*. There is therefore a difference between many of the forms which a child is likely to hear in speech and their printed forms. For example, *going to* is likely to be pronounced, especially when followed by a verb, as:

/gɒnə, gənə, gəntə/.

Except in very formal speech, it is rather unlikely to be pronounced

/gəuɪŋ tə/

unless in a different context, not before a verb, as in *I'm going to London*, where *going* is itself a main verb. And it is most unlikely to be pronounced

/gəuɪŋ tu·/

unless in a contrastively stressed example where there has been some previous misunderstanding: *I said I'm going to London, after I've come back from Cardiff.* Conversely, the spelling *gonna* will only be found in stereotyped indications of casual speech, in, say, a novel.

A principle which a beginner has to learn therefore is to identify the range of pronunciations of a word or phrase in normal conversation with the fully stressed citation forms represented by the spelling system.

Spellings correspond most closely to the ideal pronunciation of words in isolation, or to the pronunciation towards which a speaker may tend if required to repeat a message clearly down a bad telephone line.

The English writing system has not always followed this principle. In Middle English, post-1066, the word for *you* (singular) was

subject þu /θuˑ/   object þe /θe/

But it showed a strong tendency for the initial /θ/ to assimilate to the final consonant of the preceding word, and one finds written forms such as

artu   from *art þu*
and te   from *and þe*

But after about 1370 there was a growing tendency to regard the writing as logographic, in the sense of expecting a single spelling to stand for any word in all circumstances, and such alternative forms become rare in written records (Strang, 1970, p. 263).

In spoken English words are subject to different kinds of variation. (Gimson, 1970, is a standard textbook and source of data on the pronunciation of English and much of the following discussion is based on this source. Brown, 1977, is also full of very good examples and data on the pronunciation of contemporary standard English, and this book has also been fully consulted.) The simplest type of variation is the variable pronunciation of isolated words, within a single accent. Thus *economics* can be pronounced /ɛkənɒmɪks/ or /iˑkənɒmɪks/. Other examples are

privacy   /praɪvəsɪ/, /prɪvəsɪ/
patriot   /pɛɪtrɪət/, /pætrɪət/

Gimson (1970, p. 301) estimates that 15 per cent of the thousand most common words in English admit this kind of phonetic variability. This is variation within what would normally be considered a single accent.

A second very common type of variation is due to words being pronounced differently according to the phonological context in which they occur. There is a strong tendency in English, for example, for phonemes to change at word boundaries. In isolation *can't* is pronounced /kɑˑnt/. But it regularly has alternative forms such as

/kɑˑŋ/ as in /aɪ kɑˑŋ gəu/   *I can't go*
/kɑˑm/ as in /aɪ kɑˑm pɒsəblɪ/ *I can't possibly*

Assimilation of this type is most common in syllable- or word-final position. Initial consonants are rarely changed, implying that they are more important in identifying words. Most often, it is the point of articulation which is changed, while manner of articulation (e.g., plosive,

119

fricative, affricate, nasal) and voicing remain constant. The majority of assimilations involve an alveolar sound before a labial or velar. That is, final alveolars, /t, d, n, s, z/ are particularly unstable in final position before a labial /p, b, f, v, m/ or velar /k, g, ŋ/. Of these, /t, d, n/ are involved in the great majority of assimilations. It is also interesting that the set of alveolar phonemes /n, t, d/ are, in that order, the three most common consonant phonemes in English. Table 2 gives the relevant consonant phonemes for English. (See also Appendix B for a definition of the terms used.)

TABLE 2

manner of articulation	point of articulation				
	labial	dental	alveolar	post-alveolar	velar
plosive or affricate	p b		t d	tʃ dʒ	k g
fricative	f v	θð	s z	ʃ ʒ	
nasal	m		n		ŋ

Typical assimilations are therefore:

a fat man	/ə fæp mæn/	/t/	before labial
hot coffee	/hɒk kɒfɪ/	/t/	before velar
a bad boy	/ə bæb bɔɪ/	/d/	before labial
a good girl	/ə gu·g gə·l/	/d/	before velar
handbag	/hæmbæg/	/n/	before labial, with additional elision of /d/
handkerchief	/hæŋkətʃi·f/	/n/	before velar

The phonemes /t, d/ are also often prone to be elided. When /t, d/ occur in the centre of a three-consonant cluster, it is rare to hear them at all in fluent speech even though they may be markers of the morpheme *past*. For example:

he hopped down	/hi· hɒp daun/
and bagged three ducks	/əm bæg θrɪ· dʌks/

People are often astonished or simply sceptical when such phenomena are pointed out to them. This is presumably because for highly literate speakers words comprise complex audio-visual images, and it is very hard indeed to make people hear what is actually said, independently of expectations induced by the spellings. For example, my experience in teaching linguistics to students is that it takes them one or even two years before they cease entirely to get confused between phonemes and letters. In addition, the kinds of assimilation illustrated above are changes in the shape of words which do not affect meaning. Since in conversation we are normally listening for meaning, such changes are irrelevant and are therefore to be ignored. I emphasize that the phenomena I am discussing are not merely found in casual, rapid, very informal conversation. Brown (1977) has documented such phenomena of elision, assimilation and vowel reduction, using data from BBC news broadcasts and radio discussions, that is, relatively formal speech, often scripted, where such phenomena nevertheless pass unnoticed every day. It is therefore unhelpful to dismiss such phenomena as careless, or as indicating the moral decline of the BBC, since all native speakers produce them in every situation, although they are obviously even more extreme in casual conversation. (See 2.6 on the unnoticed prevalence of dropping aitches which occurs in everyone's speech.) All languages undergo assimilatory processes of one type or another, and this has long been known to be an important factor in language change.

There are two important general points to conclude here from such examples. First, an orthography is not at all the same thing as a transcription, and those who argue that English spelling ought to be more consistently phonemic are ignoring this fact. Second, someone learning to read and write has to appreciate that a single spelling corresponds to a range of pronunciations and differs in form and function from corresponding transcriptions.

The range of pronunciations of individual words is most extreme with grammatical words (also known as structural words, function words and functors), that is, pronouns, articles, auxiliary verbs, prepositions, and conjunctions; as opposed to lexical words (or content words), that is, nouns, adjectives, verbs, and adverbs. The range of pronunciation which grammatical words undergo often means that the contrast between them is eliminated. Pronunciations such as the following are common:

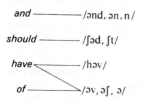

and ——————— /ənd, ən, n/

should ——————— /ʃəd, ʃt/

have ——————— /həv/

of ——————— /əv, əʃ, ə/

In appropriate phonological contexts, *have, of, are, a, or, her* may all be pronounced as /ə/. Further, although English writing gives such items the status of words by placing them between spaces, many cannot occur in isolation in speech, unless they are elicited in a linguistic discussion, for example. Thus, there is no occasion, apart from such citation forms, on which one can say *and* and nothing else. The word can occur only between or before other words. This fact, that certain words cannot meaningfully be read in isolation, is sometimes not taken into account in reading schemes. For example, the smallest sensible context for *and* is some frame equivalent to *Bill   Fred*. (See Gudschinsky, 1974.) *And* is simply not a normally pronounceable item in isolation, and the pronunciation /ænd/ is rare except in contrastively stressed contexts such as: *I said Bill 'and Fred, not just Bill* . It is clear that learners can become confused about grammatical words, since one finds mistakes of the type: *I should of gone*.

Since many words can have more than one pronunciation according to their phonological context, it follows that for any sentence we can propose a range of phonemic transcriptions depending on the speed and style of utterance. Thus a speaker might say: *I should have gone back to London on Wednesday* at different tempos and varying degrees of casualness, and three corresponding broad or phonemic transcriptions out of a range could be:

/aɪ ʃʊd həv 'gɒn 'bæk tə 'lʌndən ɒn 'wɛdn̩zdɪ/	(1)
/aɪ ʃəd əv 'gɒn 'bæk tə 'lʌndn̩ ən 'wɛdn̩zdɪ/	(2)
/aɪ ʃt əf 'gɒm 'bæk tə 'lʌndn̩ n̩ 'wɛnzdɪ/	(3)

(1) might be produced in a very formal social setting where the speaker is paying attention to the way he is speaking; (2) is still rather slow speech, but slightly less formal; and (3) is more normal, casual speech, although still by no means extreme. All three transcriptions are at the same level of abstraction: phonemic. That is, the same sentence can be represented by different phoneme strings. Other such phonemic transcriptions could also be proposed for the same sentence. Precisely the same phenomona can be documented for other languages. For example, Dressler *et al.* (1976) discuss phonological differences between careful and rapid speech in the German spoken in Vienna, and give a similar set of transcriptions for a single sentence, showing entirely comparable processes of assimilation and elision.

One type of transcription, then, is an attempt to fix the phonemic features of an utterance as it might be spoken by an individual at a point in time. It is a representation of some aspects of a unique event. Conventional writing, on the other hand, aims at a much more enduring, abstract generalization, and ignores many types of variation in utterances. Linguists distinguish sharply between *utterances* and *sentences*. For example, the following sentence could be uttered by half a dozen people: *This book is about literacy*. Each of the speakers would be producing different utterances of the same sentence, and the different utterances might differ in speed, pitch, intonation, and so on. The same distinction is made by philosophers who distinguish between *types* and *tokens*. Tokens are actual instances or occurrences of abstract types.

Thus one can have an infinite number of utterance-tokens of the same sentence-type. Transcriptions represent some aspects of utterance-tokens, but conventional writing systems represent sentence-types.

Nevertheless, phonemic transcriptions represent only aspects of utterances, and are themselves still highly abstract and ignore, in their turn, sub-phonemic, allophonic variation (see 2.6). Since allophonic variation is also ignored by English spelling, and by orthographies in general, this point does not concern us here.

One of the most general and important points to have emerged in this section is that spoken English, at least at the levels of phonology and morphology, varies much more than written English, and varies much more than literate people generally realize. In contrast to spoken language, written language is the product of much idealization and often deliberate formalization.

We have also raised here another important general point which we have touched on in several places before: that the conventions of our writing system impose on us a particular segmentation and analysis of language. This segmentation is only one possible segmentation amongst many, but it follows that learning to read necessarily involves accepting the analysis of language provided by the writing system.

We have already briefly cited (2.1, 5.1) work by Reid (1958, 1966) and Downing (1969), who found that young children learning to read are often very confused about the nature and purpose of reading. More precisely, such studies have found that children are usually confused and vague about such terms as *letter, word* and *sentence*. Francis (1973) confirmed these findings with five- to seven-year-old children. She suggests that this is not simply because such terms refer to abstract concepts, but because the concepts themselves are complex and not clearly definable; and because it is only through learning to read that children come to develop an analytic view of language as something which is segmentable into such units. She argues that it does not occur to children to analyse speech. But in learning to read, they are forced to recognize hierarchically related units: letter, word, sentence. Further, these units are in any case only fully applicable to written language. This is clear with *letters*; but also words are divided off by spaces in our writing system, but not in speech; and sentences are similarly divided off unambiguously by the conventions of our writing system, but not clearly definable units in speech.

There is also considerable and more direct evidence that children beginning to read have difficulty in understanding the convention of word boundaries in written English, and do not necessarily perceive either written or spoken discourse in terms of discrete words in the way in which this term is conventionally used. Holden and MacGintie (1972) carried out word-recognition experiments with five-year-old children and concluded that they were 'quite unaware of the printing convention' which puts space between words. Teachers therefore cannot take for granted that children will understand reference to 'words'. Weaver *et al.* (1972) concluded on the basis of similar experiments that children beginning to read lack a precise notion of 'words', and suggest further that 'perhaps sounds become words only in written form'.

We might make such arguments more explicit as follows. It may be that it is only in learning to read that children acquire the ability to segment and analyse language consciously. Learning to read and write involves learning the kind of segmentation and analysis on which the writing system is based, but this analytic ability is seldom taught explicitly. Children therefore often have to learn two things at once, since one of them is simply taken for granted by teachers. It is worth emphasizing at this point that the segmentation which underlies our particular writing system is only one possible segmentation. The English writing system is alphabetically based, and therefore based on an intuitive notion of a phoneme, and in addition marks words and sentences unambiguously. Other writing systems may be based on syllables or morphemes, and indicate neither phonemes or words (see 3.2).

Taking this line of thought further, one may note that the development of concepts in the history of linguistics itself has undoubtedly been influenced by the segmentation underlying different writing systems (Bugarski, 1970). That is, professional linguists have been influenced in their preconceptions about how language should be analysed by their familiarity with particular writing systems and with the practical problems of developing methods of transcribing spoken language. A well-known case is the development of phoneme theory itself. The concept of the phoneme became fully explicit around the beginning of the twentieth century, largely through the practical work of men such as Ellis, Bell and Sweet who were tackling practical problems of orthography and transcription: in attempting spelling reforms, devising shorthand methods, and in examining foreign language teaching problems. The phoneme concept clearly underlies, in an intuitive and inexplicit way, alphabetic writing systems, but the concept became clear only through struggling with the inconsistencies of practical alphabets.

Thirty years later, however, J. R. Firth (1957) argued that an alphabetic writing system or a phonemic transcription imposes an arbitrary segmentation on the stream of speech, and that it completely misses various features of speech which continue unbroken across larger segments, including syllables and words. Firth makes it quite explicit that his criticisms of phoneme theory are a result of his familiarity with Indian syllabic writing systems. Firth developed a 'prosodic' theory of phonology which is a radical alternative to phoneme theory.

In the same connection is it significant that the very advanced work on Sanskrit carried out by Indian grammarians around 500 BC concentrated on problems raised by the type of writing system they had. They considered in detail the question of whether 'words' were an artefact of analysis and whether sentences were not rather the basic unit of language; and they are mainly known for the discussion of *sandhi* phenomena: that is the changes which words undergo in connected speech across their boundaries. The Sanskrit term is still used by linguists in this sense. In Europe, questions of sentence structure have been tackled seriously only in very recent times: it has been 'words', which are the units marked most clearly in our writing system, which have been the focus of linguistic analysis since the Greeks and Romans to the twentieth century.

6.3   Standard and non-standard English and accents

We need at this point to explore in a little more detail the relationship between the standardization involved in the development of writing systems, and written and spoken English. The relationship between standard and non-standard English is in any case central to an understanding of literacy for two main reasons. First, standard English is often regarded as the language of formal school education; and second, the concept of standard English is arguably only fully applicable to written English.

The relation is complex for English since we have to discuss separately accent (pronunciation) and dialect (grammar and vocabulary). And whilst it is relatively clear what is meant by standard English grammar and vocabulary, spoken or written, there is no single standard accent, even within Britain. Since spelling is highly standardized, it follows immediately that different accents have different, though roughly equivalent, relationships to spelling.

The term standard English (SE) is widely used but often not clearly defined. Various other terms are also widely used as synonyms of SE, including 'the Queen's English', 'BBC English' and 'Oxford English'. These terms do no particular harm if they are just alternative labels, although they do imply a rather out-dated view of the sociolinguistic situation in Britain. The BBC has used announcers with regional accents for some years, and it is simply not true that either the Royal Family or the inhabitants of Oxford provide a standard for present-day English speakers. What SE should not be confused with, however, is Received Pronunciation (RP). This is a term used by linguists to refer to a particular accent which has, or at least used to have, high social prestige.

It is useful to retain the term SE to refer to a dialect, that is an amalgam of syntax and lexis.

An interesting sidelight was recently thrown on the BBC's attitude to RP and on the status of RP as that variety of English accent best known abroad, by radio interviews with Wilfred and Mabel Pickles, well known for their radio programme *Have a Go* which ran from 1946 for many years (Radio 4, 5 p.m. News, Monday 27 March 1978). Wilfred Pickles was well known for his northern Yorkshire accent. In the early 1940s, when it was feared that Britain might be invaded by Germany, Pickles was moved from the north to London, to read the News. The reason, which was not advertised at the time, was the feeling that the German propaganda machine might well be able to imitate convincingly an RP accent and therefore mislead people with counterfeit news broadcasts; but that a Yorkshire accent would not be able to be successfully imitated and listeners would know that they were listening to a genuine broadcast. Pickles reported that he was popular in the south, but not in the north: he realized that in the north people were complaining that they sent their children to school to learn to 'talk properly', only then to have them hear regional accents on the BBC. It is a finding in many sociolinguistic surveys in many parts of the world that speakers regularly down-grade their own regional accents and dialects (see 4.4).

An important point about social and regional varieties in British English is that social class and geographical variation interact. The higher up the social scale one goes, the less regional variation there is in language. Thus educated middle-class speakers in Aberdeen and London use very similar grammar and vocabulary, but working-class speakers will differ quite sharply. This pattern is characteristic of British English, but not of all languages. In Germany, for example, there is much regional variation in dialect amongst educated middle-class speakers and no stigma necessarily attached to recognizably regional forms.

SE can be defined in various ways. Most common is probably the concept of SE as a social class dialect. That is, SE is that variety of English spoken by educated middle-class people in most parts of Britain. This definition is, of course, circular. It asserts that this social group speak SE, and that SE is, by definition, what they speak. If their language changes, so does SE. The first problem is then regional variation within SE. Educated middle-class speakers in, say, London and Glasgow will have in common the vast bulk of their lexical and grammatical systems, but they are also likely to differ in a few words and grammatical constructions. The Londoner is likely to say *I am, aren't I*. The Glaswegian is likely to say *I am, amn't I* or *I am, am I not*. Such differences are rather minor and one may either decide to ignore them, or to say that there is a separate standard Scottish English. Similar cases would arise with standard American English (cf. *I have gotten*).

One could in addition define SE geographically and historically. SE is that dialect of English which has social prestige since it is spoken by the dominant educated middle-class group in Britain (social-class dialect definition); and which is particularly associated with the south-east of England, although now much more widespread (geographical definition as regional dialect), since it developed from the language of the court in London after the Middle Ages (historical definition). It is clearly a social, historical and geographical accident that SE developed out of a regional and social dialect of London. But since it did, there is now this dialect of English which has social prestige, due to its prestigious origins and by association with its prestigious and socially dominant users. The prestige of its users rubs off, as it were, on the language.

According to the observed linguistic usage of a large group of people, we could therefore specify that some forms are used by this group and are standard: e.g., *we were* (1). Other forms are not used by this group and are therefore non-standard: e.g., *we was* (2). We have not said that (2) is ungrammatical: it is perfectly grammatical in many non-standard dialects of English, but it does not have the social prestige attached to the standard form. Conversely, (1) is not used in many non-standard dialects. To say, in a shorthand way, that (2) is 'wrong' is to make a social judgment, not a linguistic one. I think there would be a general consensus amongst native speakers of English, both standard and non-standard, that (1) is standard and (2) is non-standard, although informants might interpret the distinction in terms of 'correct' versus 'incorrect'.

To say that there is a large intuitive consensus about what SE is, is not to say that it is well-defined. SE is, for example, nowhere clearly described. It is easiest to start with what is most clearly standardized: spelling. With a very few exceptions every word in British English has only one spelling. These spellings have been codified in dictionaries since the eighteenth century, and are accepted and used in all normal publications. American English has slightly different, but equally rigid spelling conventions. Spellings in English are therefore as highly standardized as it is possible for an aspect of language to be.

Conversely, there is no standard pronunciation (accent) for English. RP used to fill the role of a socially prestigious and accepted norm. This is the accent associated with upper-middle-class speakers, and was passed on through the public school system. It has the peculiar feature that it shows almost no regional variation. But SE can be spoken in a variety of accents including RP, standard Scottish, and so on. SE is generally not spoken in a broad Glaswegian accent, but it could be, since accent and grammar/lexis are in principle quite independent. (Conversely, RP is only ever used with SE, but again this is a social fact

about language varieties in Britain: it is not a necessary linguistic truth.)
There is nothing to prevent someone saying:

	Where's Gordon gone?	(3):	SE grammar and lexis
as	/wɛəz gɔ·dən gɒn/	(4):	RP accent
or	/hwerz gɔrdən gɔn/	(5):	standard Scottish accent

But if someone says: *Where's Gordon went?* (6) then he is using non-standard grammatical forms.

In summary, there is a single standard for the written language in spelling, but not for the spoken language in accent.

The aspect of English which is next most codified, and therefore standardized, is written English lexis and syntax. Almost all the many English grammar books describe or prescribe the syntax for written English, and even worldwide there is remarkably little variation in the vocabulary or grammar of formally published material. As a result, the same books and newspapers can be read and understood in London, Karachi or Alice Springs. There is variation, of course, in local vocabulary, and less so in grammar; but really very little variation compared with what the different regional varieties have in common.

The main point for the present argument is, therefore, that the concept of SE is fully applicable only to written language, since, as I have defined it here, SE has the following characteristics. It is highly codified: the language has been subject to deliberate language planning in the form of dictionary-making, since the eighteenth century especially, and in the form of the preparation of prescriptive grammar books. There is also a set of attitudes associated with SE: the language variety is accepted by the community as a model and as a prestige norm. This codification and set of attitudes has been deliberately transmitted by the school system and as a result the norms now have considerable stability. School education has, in turn, given particular weight and prestige to written language and literacy, sometimes equating 'literate' with 'educated' *per se*. Written language is therefore necessarily on the standardization scale, since writing conventions always develop when a language acquires a writing system, and by being written down, these conventions are inevitably codified. (See Garvin, 1973, who discusses these questions of defining the concept standard language.)

6.4 Accent differences

Accents (pronunciations) can differ in various ways. An accent can be defined quite precisely in phonetic and phonological terms, according to: (1) the list of phonemes it contains; (2) the distribution (place of occurrence) of these phonemes; and (3) the phonetic realization of the phonemes.

For illustrative purposes I will compare RP (Received Pronunciation) and accents of SSE (standard Scottish English). For many purposes these can be regarded as homogeneous accents, but both are strictly speaking a range of accents. Gimson (1970) discusses changes which are currently taking place in RP, and Abercrombie (1977) analyses what he calls the basic Scottish phoneme system and a series of other systems which are modifications of SSE in the direction of RP. There is further data on SSE and non-standard Scottish accents in Speitel (1975).

1 *Phoneme inventory*: SSE accents regularly have a velar fricative phoneme /x/ which is used in words such as *loch* and *Buchan*. Thus SSE distinguishes between *loch* and *lock*, whilst RP does not:

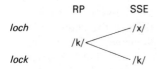

At this point in the system, SSE simply has an extra phoneme. Apart from a few differences of this type, the consonants of British English accents are remarkably uniform, but there are many such differences in the number of phonemic contrasts available in vowel systems. Contrasting RP and SSE further we find:

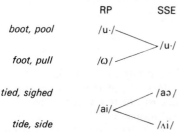

That is, SSE does not distinguish *pool* and *pull*. Conversely, SSE accents do distinguish *sighed* and *side* and similar pairs, where the mophologically complex word (verb plus *past*) has a different phoneme from the morphologically simple form.

2 *Distributional differences*: In other cases, two accents can have the same phoneme, but certain phonemes may be distributed differently. For example, both RP and SSE have an /r/ phoneme. In RP, it occurs only before vowels, but in SSE it can occur before and after vowels in the same syllable. Thus:

	RP	SSE
run	/rʌn/	
urn	/ə·n/	/ɛ·rn/
are	/ɑ·/	/ɑ·r/

Similarly, both RP and SSE have the phonemes /a·/ and /æ/. Sometimes they correspond in their occurrence in words; elsewhere RP has /a·/ where SSE has /æ/, for example:

	RP	SSE
gas, hat	/æ/	
bar, car	/ɑ·/	
bath, path	/ɑ·/	/æ/

Another example of distributional differences occurs with /s/ and /z/ phonemes in words such as *houses* and *housing*, where SSE accents often have /s/ word-medially.

3 *Phonetic realization*: Accents may have the same phonemic distinctions but differ in the phonetic realizations of the phonemes. For example, both RP and SSE have an /r/ phoneme. In RP it is never trilled, but in some SSE accents it is. Similarly, RP and SSE have the same vowel phoneme in words such as *no, know, bowl, cold*. But whereas in RP it will be a diphthong /əu/ or /ɔu/, in SSE it will be a monophthong or nearly so, /o·/.

The implications of accent differences such as these for learning to read and spell are probably as follows. Suppose a child pronounces the following pairs or triplets of words identically:

our, are	/ɑ·/
tower, tar	/tɑ·/
sure, shore, Shaw	/ʃɔ·/
for, four	/fɔ·/.

Such pronunciations are used by some but not all RP speakers. RP, as we have said, covers a range of accents and is at present changing in precisely words such as these. Such lack of one-to-one correspondence between pronunciation and spelling will probably constitute a teaching problem. However, the main point is that speakers of different accents will all have comparable problems: not the same problems, because accents differ and the problems will occur at different points, but the problems will be similar in kind. For most Scottish children, spelling differences in *watt, what*; *Wales, whales*; *witch, which*, will correspond to a difference in pronunciation; for most English children they will not. Many Norwich speakers pronounce differently the vowels in pairs such as: *nose, knows*; *moan, mown*; *toe, tow* (Trudgill, 1975, p. 49). And so on: one could go on detailing such distinctions which will appear at different points in the accent system.

There are probably two main implications of such accent variations. The reason why speakers with different accents have different but comparable problems is that English spelling is not consistently phonemic. If spelling was phonemic, it would by definition relate to a particular accent. One alphabet which is considerably more phonemic than conventional orthography is the Initial Teaching Alphabet (ITA). ITA is not consistent with the phoneme system of any single accent, and is not, in fact, consistently phonemic. However, it is biased clearly in favour of the accents used by middle-class speakers from southern Britain. Trudgill (1975, pp. 50-2) gives interesting examples of the confusions which can arise for speakers with other accents.

Since all accents have comparable problems when conventional orthography is used, these problems will probably have to be explained to learners. This implies that the teacher has to know the accent system of the pupils, and this is not always easy, especially if the teacher's own accent does not entirely correspond to the pupils', as is quite likely. It would be quite normal to expect three overlapping systems: the teacher's phoneme system, the pupil's phoneme system, and the phonemic distinctions marked by the spelling. For some of the time all three will correspond, but often they will not.

It is most important then for teachers to distinguish between differences in pronunciation and mistakes in reading. Suppose a child speaks an h-less accent of English, that is an accent which regularly has no word-initial /h/ phoneme in words such as *horse, house* or *hat*. Many regional and working-class accents from all over Britain are h-less. The child is likely to read a sentence such as: *Harry hates horses* (1) as *'arry 'ates 'orses* (2). This would be a correct reading at word level in his normal pronunciation. If the child is corrected by the teacher insisting that (1) should be: *Harry hates horses* (3), the only way to interpret this is that the teacher is correcting his pronunciation, not his reading, which is perfectly correct.

We are talking here about accent, but precisely analogous issues arise at other levels of language. Suppose a pupil reads: *Where's Harry gone?* (4) as *Where's Harry went?* (5). Reading (5) would prove that the pupil has understood (4) and has in addition translated (4) into his own non-standard dialect. If the teacher wishes to correct (5), he or she would have to distinguish between attempting to change the child's grammar, and explaining that there is a conventional correspondence between standard English and written English. At the level of meaning, (5) is perfectly accurate, and a comment that it is 'wrong' without further explanation could only be confusing, or be taken as a criticism of the child's native language.

It should probably be taken as a teaching principle that children's grammar or pronunciation should not generally be corrected while they are learning to read, since this can only confuse two tasks with one. If their language is to be corrected while they are reading, then this should be restricted to a particular period when it is explicit that their grammar and accent are being judged and not their comprehension.

There are three possible solutions to the problem of a mismatch between a child's dialect or accent and the language of reading books.

1   The child may be taught the standard language before being taught to read. In practice this turns out to be impossible, since the influence of the child's peer group will be towards the non-standard language, and this influence will be so strong that it will outweigh any English lessons in school. If learning to read has to wait until the child has acquired the standard language, this will never happen; or learning to read will, at best, be retarded by years.

2   Reading books can be prepared in non-standard dialects. This is expensive, and more important perhaps, it is an artificial solution, since such books have no wider utility: they are not 'real' books.

3   Children can be taught to read with books written in the standard language, but allowed to translate into their own dialect and accent as they read aloud. This is the solution which is often the most realistic. It does not involve criticism of the child's own language; it does not require special and artificial teaching material. What it does mean, however, is a change in the way many teachers view the use of non-standard dialects in the classroom.

6.5   Non-standard English, accents, and reading ability

There is a particularly neat set of experiments by Labov (1970) which provide a detailed study of the relation between non-standard dialect and reading failure, and which relate closely to several points we have discussed in detail above:

1   the morphophonemic nature of English spelling (Chapter 3);
2   in particular the morphophonemic representation of grammatical morphemes such as *-ed* (3.5);
3   the relation between English spelling and regional and social class accents (6.3);
4   the relation between the variability of spoken language and the categorial behaviour demanded in reading (6.2): and
5   whether such differences in dialect or accent do, in fact, cause reading problems at all.

Labov claims to provide a precise answer to (5): namely, that linguistic differences are not in general the primary cause of reading problems, although there are particular problems which may be caused by such differences.

Labov's data are from speakers of Black English Vernacular (BEV), that is, the non-standard dialect of English widely used in the USA, especially by black youths in inner city areas of New York, Chicago and other large cities. BEV has many phonological and grammatical characteristics which distinguish it noticeably from standard dialects of British and American English. (Labov, 1972b, gives detailed descriptions of many features of BEV.) Only one characteristic concerns us here. BEV contains a rule which simplifies consonant clusters in word-final position: for example, *past* and *went* will often, but not always, be pronounced /pas/ and /wɛn/. What more particularly concerns us, is the tendency to delete word-final /t/ or /d/ which may be the phonological marker of the past tense morpheme, indicated by *-ed* in the writing system. (We noted above, in 6.2, that /t/ and /d/ are often deleted in accents of standard English when they occur in the middle of a consonant cluster.) Deletion of word-final /t/ and /d/ is not invariable in BEV, however, but becomes more or less likely depending on the environment. Deletion is more likely if there is another consonant before the /t/ or /d/. That is, it is more likely in *past* and *raved*, than in *wet* and *showed*. Deletion is more likely if there is another consonant following the /t/ or /d/, rather than a following vowel. That is, it is more likely in *passed by* than in *passed over*. Deletion is more likely if the /Ct/ or /Cd/ cluster occurs within a single morpheme, as in *past*, than if the cluster occurs across a morpheme boundary, as in *passed* (where C = consonant).

These three contexts may interact: that is, more than one factor may be relevant in a given case. There are, therefore, both phonological and morphological constraints on consonant cluster simplification in BEV. (Labov claims that what are involved are highly systematic variable rules. Readers requiring further details on the kind of rule involved should consult Labov, 1970, 1972b.)

Labov's general argument (1970, p. 223) is that such linguistic differences are not generally the primary cause of reading failure. He argues that the primary cause is the cultural clash between working-class black culture and the white middle-class culture of the school. In other work, Labov (1969b) shows that reading ability correlates with peer group membership. For the black adolescent males he studied in south central Harlem, New York, core members of the street culture scored significantly lower on reading tests than boys who were more peripheral members of street gangs and more influenced by the norms of the schools.

However, there are certain correlations between particular reading difficulties and particular linguistic rules of non-standard dialect, regardless of social group membership (1970, p. 225). One of these correlations occurs with the reading of the *-ed* suffix in past tense forms. The general reading ability of adolescent working-class Negro boys is low, characteristically from two to five years below grade. But their ability to read correctly *-ed* forms is below their general reading ability. As we have seen above, there is no way to test the reading of such forms by presenting isolated words. If asked to read *passed*, /pas/ might be a correct reading in BEV: such a pronunciation is simply ambiguous on its own. Therefore, the technique which Labov used was to present sentences such as: *I looked* (1) *for trouble when I read* (2) *the news.* (1) could be correctly read as either /luk/ or /lukt/. But to show that (1) has been correctly understood as a past tense form, (2) must be read as /rɛd/. Labov is therefore distinguishing sharply between pronunciation (accent), reading isolated words, and understanding meaningful sentences. He is taking 'reading in the full sense of the term – deciphering meaning from symbols on the printed page and project- ing this meaning on other elements that have been deciphered' (p. 223). He is therefore pointing out that understanding at one point in a sen- tence may only be evident from what is said at some other point, and that one cannot use pronunciation alone to decide whether *-ed* forms are being correctly read.

Various other controls on what the boys could read were used. For example, he used sentences such as: *Last month I read five books*, to check that the boys could transfer tense information from one point in a sentence to another, when it did not depend on an *-ed* form. He found a high level of success in this text, but a much lower level of suc- cess in the *-ed* problem. The general conclusion is that 'the reading of the *-ed* suffix is not correlated with general reading skill' (p. 227).

Labov argues (pp. 244-5) that a source of confusion may be that whilst the relevant rules of the spoken dialect are variable, reading the *-ed* suffix requires categorical behaviour. As we have seen in detail, in Chapter 3, English spelling is based on a principle of one-spelling-one- meaning, and the *-ed* suffix must be understood as *past* every time it is encountered.

6.6   Conclusions

We have come back once more to the complex relations between written and spoken language, which we have now interpreted as a relation between a written system which is relatively invariant and a spoken system which is inherently variable. Such relations are likely to cause problems of detail for readers, but it is unlikely that accent or dialect differences are a major cause of reading failure in themselves. They may cause general problems, however, if they shake the beginner's confidence that the written language is rule-governed. And further, considerable confusion may be caused by a teacher who confuses accent differences with reading mistakes, and who, in attempting to correct reading mistakes, is interpreted by the child as criticizing an accent.

Part three

Explanations of reading failure

Chapter 7

Initial literacy and explanations of educational failure

There is nowadays probably a general consensus in educational think-ing that education should be child-centred, in the sense that learning is most effective if it is based on the child's own experiences. Teaching has to start from where the child is, because there is, logically, nowhere else to start. The well-known statement by Unesco (1953, p. 11) is widely accepted by educationalists:

> It is axiomatic that the best medium for teaching a child is his mother tongue. Psychologically, it is the system of meaningful signs that in his mind works automatically for expression and understand-ing. Sociologically, it is a means of identification among the members of the community to which he belongs. Educationally, he learns more quickly through it than through an unfamiliar linguistic medium.

We have discussed from various points of view ways in which some-one learning to read inevitably draws on his existing knowledge of language. Once a person can read fluently, then reading may be a way of acquiring new ideas or even new styles of language itself. But in the initial stages this could only be a distraction from the main task, which is to learn how to proceed from written language to a form of language which the reader knows already. This suggests a definition of reading as decoding from writing to a form of language which the reader is already able to understand. Note that this definition does not necessarily imply a decoding-to-sounds view of reading. On this definition, a person has not learned to read Russian if he has learned to decode and pronounce words written in Cyrillic script. Also the definition does not cover those cases in which a fluent adult reader might understand written language directly, without the intervention of spoken language.

In the initial stages, then, it is plausible to assume that any mis-matches between the child's spoken language and what he has to read, or between his experience and the content of his books, are likely to be obstacles to learning. It would now be accepted as axiomatic therefore by most educationalists that the best medium for teaching initial literacy is the child's own native language, and there has been considerable interest recently in preparing teaching materials which reflect the child's own interests and experience of language. Otherwise one is asking the child to learn a foreign language or dialect at the same time as he is learning a new skill.

In ways that we are familiar with from earlier chapters, the short-term educational and psychological goals often come into conflict with wider social, economic and political factors; and in the long term it may be to the child's advantage to learn to read and write in a language or dialect which is not his native variety. Initial literacy in the vernacular could not therefore simply be accepted as a panacea.

7.1 Possible sources of reading failure

Logically, there is a restricted number of places in which to search for the cause of reading failure. If someone fails to learn to read, then the cause must lie in: (1) the pupil; (2) his family or social background; (3) the teacher or the school; (4) the medium, primarily the writing system; (5) the materials, for example the content of the basal readers; or (6) the method; for example, phonic versus whole-word. Either there is something wrong with one of these factors, or there is a mismatch between them, for example, a difference between the child's spoken language and the written language of books.

There is no logical reason, of course, why different causes of different types (for example, medical plus social) should not contribute together in a particular case of reading failure, and this is probably what most commonly happens. It is likely that many cases of reading failure have several different causes, because, conversely, for every factor that is said to contribute to reading failure, it is probably possible to find a child who ought to be at risk, but who can read tolerably well (Merritt, 1972). That is, one finds children with low IQ, or with emotional disturbances, or from impoverished home backgrounds who can read. Interest in possible psychological causes and medical causes of reading difficulty began around the end of the nineteenth century and the debate still continues over whether reading ability is affected by constitutional or biological factors, whether inherited or not. (For a review of the controversy over the concept of dyslexia or specific reading disability, see Reid, 1968.) More recently, other factors such as emotional disturbance and social under-privilege have been suggested as causes.

One possibility is that the cause lies in the pupil: there is something wrong with Johnny. There are several sub-possibilities: (a) The cause may be medical, hereditary or not. Such factors are not discussed in this book. Terms such as 'word-blind' or 'dyslexic' imply a medical view even if, on inspection, such terms turn out not to be used in a precise medical sense. (b) The cause may be psychological: for example, the pupil may be emotionally disturbed or have a personality disorder. Again, this will not be discussed here in any detail. Note simply that it is often not clear which is the cause and which is the effect. Because of the high value placed on literacy in our society failure to learn to read can cause or worsen anxiety and emotional disturbances. This point, of course, questions the very distinction between psychological and social causes. (c) The cause might lie in the pupil's language. There is nothing 'wrong' with the language of any normal child, but this language may differ sharply from the language conventionally used in books. Aspects of this question were discussed in Chapter 6, and the notion of verbal deprivation is discussed below.

A second possibility is that the cause lies in Johnny's family: for example, there are no books in the home or his parents do not read to him. The correlation between social class and reading failure is well documented. Kellmer-Pringle *et al.* (1966) grouped 11,000 seven-year-olds into three categories: good, medium and poor readers, on the basis of their performance on the Southgate word-recognition test. The following percentages of poor readers were then found:

social class	I, II	7.1 per cent
	III	18.9 per cent
	IV, V	26.9 per cent

But such correlations are now so widely known that they may be taken for granted and exaggerated. Vernon (1971) warns that teachers may overestimate the reading ability of middle-class children and underestimate the ability of working-class children. That is, such a correlation is so widely known that it may become self-perpetuating, since teachers expect it and their expectations influence their perceptions. This point questions a clear-cut distinction between social factors and people's attitude to social factors; this is discussed in more detail below. A social pathology model (that there is something wrong with Johnny's family) may in turn be held to explain a language deficit (that there is something wrong with Johnny's language).

A third possibility is the teacher. There has been surprisingly little research on the influence of teachers on learning to read, but the research that has been done appears to show that differences amongst teachers are far more important than differences between materials and methods (Harris, 1969; Goodacre, 1971). This finding is important, but it is not at all clear what to do with it, since it throws us back on what we knew already: that there are good and bad teachers. It does perhaps usefully throw doubt on the panacea view of teaching literacy: that if only we can develop yet another better method the problems will be solved. It argues in addition for having better informed and trained teachers.

A fourth possibility is the medium. The writing system has been discussed in Chapter 3, and some relationships between spelling conventions and pronunciations have been discussed in Chapter 6. The large debate over ITA is obviously relevant here, but again beyond the scope of this book. (Main references are Pitman and St John, 1969; Southgate, 1969.) The argument here is that English spelling is difficult or irregular and can confuse the beginner. The two possible solutions are to reform English spelling, which as we have seen is impossible in practice; or to introduce pupils to reading via an easier system (e.g., ITA) and have them transfer later.

Fifthly, the materials may be socially inappropriate, being middle-class, racist, or simply boring to children. There may be a mismatch between the reading primers and the children's interests or experiences, in terms of language or content. Many reading schemes are now very conscious of the phenomenon of the 'invisible Black child' or the 'invisible working-class child' who never sees himself portrayed in books. Children must of course be treated equally, but this is not to say that they must be treated as the 'same', ignoring cultural differences. Ignoring or disregarding a child's native language variety or home experiences may amount to rejecting them. One way of ensuring that learning to read is child-centred in both languages and content is to have the pupils construct their reading material themselves. *Breakthrough to Literacy* (Mackay *et al.*, 1970) uses one version of this language experience approach in which children use sentence-makers to construct their own sentences and stories.

Sixthly, there is a multitude of methods on which there is a huge literature, again outside the scope of this book. I will merely note two points. First, most children will learn to read by any method. Second, many methods which have been promoted from time to time are little more than gimmicks. Two of my favourites are as follows. One method tried in the eighteenth century (Pitman and St John, 1969, p. 20) was to make letters out of gingerbread: the pupil was allowed to eat them when they were learned. Another method based on reward, which misfired, was experienced by the daughter of a friend. The girl was making slow progress through reading books. Her parents discovered the reason: as a reward for finishing a page in a reader, pupils were allowed to colour in a picture on the opposite page. The girl could read well, but was extremely slow and indecisive about colouring, and was not therefore making much progress in reading!

142

7.2 Deprivation theory

We will discuss now in more detail one particularly influential approach to explaining children's educational failure. This is deprivation theory, a version of the view that educational failure results from a mismatch between children's language and experience, and the language and experience demanded by schools. It sets out to be a theory of the relationship between children's language, social class and educational success. The debate over such a theory is obviously of particular relevance to the acquisition of literacy, but has wider relevance to theories of educational success and failure, and is therefore an appropriate topic for the last main chapter of this book.

Over the past ten or twelve years it has been proposed that an explanation for the failure of certain children in the formal school system is that they are 'deprived'. 'Deprivation' is taken in different ways. It may refer simply to material deprivation: children from home backgrounds where unemployment, poverty and overcrowding are severe, are likely to be at risk at school. They will arrive at school tired and undernourished, and with more immediate problems than learning to read. But generally, deprivation theory is taken to refer to cultural or linguistic deprivation. It is argued that children's cultural and/or linguistic experience is somehow impoverished and therefore does not prepare them to learn what the school has to offer.

It is widely known that children from lower socio-economic class groups are less likely to do well at school than children from middle-class homes. Such trends are depressingly well documented, both for educational success in general, and for reading success in particular. For example, Davie *et al.* (1972) found that in Britain the chances of an unskilled manual worker's child being a poor reader at seven years are six times greater than those of a professional worker's child; and that an unskilled worker's child has fifteen times more chance of being a non-reader at seven years. The general trend of such findings is well enough known, and we do not have to discuss here the precise correlations which have repeatedly been found between social class and educational success. What I propose to discuss here is the logic behind one type of explanation which has been given of such findings.

One explanation of such findings which has been particularly influential since the mid-1960s is the so-called theory of cultural, social or verbal deprivation. This is an environmentalist theory: that the early social and family environment is particularly crucial to school success; and that those children from working-class or minority ethnic backgrounds who fail do so because they lack early childhood experiences which are thought to be important for school learning, and because the lack of these experiences leads, for example, to poor motivation, poor attention span, poor language development, unfamiliarity with values which schools regard as important, and so on. The debate over cultural deprivation, and consequent attempts to improve deprived children's school performance by putting them through programmes of 'compensatory' education has been a major issue, particularly in the USA since the 1960s, when the concern over the failure in schools of working-class and ethnic minority children coincided with a focus on civil rights and with the War on Poverty programmes launched by President Lyndon B. Johnson in 1965. 'Head Start' was a federally funded programme for pre-school children from poor families, and the term 'head start programme' has come to be used more widely for such interventionist or compensatory programmes. Between 1965 and 1970 $10 billion (£4,000 million) were spent on the education of the poor and minority groups in the USA (Moss, 1973, p. 30).

By the late 1960s, data were becoming available about the success of such programmes. The general effect appeared to be an initial spurt in measured intelligence, followed by a plateau or decline, and therefore no long-term improvement, although there is also some evidence that although large-scale programmes have failed, small-scale experiments have had some success (Labov, 1969a; Baratz and Baratz, 1970). At this time, severe criticisms of the logic of deprivation theory and compensatory programmes also began to appear. Labov's famous paper on 'The logic of non-standard English' was first published in 1969: in it he argued that the concept of verbal deprivation was a myth with no basis in fact.

In Britain, a particularly notable event was the publication in 1972 of a report from the Department of Education and Science on Educational Priority Areas. And the work of Bernstein and his colleagues has been published in a steady stream since the late 1950s. This work has a problematic relationship to deprivation theory (see below), and Bernstein himself has published an article attacking the concept of compensatory education (Bernstein, 1969). But the work has been assumed by many people, particularly in the USA, to be a theory of linguistic deprivation.

The debate over cultural deprivation has, therefore, continued since the 1960s, but it shows little sign of diminishing. First, work is still being regularly published in the area. Taking just two British examples: work is still being published from the Sociological Research Unit at the London Institute of Education, where Bernstein's work on restricted and elaborated codes was originally done (e.g., Hawkins, 1977); and work which is increasingly influential is Joan Tough's work in Leeds on what she calls advantaged and disadvantaged children (e.g., Tough, 1977). Second, the general debate in such areas always lags at least five or ten years behind the published research, and much of the published commentary on this area is simplified and misinformed (see below). For example, Bernstein began publishing his research on restricted and elaborated codes in the late 1950s, but does not appear to have much influence amongst teachers till about the late 1960s. Third, the debate does not seem to have made much progress lately and may have reached something of a deadlock, which we will attempt to analyse in this chapter.

In addition, ideas of language deficit have often been seized upon to explain the educational problems of children in many parts of the world. Holmes (1976) points to evidence that teachers and educational administrators in New Zealand tend to regard Maori children's language as impoverished and deficient, and that they use this belief to explain why Maori children often fail in school. Gardiner (1977) discusses a similar phenomenon in Australia, arguing that most of the special education programmes for speakers of non-standard dialects have been based on theories of linguistic and cognitive deficit. Some Aboriginals have as their native language one of the many indigenous Australian languages, and may be monolingual in this or bilingual in it and in a variety of English (see 4.7). But varieties of non-standard Aboriginal English have developed in contact situations between Aboriginals and English speakers; and Aboriginal English now also serves as a lingua franca between different groups of Aboriginals with different indigenous languages. Many Aboriginal children now have a non-standard variety of English as their only language. In line with trends in the USA, the trend has been towards earlier and earlier intervention via language programmes based on a notion of deficit and deprivation. Gardiner argues on the contrary for a difference theory which recognizes the legitimacy of the child's own dialect in the classroom.

7.3 The stages in the debate

It should be emphasized first that the whole area of deprivation theory, and the debate about whether the concept is a myth or not, often appears almost hopelessly confusing. It is not entirely clear what deprivation theory is: there appear to be several versions of the theory, and it is not certain that it is a genuine theory at all. It is not clear who holds versions of the theory. For example, does Bernstein hold a version of deprivation theory, and whether he does personally or not, does his work necessarily imply it?

One of the disturbing things about the area is that some people believe they know the truth about what is going on. My own view is, rather, that a lot of the discussion is speculation unsupported by much relevant fact. The only thing which seems certain is the importance of people's beliefs in this area, and that if teachers let children know that they think they are deprived, deficient or inferior, then the children are likely to act in fulfilment of their teachers' (and their own) beliefs. The gist of the argument in this chapter is that the debate may now have gone full circle, and that there is probably no way out of the circle until we have more facts.

There appear to have been various stages in the development of the debate over deprivation, and I will attempt to separate these out, as logically distinct positions. I will list these stages briefly, and then discuss each. Stage 1 is the deprivation hypothesis: that the concept of deprivation or deficit can explain why some children, usually from working-class or minority ethnic backgrounds, fail at school. In stage 2, the concept of deprivation is taken for granted by some people, and becomes a 'fact' which can be taught on courses to other people. At this stage, the concept is often simplified. In stage 3, the notion of deprivation is criticized and said to be a myth, an illusion or simply meaningless. In stage 4, the notion that it is myth comes to be accepted as a fact by some people. And it is taught on some courses, argued in books and so on, that it is fact that it is a myth. At this stage, the phrase 'the myth of deprivation' becomes the title of books, articles and conferences. Beyond this, it is pointed out that whether it is a myth or not, the same children still fail at school, that perhaps it is a 'useful myth', and that there are, in any case, many further complications, including the relation between the theory and practical policy decisions in education.

I do not intend to imply that these have been chronologically separate stages, but that they are useful logical distinctions. Some of the stages are collapsed into single books and articles, some people still believe that deprivation theory is a genuine hypothesis which can be tested, some people believe that it is fact, others believe that it is meaningless, and so on. However, I will develop these so-called stages, as a framework for making some comments on them.

7.4 Stage 1: deprivation theory

In stage 1, deprivation theory is put forward as a testable hypothesis or explanation for why some children fail at school. In order to explain why children from certain social-class groups are likely to do poorly at school, it is proposed that these children are deprived of something necessary to their intellectual development. Different versions of this view are proposed by Bereiter and Engelmann (1966), Deutsch *et al.* (1967), Jensen (1969) and others. (Dittmar, 1976, and Moss, 1973, review much of this work.) A deprivation theorist claims that children who fail at school are typically either exposed to an inferior variety of language, or not exposed to enough language, or exposed to a social or family background which is impoverished in some way. In extreme forms such a view may amount to what Wax and Wax (1971) call a 'vacuum ideology': the belief that some groups do not possess any meaningful culture at all. Such a theory typically contains other underlying assumptions, such as that certain varieties of language are inferior to others, that cognitive development is dependent on linguistic and social experience, and so on.

We ought to start from at least a clear working definition of what deprivation theory is, but this is not easy. It is clear what the theory is in general terms, and this has just been stated. But many different deprivation theories have in fact been put forward, often referring to earlier and earlier stages in the child's development. It was proposed, for example, that so-called linguistic deprivation might be remedied by 'head start programmes' of compensatory education. The programmes were not as successful as hoped, and it was then argued that the intervention had come too late: it was 'inadequate mothering' that was to blame, and the mother rather than the child who required compensatory education. And so on. If the concept of deprivation is moved back far enough, we presumably have to give compensation in the womb, or to engage in genetic engineering, and have then moved from an environmentalist to a genetic hypothesis. (These stages in the formulation of the theory are documented by Labov, 1969a, and by Baratz and Baratz, 1970.)

In addition, deprivation theories have been proposed in two general forms. One is:

If lower working-class or ethnic minority children are given programmes of compensatory education, this will improve their performance at school.

This is an interesting and genuine hypothesis which is open to test. It has been tested, but unfortunately, as we have already indicated, it is only true in a very limited way, if at all. A second formulation is:

Lower working-class or ethnic minority children are not equipped to succeed at school, because they are deprived.

This is not a genuine hypothesis, because it is so vague. The term 'deprived' is not defined, and may simply be factually inapplicable. Conversely, no one has ever succeeded in discovering just what characteristics are necessary for success at school.

The fact that deprivation theory exists in many versions may account for its persistence. Before a theory can be definitively criticized and refuted, it must at least be stated clearly. If a theory is stated in different

147

forms or ambiguously, to any criticism one can say: that criticism does not apply to this version of the theory. And if theories exist in several different forms, relating to whole languages and cultures, then any criticism either appears blunt (because it is not attacking anything precise) or trivial (because, in order to attack something precise, it chooses one aspect of one theory and ignores everything else).

Two other confusions might be mentioned briefly here. First, there is some confusion over whether the terms 'deprivation' and 'deficit' mean the same. Most writers appear to use the terms synonymously. On the other hand, some argue (e.g., Levitas, 1976) that a deficit is something to do with an individual who lacks something, whereas deprivation involves someone else: someone is deprived of something by (being exploited by) someone. Little is normally made of this distinction, however. A more important terminological distinction may be between 'deprivation' and 'disadvantage'. The term deprivation implies that there is a lack in the child or in his family, whereas the term disadvantage could more easily be taken to imply that there is nothing wrong with the child, but that his social experience puts him at a disadvantage because it is different from what is expected by schools and may be stigmatized in schools. This is important also, therefore, in the statement of the theory, for we have in fact different accounts of where the deprivation is: is it in the child, in the child's language, or in the child's family? If it is maintained, on the contrary, that there is no such lack, then we have in fact a 'difference' theory: that it is cultural and linguistic differences which cause problems.

Second, there is considerable confusion over who holds versions of deprivation theory and who does not. In particular, it is not clear whether we are here talking of Bernstein or not. Bernstein has stated explicitly that he does not believe that working-class language is deprived (Bernstein, 1971, p. 221), and that he does not accept the theory underlying compensatory education (Bernstein, 1969). But Bernstein's work has been used, particularly in the USA, to provide a theoretical justification for programmes of compensatory education. And many people clearly associate Bernstein's theory of restricted and elaborated codes with deprivation theory (e.g., Dittmar, 1976; Flower, 1966, p. 110); and papers have been published which argue that Bernstein's position necessarily involves his holding a version of the theory (e.g., Gordon, 1976). Hawkins, an ex-colleague of Bernstein, has published a book in the series from the Sociological Research Unit at the London Institute of Education (Hawkins, 1977). He argues (p. 191) that all children from all social classes, who have English as their native language, must be assumed to share the same knowledge of grammar, or competence. He agrees with linguists who argue that to talk of deficits in grammatical competence does not make sense: any normal child of school age is competent in the grammar of his native language. But Bernstein's theories are about language use (linguistic performance) not about knowledge (linguistic competence), therefore:

Bernstein's model *does* involve a 'deficit', but ... Bernstein's deficiency would not be in linguistic competence but in some other kind of competence which involves the actual use of language (p. 192).

A more general complicating factor in the debate is as follows. In the debate over cultural and linguistic deprivation, there is no disagreement over certain facts, but there is severe dispute over how these facts should be interpreted. There are two facts (and possibly only these two) which are not in dispute. These are: *Fact A*: the language of working-class and middle-class speakers is different. *Fact B*: working-class children do less well at school than middle-class children.

Fact A is simply a well-known fact about linguistic diversity in a complex, urbanized, class-stratified society such as Britain or the USA. It is a standard sociolinguistic finding from all over the world that social groups are differentiated by their language. *Fact B* does not mean that no working-class children do well at school. It is a statistical statement about a group of children, and claims that on average a working-class child has less chance of, for example, getting to university than a middle-class child.

I assume that these are accepted facts. No one who criticizes Bernstein, for example, ever denies that there are differences in the language used by working-class and middle-class pupils. But because these facts are massively documented, some people assume that their implications are obvious. This is not so. There is considerable debate about how, if at all, the facts are related, and there are several possibilities.

One possibility is that *A* causes *B*. This is a version of deprivation theory: differences in language cause differences in educational attainment in a direct way, because differences in language causes differences in intellectual ability. The view that language has a direct causal effect on thinking is also known as the Sapir-Whorf hypothesis (after two American linguists working from the 1920s to 1940s). Bernstein has certainly argued a version of this theory in places, and cites Whorf as one of the major influences on his work (Bernstein, 1971, p. 195). (See 5.6.)

A second possibility is that *A* causes *X* which in turn causes *B*. That is, *A* and *B* are causally related but only indirectly. *X* might be intolerant attitudes provoked by language differences. Thus: language differences provoke social stigma (say, amongst teachers), these attitudes are conveyed to pupils, and that is what causes educational problems. Either the pupil feels rejected or the teacher does not expect the pupil to do well, and the prophecy becomes self-fulfilling. A version of this view is held by Labov: that language differences are mainly important because they are a focus or symbol of cultural attitudes and prestige (.e.g, Labov, 1972b). This is a version of difference theory: it is differences in the culture and language of social groups which cause problems, due to the way in which these differences are interpreted.

Other interpretations are also open. For example: *X* causes both *A* and *B*. That is, *A* and *B* merely correlate, but neither causes the other. In this case, *X* might be a cluster of values or beliefs, held by a social group. On the one hand, an individual's beliefs and values determine his interest in school: some people are just not interested in succeeding at school. On the other hand, language is a powerful symbol of group identity, and different social groups often make efforts to keep their language recognizably distinct from that of other groups.

Another way of expressing these points is that I do not think there is any genuine disagreement that language is somehow crucially related to educational success. But there is considerable disagreement about whether language is a primary or secondary factor. Those who claim it is a primary factor claim that language ability causes intellectual success or failure. Those who claim it is a secondary cause claim that it is the social prestige and stigma of different language varieties which causes the problems. I suspect that this may be the single most important area of confusion. One has to distinguish sharply between (a) the internal linguistic organization of a language variety, and (b) external social factors such as attitudes towards that variety in the community. One therefore has to be prepared to make such statements as: this minority language or non-standard dialect is structurally very complex and equivalent to standard English in this respect; but its prestige in the community is low and reflects the fact that its speakers are socially stigmatized. People often find it very difficult to keep distinct (a) the linguistic and (b) the social characteristics of a language variety; or to keep distinct (a) a language variety and (b) its speakers. The prestige of speakers often rubs off on their language.

The main point which has been made in this section is that the data on which deprivation theory has been based are open to very different interpretations.

7.5   Stage 2: deprivation theory as fact

In stage 2, deprivation theory becomes reified: that is, it is accepted as a fact and taken for granted. By being accepted as a fact it is inevitably simplified, sometimes to the point of a succinct and crude aphorism such as 'educational failure is linguistic failure'. The concept becomes institutionalized (Keddie (ed.), 1973) by being taught as a topic on courses, for example, to student teachers. And 'apocryphal Bernstein' (Rogers, 1976) becomes part of the staffroom folklore (Rosen, 1973) and flourishes in a corrupt form, particularly perhaps in the USA. The concept of deprivation is presented in simplified fashion, as though it was a fact, in several books which are widely used by courses for student teachers, including Creber (1972), Flower (1966), Herriot (1971), Shiach (1972) and Wilkinson (1971). This is despite the fact that the concept is under serious cricitism from many linguists at present and certainly has no general acceptance. (Trudgill, 1975, pp. 95ff., usefully documents such crude simplifications of deprivation theory by educationalists.) In addition, work is cited in a form which is grossly out of date. For example, in work on reading Vernon (1971) cites only a Bernstein article published in 1958, in support of an argument about social class and language differences, although Bernstein has fundamentally altered his theory between then and his papers on codes theory published up until 1973.

When discussing this area, I am therefore never certain whether to discuss deprivation theory in so far as I understand it; or whether to discuss people's misunderstandings and oversimplified or inaccurate presentations of it. Sometimes I feel I ought simply to discuss it as a scientific hypothesis, and ignore misrepresentations of it: this is the argument that bad books should not be reviewed, but just forgotten. At other times I feel it is more important to combat the caricatures of the theory, since this is possibly what more people are exposed to. And then also the two positions sometimes appear inseparable, since if people believe the simplified versions of the theory, then this becomes a factor which can affect the theory. A consequence of believing the theory may be to make it fact, since we are now in the realm of self-fulfilling prophecies. If children are believed to be deprived, they may act as though they were. It is no longer clear whether they fail because they are deprived, or whether they act as though they were deprived because this is what people expect of them. They may actually act differently, or teachers and others may just perceive them as acting differently. Vernon (1971) points out that the correlation between socio-economic class and reading failure is so well known that teachers sometimes exaggerate it. The statistical differences in reading attainment may be consistent and predictable for social groups, but they may be quite small, and teachers may overestimate the ability of middle-class children and underestimate the ability of working-class children, thus contributing to the difference.

It is obvious that in teaching anybody anything, one often starts out with a complex series of hypotheses which are only partly corroborated by contradictory evidence, and one ends up having conveyed to at least some of the people something like 'educational failure is linguistic failure', which is easy to remember (although the aphorism makes at least as much sense, *a priori*, in reverse). But when social scientific theories are open to simplification and misinterpretation in this way, in an area which is of practical importance to all children, the researcher is in an awkward position. Ultimately, I suppose one has to adopt the position that one cannot legislate for fools, or for people who do not read books carefully. But the researcher in this area does have a particular responsibility to be as clear and explicit as possible, and to be sure of the facts before erecting a high-level theory on dubious data.

A particularly confusing set of work from this point of view is Joan Tough's. On the one hand, she goes to some lengths to point out explicitly the limitations in her data and the difficulty of interpreting the data. On the other hand, she is prepared to assert that she has identified fundamental differences in different groups of children. Tough (1977) puts forward the view that educational disadvantage is 'to some extent' a 'reflection' of disadvantage in the linguistic environment of schools (p. 1). This is a vague statement, but is the way in which versions of deprivation theory are often stated. In the book, Tough presents language data from sixty-four children from advantaged and disadvantaged homes, and claims (p. 25) that there are clear differences between the children from the two groups on all the linguistic features she investigated. She believes that these differences can be compensated for by a programme of language training.

She is careful to point several times to difficulties in interpreting the kind of data she has. She emphasizes (pp. 27, 28, 30, 87, 168) that her data refer to the frequency with which the two groups of children choose to use various features in which she is interested. That is, the data refer to the children's performance: what they do actually say, not to their competence or knowledge or what they might say if the situation was different. This is an important point and it occurs in most of the data on social class differences in language, including Bernstein's work which she cites in this context (p. 30). A standard finding is that one does not discover absolute differences in usage of the same linguistic feature between social groups. It is found, for example, that working-class boys use more pronouns and fewer complex noun phrases than middle-class boys. But both groups use both constructions. This proves that both groups know and can use both forms. But one group does use one choice less often. Such data arguably have to do with preferred style of language in certain social settings, since it is difficult to see how a statistical tendency to use more of a linguistic feature can affect intellectual development.

Yet despite Tough's frequent discussions of the nature of the data, she believes she is dealing with constraints on intellectual ability. Thus, in spite of her own warnings and caveats, the message inevitably gets through that we have two groups of children who differ linguistically in an important way which is crucial for their education success. (See Note at the end of this chapter.)

Again it must be emphasized that widely different interpretations may be placed on such data. Hawkins (1969) published findings about social-class differences in pronoun usage, arguing that such differences 'may well have important cognitive consequences'. But in a subsequent book, Hawkins (1977) presents a reanalysis of the same data, which reveals that the differences were much more complex than he earlier implied, and in the later book he has dropped all references to possible direct cognitive consequences. (See also Stubbs, 1978, which reviews Hawkins, 1977.)

7.6   Stage 3: deprivation as myth

Stage 3 is the argument that deprivation is a myth. This is argued by Labov (1969a), Baratz and Baratz (1970), Keddie (1973) and others. Two lines of argument are open here. One can try to show that children claimed to be deprived are, in fact, not deprived and really share a rich culture and/or language. Alternatively, or in addition, one can try to show that statements about cultural and linguistic deprivation do not make sense. One has then the unfortunate situation in which one group of social scientists see themselves as attempting to clear up the confusion caused by another group. Much of the argument that deprivation theory is a myth hinges on showing that statements such as *This child is deprived* are meaningless, and are therefore 'semi-philosophical' (Davies, 1977, p. 4) discussions of whether it is appropriate or semantically anomalous to make such statements.

One way of refuting a deprivation theory is to argue that, in principle, there is no such thing as a primitive language or a deficient culture. The argument runs: this piece of language or behaviour only appears deficient when seen out of context or in the wrong context; for example, in an artificial experimental situation or in comparison with middle-class norms. But when it is seen in its own context, it is in fact complex, subtle, interesting and functional. This is a classic argument used by anthropologists. It runs: the behaviour of this tribe may appear primitive to you; but that is only in comparison with your culture, and this is not a relevant comparison. Also, as an outsider, you do not fully appreciate just how complex the culture is. It is also an important argument of linguists, where it runs: this language may appear strange, exotic or primitive to you; but that is only because you are viewing it in terms of your own language and trying to force onto it the categories of standard English, Latin or other language, instead of analysing it in its own terms.

Such arguments therefore hinge on taking a relativist position, that is, a culture-specific frame of reference, and arguing that cultures and dialects must be analysed as self-contained wholes, in their own terms, without imposing alien categories and norms on them. The major problem which then arises is whether it is appropriate to regard social and linguistic systems as idealized wholes in this way, or whether they have to be seen in their wider context. The only answer seems to be that they have to be seen in both ways.

One stage in the quasi-philosophical debate over the meaning of terms is the argument that 'no group can be deprived of its own culture' (see Keddie, 1973). But this appears to be a trick argument (Levitas, 1976, p. 109). First, it is not true. A group can be deprived of its own culture if its culture is systematically destroyed by another group. Governments have made attempts with different degrees of success to eradicate whole languages: for example, Scottish Gaelic after Culloden in 1745, Welsh in the nineteenth century, or Australian Aboriginal languages until only a few years ago. Second, if a group is denied access to power, knowledge or resources which are available to others in the wider community, then arguably they are not deprived of their own culture, but this is a weak argument since they are deprived of benefits which others have, deprived of access to 'mainstream' culture, and so on. Third, the relativist argument risks confusing the inherent value and complexity of some culture or language variety, with the social value attributed to it by its users or others, or the social value which it has in the wider social and economic community.

The problem, for which sociology has not yet found a principled answer (Edwards and Hargreaves, 1976), is: how much context is relevant? If some behaviour 'makes sense' in its own terms, is this enough? Is context to be defined in terms of the participants' own short-term goals? Who is qualified to judge short- or long-term goals? The relativist view, that sub-cultures are just different, seems to imply that they are self-contained wholes, which do not interact; but this is clearly false. Again, the distinction has to be maintained between the internal organization and complexity of sub-cultures and language varieties, and the external social pressures on them; but both have to be recognized.

We run here into the political implications of deprivation theory and difference theory. Those who argue that non-standard dialects, working-class culture and so on, are not inferior, just different from standard language or middle-class 'mainstream' culture, appear to be adopting an egalitarian, 'radical' point of view. They are asserting the inherent value of minority language and culture, and sometimes, as Labov (1969a) does, combining this with an explicit attack on the empty verbosity of middle-class culture. However, one has to strike a balance between asserting the inherent value of some set of customs or language, and recognizing their survival value in the wider economic community. Linguists and anthropologists may wish to preserve minority customs, but they may thus be condemning people to live in 'museum cultures' (Bull, 1955).

The problem is clearer with specific reference to the acquisition of literacy by a small ethnic group. We have mentioned already (4.7) the case of the Eastern Eskimo in Canada who have been literate since the end of the nineteenth century. At that time a syllabic writing sytem, with no relation to the Roman alphabet, was introduced to them from the Cree Indians. The syllabary is well suited to the language, probably better suited than a Roman alphabet would be, and the Eskimo use it. In the narrow context of Eskimo society the syllabary appears ideal, but it is clearly not ideal in the wider social and economic community of Canada. This has nothing to do with the inherent value of the syllabary. If the Eskimos are left with their syllabary this will probably help their short-term goals of learning to read, but it will damage long-term goals of social and economic integration into Canadian society.

Analogous problems arise in asserting the inherent value of minority languages such as Welsh and Scottish Gaelic, or non-standard dialects of English. If individuals have access only to a minority language or culture, they are at a clear disadvantage in the wider community. This causes particularly difficult teaching problems. The child who speaks a minority language or non-standard dialect must be given access to the majority or standard language variety, without his own language being denigrated.

Finally, relativist positions which assert the value of minority cultures have been attacked as reactionary, on the grounds that they smooth over political and social differences and avoid conflict. Dittmar (1976) argues that such views maintain the *status quo*: by persuading working-class and ethnic groups of the inherent value of their language and culture, social science is used to 'pacify the ghettoes' (p. 249), just as anthropology was used to pacify the American Indians in the nineteenth century, so he claims. In a similar way, Levitas (1976) argues that a relativist cultural position denies deprivation, and by denying it, condones it. Another confusion in the debate is therefore over who is 'radical' and who isn't!

7.7 Stage 4: myth as fact

Stage 4 is the reification of the myth. That is, it is believed, and taught on courses, that it is a fact that deprivation is a myth. The phrase 'the myth of deprivation' itself acquires the status of an aphorism, and the term 'myth' appears in the titles of books (e.g., Ginsburg, 1972; Keddie,

1973), the titles of articles and chapters in books (e.g., Jackson, 1974; Stubbs, 1976), and the titles of conferences (Edinburgh, October 1977).

Again, there is the danger of simplification, but now we are in a position of being able to caricature both sides at once, since the reification of the myth is, logically, at least the fourth potential stage in the debate. For example, many departments of education give the status of fact to some version of Bernstein's theories. Conversely, it is taught by other departments that Labov's work has refuted, negated or provided a definitive critique of Bernstein's views. But neither of these positions is true. The findings of Bernstein and his colleagues are interesting: no one doubts that there are differences in the language of working-class and middle-class children. The problems arise over how to interpret these findings: are they just artefacts of the experimental situation? do they have anything to do with cognition? are the findings explained by Bernstein's theories or do the findings actually refute the theories? (See Stubbs, 1976, 1978.) Neither is it the case that Labov's work directly refutes Bernstein's. At most one can say that his findings about language use in natural situations and his detailed syntactic analyses of non-standard dialects of English complicate the issue and provide more awkward facts for Bernstein to explain. But Labov's work has been done with American negroes and other minority ethnic groups in the USA: it is not clear that this work can be extrapolated to Britain. And whereas Labov's work is naturalistic and involves detailed linguistic analysis, Bernstein's is mainly experimental and involves high-level theory about social-class structure. The two bodies of work are therefore not directly comparable in terms of either data or theory. Bernstein and Labov are therefore only 'apparent protagonists' (Davies (ed.), 1977, p. 4), and have never discussed each other's work in any detail, although they have made brief and critical references to each other. A typically over-simplified reference is by Tough (1977, p. 31) who says: 'There have been many criticisms of Bernstein's work, most notably by William Labov.' This is inaccurate.

7.8 Conclusions

I have suggested that the debate has gone full circle and that none of the four 'stages' represents a coherent position. Much of my own discussion has been semi-philosophical: about whether certain statements are meaningless or mythical. It is difficult to see how the discussion can be anything but semi-philosophical until we have fresh facts to argue from, and these facts will have to come from direct observation of real language in use in classrooms, schools, pupils' peer groups and families.

Much research in this area (including, for example, the whole of Bernstein's) has been based on the observation of language use in artificial experimental situations, and the relation between such artificial language use and language use in real, everyday situations is at best tenuous and difficult to interpret.

The main problems with the concept of deprivation are versions of the question: which context is relevant? Contexts tend to be differently defined by different professional groups, and linguists, psychologists, sociologists and educationalists each look at language and see something different. Linguists are trained to see a language or dialect as a highly organized, largely autonomous system. And they maintain as a principle that any notion of a simple or primitive language is a myth: from the point of view of language structure, all languages and dialects, standard and non-standard, are just very complex and therefore equal. From the principle of the primitive language myth, it follows that all language varieties are potentially functionally equal. For example, Eskimo, Jamaican Creole and standard English are potentially equal as media of education: it is a social and historical accident that standard English is a world language and Eskimo is not. But linguists have sometimes been slow to recognize the actual socio-symbolic and functional differences between language varieties.

Sociologists, psychologists and educationalists, on the other hand, are interested in language as an explanation of educational failure, having in the past tried IQ, home backgrounds, social class, and other reasons. They have therefore had a tendency to ignore the organization of language itself, and to jump directly to its purported relation with cognition. The linguistic naivety of many intervention programmes, especially in the USA, has been due to their having been organized by educationalists and psychologists, who have had no real understanding of language and have committed the most elementary blunders (Labov, 1969a).

We are used to thinking in such simple causal chains as (a) deprivation causes (b) educational failure. But such causal chains could only possibly operate within closed systems, where (a) and (b) do not interact with anything else. However, it is obvious that educational failure could not have a single, well-defined cause, since social class, measured IQ, language differences, family environment, social class and various other factors are all known to interact. Different professional groups attempt to create their own closed systems.

An unquestionable principle must be that every individual pupil and his or her language and culture must be treated with respect. Further, every individual pupil must be encouraged to have confidence in his or her language and culture. They must also have access to standard English and mainstream culture, but not at the expense of denigrating their

157

own family and background. Children must be treated as equal; but this principle cannot be interpreted as meaning that cultural differences can be ignored. In reading material, for example, this can lead to the phenomenon of the 'invisible' black or working-class child: if all reading matter shows white middle-class characters, some children will never see themselves portrayed in books. Refusing to recognize a child's language or background can be tantamount to rejecting or attacking them.

The main priority must be to increase teachers' understanding of linguistic and cultural diversity. They must appreciate the complexity of all language varieties, standard or non-standard; the types of diversity, regional, social and stylistic, which they will encounter; the forces which maintain the diversity and the forces which maintain the standard language. When the complexity of any normal child's linguistic competence is understood, it is impossible to maintain a position of linguistic or cultural intolerance. The main priority must therefore be to increase teachers' understanding and tolerance, since one of the few things about which there is no doubt in this murky area is the effect of people's beliefs.

Note 1

There are many other criticisms which can be made of Tough (1977). Wells (1977) reports a failure to replicate Tough's findings on his own data, and provides other serious criticisms of the book. The book also contains many statements about linguistics which are simply wrong. Some examples are:

> It is argued (by Chomsky that) the speed of language acquisition is dependent on the child being able to acquire and operate rules, rules that it seems are innate (Tough, 1977, p. 17).

This is contradictory: if rules are acquired, they cannot be innate. Chomsky nowhere argues that the syntactic rules of particular languages are innate.

> The concept of transformation (in Chomskyan grammar) ... refers to each change that must be made to the underlying 'S' ... in order to produce an utterance in which particular features of speech show the relations between parts of the sentence required by the grammar (p. 18).

This is meaningless: in particular it confuses utterances (actually produced by speakers) and sentences (abstract objects generated by the grammar).

... kernel sentences (Chomsky, 1965) ... (p. 19).

Chomsky has dropped the term 'kernel sentences' by 1965.

Chapter 8

Summary and conclusions

8.1 Summary

Despite a vast amount of study since the end of the nineteenth century, reading and literacy are still very confused research areas. Literacy involves not only psychological processes in the individual reader. It is also a linguistic process, closely dependent on the reader's knowledge of his language; and it is a social process which has different expectations and values attached to it in different communities. Detailed experimental studies on small aspects of reading are of course necessary, but work on literacy is just as much in need of attempts to integrate findings from widely different disciplinary areas (Chapter 1).

A systematic theory of literacy must be based, first of all, on an account of the relationship between spoken and written language. If we do not know what this relationship is, then we have no way of stating just what children learn when they become literate. We must in fact distinguish different types of relationship: chronological, social and logical. And we must recognize further that written and spoken language may be differently related in different communities or at different periods in the history of one community (Chapter 2).

The relationship between the English writing system and units of spoken English is complex. However, although there are inevitably residual problems, the English spelling system is now quite well understood. It is inadequate to regard it simply as illogical or out of date. Often such views result from trying to see English spelling solely in terms of letter-phoneme correspondences. It is based on such correspondences, but it is also a mixed system and is based on more abstract relations between orthographic symbols and morphemes. Although the principles underlying the system are fairly clear, the implications for the teaching of reading are not, since the spelling system, although highly organized, is, it must be admitted, highly abstract and complex,

160

and some of its features are almost certainly beyond the linguistic competence of young children. English spelling is a good system for its native users and fluent adult readers, but it is not ideal for children or beginners (Chapter 3).

Although writing systems are partly independent of spoken language (writing is not speech written down), a writing system cannot be regarded as an autonomous, purely linguistic structure. Any writing system is subject to many social, attitudinal and technological pressures, and is related to other writing systems in neighbouring areas which are politically and culturally important. This can be illustrated from a wide range of countries. Such pressures are particularly powerful in the case of an international language such as English, and partly explain the inertia against English spelling reform (Chapter 4).

Although linguists agree that all languages are structurally very complex and in that sense equal, they would also admit that when a language acquires a writing system it is functionally more powerful as a means of communication than a language with no written form, since writing systems facilitate recording, bureaucratic and intellectual tasks. Many of these administrative and intellectual functions which written language serves are very far beyond the needs or experience of young children; writing has no social use for many children (Chapter 5).

All languages show stylistic differentiation according to social function and context, and all languages with writing systems show differentiation between spoken and written forms. Demands that English spelling should be more consistently phonemic are often based on a misunderstanding of the relationship between a transcription and an orthography, and a failure to appreciate that spoken language is subject to much more variation than written language. Although written and spoken English are, of course, the 'same language', and share the vast bulk of their vocabulary and grammar, there are nevertheless a large number of formal differences between them in phonology/orthography, morphology, syntax and stylistic conventions. Many of these differences stem from the functional differences between written and spoken language, in particular from the permanence of written text, and from the fact that written texts have to be comprehensible independently of context. The most general formal difference between written and spoken language is that spoken language is open to several different kinds of variation, whereas written language is relatively much more uniform. This distinction is important to an understanding of the concept of a standard language, which is central to formal education, and to literacy in particular, since the concept of standard language is arguably only fully applicable to written language (Chapter 6).

One type of explanation of reading failure, and of educational failure in general, that has been put forward frequently in the past ten or fifteen years, is the concept of 'verbal deprivation'. This suggests that the language a child brings to school can determine his success or failure at school; but formulations of the theory are confused, and the data are open to many different interpretations. There is general agreement that a child's language is important to his or her educational success, but it is probable that features of the language itself are less important than the attitudes of teachers and others to the language and therefore to the child (Chapter 7).

8.2 Conclusions

This book makes no claim to provide a well-defined theory of literacy: it is evident that we are still a very long way from such a theory. On the other hand, I have attempted to make clearer the pre-requisites for such a theory. I have argued that much work in the past has been rather narrow, tending to concentrate in particular on reading as a psychological process, but often ignoring the linguistic organization both of written language and also of writing systems, and ignoring also the social purposes of written language and of literacy.

The argument has several times had to stop short because of lack of data, and we require detailed information and analysis from areas including:

(a) studies of the lexical and grammatical differences between different varieties of written and spoken English;
(b) observational studies of children's spoken language in real social settings, particularly classrooms, homes and peer groups: that is, of the language which children bring with them to school when they are beginning to acquire literacy;
(c) observational studies of children actually learning to read in the classroom; and
(d) ethnographic studies of the place of reading and writing in different cultures and societies.

Until we do understand much more about the relationship between written language and the social contexts in which it is used, we shall have to continue to admit that we do not understand literacy or what happens when children do or do not succeed in learning to read and write.

8.3   Topics for investigation: literacy and classroom practices

The best way to end the book may be to suggest some practical ways in which readers could investigate, in classrooms and elsewhere, many of the topics which have been discussed. This will emphasize that there are many aspects of the acquisition and use of literacy on which basic information is lacking. In particular there are very few studies of literacy which are based on observation of what actually happens in classrooms.

I hope this book will be read by student teachers, practising teachers and other educationalists; and there are many ways in which they can collect valuable information. Students on teaching practice, for example, often find themselves spending lessons sitting at the back of classrooms 'observing', but unless they have some particular problem in mind in order to focus their observations, such periods may be rather pointless. On the other hand, if they are looking for something in particular, such observation periods can be highly informative.

In discussing the bases of a sociolinguistic account of literacy, I have emphasized at many points that reading and writing always take place in cultural and social settings, and that the functions of literacy must be included in any such account. My own discussion, however, has not been based on the observation of readers and writers in particular social settings such as classrooms. It must be admitted, in fact, that this is a major gap in work on literacy, and that very few studies are based on direct classroom observation of children actually learning to read and write in real lessons. (Lack of classroom observation is a general lacuna in much educational research, at least up until the last ten years. Stubbs and Delamont, 1976, and Stubbs, 1976, discuss this general lack of classroom observation in educational research and propose various appropriate research methods.) On the other hand, many of the ideas which I have discussed could inform classroom observation, and I will suggest some of these.

1 *Types of written material in use*: What types of written material are in use? These may include books, pamphlets, worksheets, posters, writing on the blackboard, material combining text, diagrams and pictures, and so on. Is the language in different types of material significantly different (cf. 4)? And do pupils use different strategies for handling different material (cf. 3)?

2 *Uses of written material*: Pupils can be directly observed to see how they actually use material. For example, is it read aloud to the class by the teacher or pupils? Is it first read aloud, then studied by pupils silently, or then discussed by the class? Is it used as reference material? Or copied verbatim into exercise books? Or learned by heart? Or paraphrased? Does the teacher discuss different uses to which it might be put?

3 *Pupils' reading strategies*: Direct observation of pupils may also be able to reveal different approaches to written material. Is it read at unvarying speed from beginning to end? Are contents pages and indexes

used? Are passages re-read, skimmed, marked, copied out? Are different strategies used with different kinds of materials?

4 *Styles of language*: Do the styles of langue vary significantly in different types of material? How do these styles compare with the spoken language of the pupils or teacher? Or with the pupils' own writing? Does the stylistic variation cause pupils difficulty? Are they encouraged to translate from one style into another, for example, by being required to explain things 'in their own words'?

5 *Functions of pupils' writing*: Does their writing have a genuine function? If so, what is it? Does it have a real audience, or is it only written for the teacher? Do pupils read each other's writing?

6 *Teachers' reactions to pupils' writing*: What kind of comments do teachers make on pupils' writing? Does this vary between different subjects? Is their writing genuinely analysed by teachers?

7 *Spelling errors*: Pupils' errors could be analysed to see if there are particular principles which they have not grasped, and if certain types of error are common. How do teachers respond to such errors?

8 *Teachers' explanations*: Do teachers explicitly discuss with pupils any of the above points about the forms and functions of written and spoken language? Are pupils themselves consciously aware of any such points?

9 *Pupils' reading outside school*: Pupils could be interviewed to discover what they read outside school. For example, it may be found that they regularly read material which is difficult if they have particular interests and expertise in the subject matter: e.g., periodicals on angling, football or motor cycles.

Further, many of these questions may be adapted as appropriate to observations outside schools. Ethnographic observations could be made of how written material is used in railway carriages, dentists' waiting rooms, public libraries, shops, cafés, government offices, streets and homes.

A sound sociolinguistic theory of literacy will have to be based on a great amount of such observations of reading and writing in social settings, and such ethnographic work has hardly been started. I hope that some of the readers of this book may use it as a starting point for making such observations of the uses to which literacy is actually put.

Appendix A

Symbols used in transcriptions

/ /   Broad or phonemic transcriptions are conventionally enclosed in diagonal slashes.

[ ]   Any other transcription is enclosed in square brackets.

/' /   Where relevant, a stressed syllable can be indicated by a short upright stroke before it. If stress is not relevant to the argument it can be omitted.

/" /   Emphatic or contrastive stress can similarly be marked, if relevant, by a double stroke.

Consonants

/p/	pin	/l/	lick
/b/	bin	/r/	written
/f/	fin	/tʃ/	chick
/v/	vote	/dʒ/	gin
/m/	mitt	/ʃ/	shin
/θ/	thin	/ʒ/	pleasure
/ð/	this	/k/	kin
/t/	tin	/g/	give
/d/	din	/ŋ/	sing
/s/	sin	/j/	young
/z/	zoo	/w/	win
/n/	nil	/h/	hat

Vowels (Transcriptions are given here for Received Pronunciation)

/i/	beat	/ɛi/	bay
/ɩ/	bit	/ai/	buy
/ɛ/	bet	/ɔi/	boy

Appendix A

/æ/	bat	/əu/	toe
/ʌ/	but	/au/	bough
/ɑ·/	bar	/iə/	beer
/ɒ/	pot	/ɛə/	bear
/ɔ·/	saw	/uə/	sure
/u·/	soon		
/ɷ/	book		
/ɜ·/	bird		
/ə/	butter		

Appendix B

Points and manners of articulation

1 Points of articulation

Articulation refers to the movements of the vocal organs in speech.

Point or place of articulation refers to the place in the vocal tract where the vocal organs come together to form a complete closure or partial constriction, in the production of a consonant. (Points of articulation are generally only specified for consonants, where there is a relatively narrow point of closure or constriction. For vowels, the constriction is wider and therefore not easy to specify.)

Points of articulation referred to in the text are as in the accompanying diagram of the vocal organs.

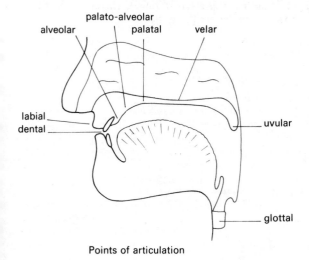

Points of articulation

2   Manner of articulation

This refers to the type of closure or constriction in the vocal tract.

Plosive
Sound produced with complete closure of the vocal tract at some point, so that no air can escape, followed by a release of the closure and there-fore a release of the air. (The nasal cavity is closed by raising the velum or soft palate, so that no air can pass through the nose.) Examples are [p, b, t, d, k, g].

Fricative
Sound produced by bringing the articulators close enough together to cause air turbulence or friction, but not close enough to stop the air-flow completely. The articulators involved may be, for example, the upper and lower lips, the upper teeth and lower lip, the tongue and the upper teeth, or the tongue and the palate. Examples are [f, v, θ, ð, s, z, ʃ, ȝ, x].

Affricate
Combination of a plosive and a fricative. Sound produced by a total closure of the vocal tract, as though for a plosive, followed by a rela-tively slow release in which friction is audible. Examples are [tʃ, dȝ].

Nasal
Sound produced with the velum lowered, so that air passes through the nasal cavity. The oral passage is closed at some point (e.g., at the lips, or because the tongue is against the alveolar ridge), therefore air passes only through the nose. Examples are [m, n, ŋ].

Suggestions for further reading

1 Written and spoken language

Brown, Gillian (1977), *Listening to Spoken English*, London, Longman. Contains a great deal of precise description of the processes of assimilation and elision in informal spoken English.

Pike, Kenneth (1947), *Phonemics: A Technique for Reducing Languages to Writing*, University of Michigan Press. The classical technical study of techniques for creating writing systems for previously unwritten languages.

Vachek, Josef (1973), *Written Language: General Problems and Problems of English*, The Hague, Mouton. A short statement of a functional approach to the theory of the relationship between spoken and written language.

2 English spelling

Albrow, K. H. (1972), *The English Writing System: Notes towards a Description*, London, Longman. Rather unsystematic, but full of brilliant insights.

Chomsky, Carol (1970), 'Reading, writing and phonology', *Harvard Educational Review*, 40, 2. Extracts reprinted in Frank Smith, *Psycholinguistics and Reading*, New York, Holt, Rinehart & Winston, 1973. Useful summary of some points which arise from Chomsky and Halle's work.

Venezky, Richard L. (1970), *The Structure of English Orthography*, The Hague, Mouton. A major scholarly study based on a computer tabulation of the 20,000 most common English words.

3 Important reviews and reference material

Downing, John (ed.) (1973), *Comparative Reading*, New York, Macmillan. General discussion of cross-national studies of reading and writing, and papers by experts on literacy in Argentina, Denmark, Finland, France, Germany, Great Britain, Hong Kong, India, Israel, Japan, Sweden, USA, USSR.

Gudschinsky, Sarah C. (1976), *Literacy: The Growing Influence of Linguistics*, The Hague, Mouton. Short review of literacy studies with particular reference to sociolinguistics, and a large bibliography of further works.

Sebeok, Thomas A. (ed.) (1963–76), *Current Trends in Linguistics*, The Hague, Mouton. An enormous collection of reference material, published in 14 volumes, each volume running to hundreds of pages. A large amount of the material is not directly relevant to literacy, but there are many articles on literacy in different countries, script reform, studies of minority languages and on the theory of reading.

4 Language in education

Keen, John (1978), *Teaching English: A Linguistic Approach*, London, Methuen. A very practical book, showing primarily what a linguistic approach can contribute to an understanding of pupils' writing.

Labov, William (1972), *Language in the Inner City*, University of Pennsylvania Press. A major collection of Labov's papers on non-standard dialects of English, including some papers specifically on reading.

Stubbs, Michael (1976), *Language, Schools and Classrooms*, London, Methuen. An introductory discussion of studies of language in education, including critical discussion of Bernstein and Labov.

Trudgill, Peter (1975), *Accent, Dialect and the School*, London, Edward Arnold. Useful introductory discussion of the relation between standard and non-standard accent and dialect, and educational problems, proposing a 'bidialectalism' approach.

Bibliography

Abercrombie, David (1948), 'Forgotten phoneticians', in D. Abercrombie, *Studies in Phonetics and Linguistics*, London, Oxford University Press, 1965, pp. 45–75.

Abercrombie, David (1977), 'The accents of standard English in Scotland', *Work in Progress*, 10, Department of Linguistics, University of Edinburgh, pp. 21–32.

Albrow, K. H. (1972), *The English Writing System: Notes towards a Description*, London, Longmans.

Alisjahbana, S. Takdir (1971), 'Language policy, language engineering and literacy: Indonesia and Malaysia', in Sebeok (ed.), vol. 8, pp. 1087–109, and in Fishman (ed.) 1974, pp. 391–416.

Andrzejewski, B. W. (1963), 'Poetry in Somali society', *New Society*, 25, pp. 22–4. Reprinted in Pride and Holmes (eds) 1972, pp. 252–9.

Ardener, Edwin (ed.) (1971), *Social Anthropology and Language*, London, Tavistock.

Asimov, Isaac (1956), 'The dying night', in A. Wells (ed.), *The Best of Isaac Asimov 1954–1972*, London, Sphere, 1977.

Baratz, Joan C. and Shuy, Roger W. (eds) (1969), *Teaching Black Children to Read*, Washington DC, Center for Applied Linguistics.

Baratz, S. S. and Baratz, Joan C. (1970), 'Early childhood intervention: the social science base of institutional racism', *Harvard Educational Review*, 40, 1, pp. 29–50.

Barber, Charles (1964), *Linguistic Changes in Present-Day English*, London, Oliver & Boyd.

Barnes, D. *et al.* (1969), *Language, the Learner and the School*, Harmondsworth, Penguin.

Basso, K. (1974), 'The ethnography of writing', in R. Bauman and J. Sherzer (eds), *Explorations in the Ethnography of Speaking*, London, Cambridge University Press, pp. 425–32.

Bell, Roger T. (1977), *Sociolinguistics*, London, Batsford.

Bereiter, C. and Engelmann, S. (1966), *Teaching Disadvantaged Children in the Pre-School*, Englewood Cliffs, NJ, Prentice Hall.

171

Bernstein, Basil B. (1969), 'A critique of the concept of compensatory education', in Bernstein, 1971, pp. 214–26.

Bernstein, Basil B. (1971), *Class, Codes and Control*, vol. 1, London, Paladin.

Bernstein, Basil B. (1973), 'Social class, language and socialization', in Sebeok (ed.), vol. 12, pp. 1545–62.

Berry, Jack (1958), 'The making of alphabets', in Fishman (ed.) 1968, pp. 737–53.

Bloomfield, Leonard (1933), *Language*, New York, Henry Holt.

Bloomfield, Leonard (1942), 'Linguistics and reading', *The Elementary English Review*, 19, 4, pp. 125–30; 19, 5, pp. 183–6.

Bolinger, Dwight L. (1946), 'Visual morphemes', *Language*, 22, pp. 333–40.

Bowers, John (1968), 'Language problems and literacy', in Fishman, Ferguson and Das Gupta (eds), pp. 381–402.

Brown, Gillian (1977), *Listening to Spoken English*, London, Longmans.

Brumby, Ed and Vaszolyi, Eric (eds) (1977), *Language Problems and Aboriginal Education*, Western Australia, Mount Lawley College of Advanced Education.

Bugarski, Ranko (1970), 'Writing systems and phonological insights', *Papers of the Chicago Linguistic Society*, pp. 453–8.

Bull, William E. (1955), 'The use of vernacular languages in education', *International Journal of American Linguistics*, 21, pp. 228–94. Reprinted in Dell Hymes (ed.), *Language in Culture and Society*, New York, Harper Row, 1964, pp. 527–33.

Burns, Donald H. (1953), 'Social and political implications in the choice of an orthography', *Fundamental and Adult Education*, 5, pp. 80–4.

Bynon, Theodora (1977), *Historical Linguistics*, London, Cambridge University Press.

Chall, Jeanne S. (1967), *Learning to Read: the Great Debate*, New York, McGraw-Hill.

Chomsky, Carol (1970), 'Reading, writing and phonology', *Harvard Educational Review*, 40, 2, pp. 287–309; extracts reprinted in Smith, 1973.

Chomsky, N. and Halle, M. (1968), *The Sound Pattern of English*, New York, Harper & Row.

Cipolla, Carlo M. (1969), *Literacy and Development in the West*, Harmondsworth, Penguin.

Clark, J. W. (1957), *Early English*, London, André Deutsch.

Clark, Margaret (1975), 'Language and reading: research trends', in Davies (ed.), 1975.

Comrie, B. and Stone, G. (1978), *The Russian Language Since the Revolution*, London, Oxford University Press.

Cook-Gumperz, J. (1977), 'Situated instructions: language socialization of school age children', in Ervin-Tripp and Mitchell-Kernan (eds), 1977, pp. 103–21.

Cottrell, Leonard (1971), *Reading the Past*, London, Dent.

Creber, J. W. Patrick (1972), *Lost for Words*, Harmondsworth, Penguin.

Crystal, D. and Davy, D. (1969), *Investigating English Style*, London, Longmans.

Davie, Ronald *et al.* (1972), *From Birth to Seven*, London, Longmans.

Davies, Alan (ed.) (1975), *Problems of Language and Learning*, London, Heinemann.

Davies, Alan (ed.) (1977), *Language and Learning in Early Childhood*, London, Heinemann.

Davies, Alan and Widdowson, H. G. (1974), 'Reading and writing', in J. P. B. Allen and S. Pit Corder (eds), *The Edinburgh Course in Applied Linguistics*, vol. 3, London, Oxford University Press.

De Camp, D. (1972), 'Hypercorrection and rule generalisation', *Language in Society*, 1, 1, April 1972, pp. 87–90.

De Francis, John (1967), 'Language and script reform', in Sebeok (ed.), vol. 2, pp. 130–50. Reprinted in J. A. Fishman (ed.), *Advances in the Sociology of Language*, vol. 2, The Hague, Mouton, 1972.

Deutsch, M. *et al.* (eds) (1967), *The Disadvantaged Child*, New York, Basic Books.

Diringer, David (1962), *Writing*, London, Thames & Hudson.

Dittmar, N. (1976), *Sociolinguistics*, London, Edward Arnold.

Dixon, R. M. W. (1972), *The Dyirbal Language of North Queensland*, London, Cambridge University Press.

Downing, John (1969), 'How children think about reading', in Melnik and Merritt (eds), 1972b, pp. 215–30.

Downing, John (ed.) (1973), *Comparative Reading*, New York, Macmillan.

Dressler, W. *et al.* (1976), 'Phonologische Schnellsprechregeln in der Wiener Umgangssprache', in W. Viereck (ed.), *Sprachliches Handeln-soziales Verhalten*, Munich, Wilhelm Fink Verlag.

Edgerton, W. F. (1941), 'Ideograms in English writing', *Language*, 17, pp. 148–50.

Edwards, A. D. (1976), *Language in Culture and Class*, London, Heinemann.

Edwards, A. D. and Hargreaves, D. (1976), 'The social scientific base of academic radicalism', *Educational Review*, 28, 2, February 1976, pp. 83–93.

Ekwall, Eilert (1965), *A History of Modern English Sounds and Morphology*, Oxford, Blackwell. (English translation, 1975, Alan Ward.)

Ervin-Tripp, E. and Mitchell-Kernan, C. (eds) (1977), *Child Discourse*, New York, Academic Press.

Evans, Harold (1977), 'Why we now make better reading', *Sunday Times*, 22 August 1977.

Ezard, John (1978), 'Program for the future – official', *The Guardian*, 21 August 1978.

Ferguson, C. A. (1959), 'Diglossia', *Word*, 15, pp. 325–40. Reprinted in Giglioli (ed.), 1972, and in Ferguson, 1971b, pp. 1–26.

Ferguson, C. A. (1967), 'St Stefan of Perm and applied linguistics', in Fishman, Ferguson and Das Gupta (eds), 1968, pp. 253–66. Reprinted in Ferguson, 1971b, pp. 197–218.

Ferguson, C. A. (1968), 'Language development', in Fishman, Ferguson and Das Gupta (eds), 1968, pp. 27–35. Reprinted in Ferguson, 1971b, pp. 219–32.

Ferguson, C. A. (1971a), 'Contrasting patterns of literacy acquisition in a multilingual nation', in W. H. Whiteley (ed.), *Language Use and Social Change*, London, Oxford University Press. Reprinted in Ferguson, 1971b, pp. 249–76.

Ferguson, C. A. (1971b), *Language Structure and Language Use*, California, Stanford University Press.

Ferguson, C. A. and Snow, C. E. (eds) (1977), *Talking to Children*, London, Cambridge University Press.

Firth, J. R. (1957), *Papers in Linguistics, 1934–1951*, London, Oxford University Press.

Fishman, J. A. (ed.) (1968), *Readings in the Sociology of Language*, The Hague, Mouton.

Fishman, J. A. (1971), 'The uses of sociolinguistics', in G.E. Perren and J. L. M. Trim (eds), *Applications of Linguistics*, London, Cambridge University Press, pp. 19–40.

Fishman, J. A. (ed.) (1974), *Advances in Language Planning*, The Hague, Mouton.

Fishman, J. A., Ferguson, C. A., and Das Gupta, J. (eds) (1968), *Language Problems of Developing Nations*, New York, Wiley.

Flesch, Rudolf (1955), *Why Johnny Can't Read*, New York, Harper.

Flower, F. (1966), *Language and Education*, London, Longmans.

Francis, Hazel (1973), 'Children's experience of reading and notions of units in language', *British Journal of Educational Psychology*, 1973, Part I, pp. 17–23.

French, M. A. (1976), 'Observations on the Chinese script and the classification of writing systems', in Haas (ed.), 1976, pp. 101–30.

Gardiner, Jennifer (1977), 'Teaching standard English as a second dialect to speakers of Aboriginal English', in Brumby and Vaszolyi (eds), 1977, pp. 165–99.

Garvin, Paul L. (1954), 'Literacy as a problem in language and culture', in Hugo J. Mueller (ed.), *Report of the 5th Annual Round Table Meeting on Linguistics and Language Teaching*, University of Georgetown, pp. 117–40.

Garvin, Paul L. (1973), 'Some comments on language planning', in Fishman (ed.), 1974, pp. 69–78; also in J. Rubin and R. Shuy (eds), *Language Planning: Current Issues and Research*, Washington DC, Georgetown University Press, 1973, pp. 24–73.

Gelb, I. J. (1963), *A Study of Writing*, revised edition, University of Chicago Press.

Giglioli, P.-P. (ed.) (1972), *Language and Social Context*, Harmondsworth, Penguin.

Gimson, A. C. (1970), *An Introduction to the Pronunciation of English*, 2nd edition, London, Edward Arnold.

Ginsburg, H. (1972), *The Myth of the Deprived Child*, New Jersey, Englewood Cliffs.

Goodacre, Elizabeth A. (1971), 'Methods of teaching reading', in Melnik and Merritt (eds), 1972a, pp. 114-28.

Goodman, Elliot R. (1960), 'World state and world language', in Fishman (ed.), 1968, pp. 717-36.

Goody, Jack (ed.) (1968), *Literacy in Traditional Societies*, London, Cambridge University Press.

Goody, Jack (1977), *The Domestication of the Savage Mind*, London, Cambridge University Press.

Goody, Jack and Watt, Ian (1962/3), 'The consequences of literacy', *Comparative Studies in Society and History*, 5, 3, pp. 304-45. Reprinted in Goody (ed.), 1968, pp. 27-68. Extracts in Giglioli (ed.), 1972.

Gordon, J. C. B. (1976), 'Concepts of verbal deficit in Bernstein's writings on language and social class', *Nottingham Linguistic Circular*, 5, 2, pp. 31-8.

Gough, Kathleen (1968), 'Implications of literacy in traditional China and India', in Goody (ed.), 1968, pp. 69-84.

Grassby, A. J. (1976), 'Linguistic genocide', in Brumby and Vaszolyi (eds), 1977, pp. 1-4.

Gray, William S. (1956), *The Teaching of Reading and Writing*, Paris, Unesco, Monographs on Fundamental Education, 10.

Gudschinsky, Sarah C. (1974), 'Linguistics and literacy', in Sebeok (ed.), vol. 12, pp. 2039-56.

Gudschinsky, Sarah C. (1976), *Literacy: the Growing Influence of Linguistics*, The Hague, Mouton.

Gumperz, J. J. and Hymes, D. (eds) (1972), *Directions in Sociolinguistics*, New York, Holt, Rinehart & Winston.

Haas, W. (ed.) (1969), *Alphabets for English*, Manchester University Press.

Haas, W. (1970), *Phono-graphic Translation*, Manchester University Press.

Haas, W. (ed.) (1976), *Writing without Letters*, Manchester University Press.

Hall, R. A., Jr. (1972), 'Pidgins and creoles as standard languages', in J. B. Pride and J. Holmes (eds), 1972, pp. 142-53.

Hall, R. A., Jr. (1975), 'Review of J. Vachek *Written English*', *Language*, 51, 2, pp. 461-4.

Halliday, M. A. K., McIntosh, A. and Strevens, P. (1964), *The Linguistic Sciences and Language Teaching*, London, Longmans.

Harris, A. J. (1969), 'The effective teacher of reading', *The Reading Teacher*, 23, 3, pp. 195-204. Reprinted in Melnik and Merritt (eds), 1972a, pp. 532-43.

Haugen, Einar (1966), 'Linguistics and language planning', in Haugen, 1972.

Haugen, Einar (1972), *Studies by Einar Haugen*, edited by E. S. Firchow, The Hague, Mouton.

Havelock, Eric A. (1976), *Origins of Western Literacy*, Ontario Institute for Studies in Education, Monograph Series 14.

Hawkins, P. (1969), 'Social class, the nominal group and reference', in Basil B. Bernstein (ed.), *Class, Codes and Control*, vol. 2, London, Routledge & Kegan Paul, 1972.

Hawkins, P. (1977), *Social Class, the Nominal Group and Verbal Strategies*, London, Routledge & Kegan Paul.

Herriot, P. (1971), *Language and Teaching*, London, Methuen.

Hertzler, J. O. (1965), *A Sociology of Language*, New York, Random House.

HMSO (1975), *A Language for Life*, Report of the Bullock Committee.

Holden, M. H. and MacGintie, W. H. (1972), 'Children's conceptions of word boundaries in speech and print', *Journal of Educational Psychology*, 63, 6, pp. 551–7.

Holmes, Janet (1976), 'Investigating subjective judgments of New Zealand English', in Euan Reid (ed.), *Abstracts of 1976 Research Seminar on Sociolinguistic Variation*, West Midlands College, Walsall, mimeo.

Holt, John (1967), *How Children Learn*, Harmondsworth, Penguin, 1970.

Householder, Fred W. (1971), *Linguistic Speculations*, London, Cambridge University Press.

Huey, E. B. (1908), *The Psychology and Pedagogy of Reading*, New York, Macmillan.

Hymes, D. (1974), *Foundations in Sociolinguistics*, Pennsylvania University Press.

Isayev, M. I. (1977), *National Languages in the USSR: Problems and Solutions*, Moscow, Progress Publishers.

Ives, S. and Ives, J. P. (1973), 'Linguistics and the teaching of reading and spelling', in Sebeok (ed.), vol. 10, pp. 228–49.

Jackson, L. A. (1974), 'The myth of elaborated and restricted code', *Higher Education Review*, 6, 2.

Javal, Emile (1897), 'Essai sur la physiologie de lecture', *Annales d'Oculistique*, 82, pp. 242–53.

Jenkinson, Marion D. (1969), 'Sources of knowledge for theories of reading', in Melnik and Merritt (eds), 1972b, pp. 102–17.

Jensen, Arthur (1969), 'How much can we boost IQ and scholastic achievement?' *Harvard Educational Review*, 39, pp. 449–83.

Johnson, Samuel (1755), *A Dictionary of the English Language*, London.

Joos, Martin (1960), 'Review of Axel Wijk *Regularized English*', *Language*, 36, pp. 250–62.

Kaldor, Susan (1977), 'Two Australian language educational programmes: a linguist's view', in Brumby and Vaszolyi (eds), 1977, pp. 82–95.

Kavanagh, J. F. and Maddingley, I. G. (eds) (1972), *Language by Ear and by Eye*, Cambridge, Mass, MIT Press.

Keddie, N. (ed.) (1973), *Tinker, Tailor: the Myth of Cultural Deprivation*, Harmondsworth, Penguin.

Keen, John (1978), *Teaching English: A Linguistic Approach*, London, Methuen.

Keenan, E. L. (1977), 'Making it last: repetition in children's discourse', in Ervin-Tripp and Mitchell-Kernan (eds), 1977, pp. 125–38.

Keller, Helen (1903), *The Story of My Life,* London, Hodder & Stoughton.

Kellmer-Pringle, M. L., Butler, N. R. and Davie, R. (1966), *11,000 Seven Year Olds*, London, Longmans.

Kochman, T. (1972), 'Black American speech events and a language programme for the classroom', in C. Cazden *et al.* (eds), *Functions of Language in the Classroom*, New York, Teachers College Press.

Koestler, A. (1976), *The Thirteenth Tribe*, London, Hutchinson.

Kohl, Herbert (1973), *Reading, How To*, Harmondsworth, Penguin.

Labov, William (1966), *The Social Stratification of English in New York City*, Washington DC, Center for Applied Linguistics.

Labov, William (1969a), 'The logic of non-standard English', in *Georgetown Monographs on Language and Linguistics*, 22, pp. 1–31. Reprinted in Keddie (ed.), 1973; in Giglioli (ed.), 1972; and in Labov, 1972b.

Labov, William (1969b), 'The relation of reading failure to peer-group status', in Labov, 1972b.

Labov, William (1970), 'The reading of the -ed suffix', in Levin and Williams (eds), 1970, pp. 222–45.

Labov, William (1972a), *Sociolinguistic Patterns*, University of Pennsylvania Press.

Labov, William (1972b), *Language in the Inner City*, University of Pennsylvania Press.

Lambert, W. E. (1967), 'A social psychology of bilingualism', in Pride and Holmes (eds), 1972, pp. 336–49.

Lawson, J. and Silver, H. (1973), *A Social History of Education in England*, London, Methuen.

Levin, H. and Williams, J. P. (eds) (1970), *Basic Studies on Reading*, New York, Basic Books.

Levitas, M. (1976), 'A culture of deprivation', *Marxism Today*, April 1976.

Lieberman, Philip (1972), *The Speech of Primates*, The Hague, Mouton.

Lunzer, E. A. and Gardner, K. (eds) (1978), *The Effective Use of Reading*, London, Heinemann.

Lunzer, E. A. and Harrison, C. (1979), 'Der Leseprozess und das Leselernen', in G. Steiner (ed.) *Die Psychologie des 20. Jahrhunderts*, vol. 7: *Piaget und die Folgen*, Zürich, Kindler.

Lyons, J. (1968), *Introduction to Theoretical Linguistics*, London, Cambridge University Press.

MacCarthy, P. A. D. (1969), 'The Bernard Shaw alphabet', in Haas (ed.), 1969, pp. 105–17.

Macaulay, R. K. S. (1978), *Language, Social Class and Education: a Glasgow Study*, University of Edinburgh Press.

McIntosh, Angus (1966), '"Graphology" and meaning', in A. McIntosh and M. A. K. Halliday, *Patterns of Language*, London, Longmans, 1966.

Mackay, D., Thompson, B. and Schaub, P. (1970), *Breakthrough to Literacy: Teacher's Manual*, London, Longmans.

McLuhan, M. (1960), 'The effect of the printed book on language in the sixteenth century', in E. Carpenter and M. McLuhan (eds), *Explorations in Communication*, London, Cape, 1970.

Magee, Bryan (1973), *Popper*, London, Fontana.

Malmquist, Eve (1969), 'Reading: a human right and a human problem', in Melnik and Merritt (eds), 1972b, pp. 341–4.

Mason, George E. (1967), 'Preschoolers' concepts of reading', in Melnik and Merritt (eds), 1972b, pp. 200–2.

Melnik, Amelia and Merritt, John E. (eds) (1972a), *The Reading Curriculum*, London University Press.

Melnik, Amelia and Merritt, John E. (eds) (1972b), *Reading Today and Tomorrow*, London University Press.

Merritt, John E. (1972), 'Reading failure: a re-examination', in Reid (ed.), 1972, pp. 186–95.

Milroy, Lesley (1973), 'Codes theory and language standardization', mimeo, Northern Ireland Polytechnic.

Milroy, Lesley and Milroy, J. (1977), 'Speech and context in an urban setting', *Belfast Working Papers in Language and Linguistics*, 2, 1, pp. 1–85.

Morgan, P. (1896), 'A case of congenital word blindness', *British Medical Journal*, 7 November 1896, p. 1378.

Morris, Joyce M. (1972), *The First 'R': Yesterday, Today and Tomorrow*, London, Ward Lock Educational.

Moss, Margaret H. (1973), *Deprivation and Disadvantage?*, Milton Keynes, Open University Press.

Nida, Eugene A. (1975), *Language Structure and Translation*, edited by A. S. Dil, California, Stanford University Press.

Nida, Eugene A. and Wonderly, W. L. (1963), 'Linguistics and Christian missions', *Anthropological Linguistics*, 5, 1, pp. 104–44. Reprinted in Nida, 1975, pp. 192–247.

O'Connor, J. D. (1973), *Phonetics*, Harmondsworth, Penguin.

Otto, Wayne (1971), 'Thorndike's "Reading as reasoning": influence and impact', in Melnik and Merritt (eds), 1972b, pp. 37–44.

Partridge, Monica (1964), *Serbo-Croatian: a Practical Grammar and Reader*, New York, McGraw-Hill.

Piaget, Jean (1926), *The Language and Thought of the Child*, New York, Harcourt & Brace.

Pike, Kenneth (1947), *Phonemics: A Technique for Reducing Languages to Writing*, Ann Arbor, Michigan University Press.

Pilliner, A. E. G. and Reid, Jessie F. (1972), 'The definition and measurement of reading problems', in Reid (ed.), (1972), pp. 20–36.

Pillsbury, Walter B. (1897), 'The reading of words: a study in appercep-
tion', *American Journal of Psychology*, 8, pp. 315–93.

Piper, H. Beam (1957), 'Omnilingual', *Astounding Science Fiction*,
February 1957. Reprinted in I. Asimov (ed.), *Where do we go from
here?*, vol. 2, London, Sphere, 1974.

Pitman, J. and St John, J. (1969), *Alphabets and Reading*, London,
Pitman.

Popper, Karl R. (1972), *Objective Knowledge*, Oxford, Clarendon.

Popper, Karl R. (1974), *Conjectures and Refutations*, 5th edition,
London, Routledge & Kegan Paul.

Pride, J. B. and Holmes, J. (eds) (1972), *Sociolinguistics*, Harmondsworth, Penguin.

Pulgram, E. (1951), 'Phoneme and grapheme', *Word*, 7, pp. 15–20.

Quirk, Randolph (1970), 'Aspect and variant inflection in English
verbs', *Language*, 46, 2, 1, pp. 300–11.

Quirk, Randolph (1977), 'Setting new word records', *Visible Language*,
9, 1, Winter 1977, pp. 63–74.

Rauch, Sidney J. (1968), 'Reading in the total school curriculum', in
Melnik and Merritt (eds), 1972a, pp. 18–26.

Reid, Jessie F. (1958), 'An investigation of thirteen beginners in reading', *Acta Psychologica*, 14, 4, pp. 295–313.

Reid, Jessie F. (1966), 'Learning to think about reading', *Educational
Research*, 9, 1, November 1966, pp. 56–62. Reprinted in Melnik and
Merritt (eds), 1972b, pp. 203–14.

Reid, Jessie F. (1968), 'Dyslexia: a problem in communication', *Educational Research*, 10, 2, February 1968, pp. 126–33. Reprinted in
Reid (ed.), 1972, pp. 130–41.

Reid, Jessie F. (1970), 'Sentence structure in reading primers', *Research
in Education*, 3, May 1970, pp. 23–37.

Reid, Jessie F. (1972a), 'Children's comprehension of syntactic features
found in some extension readers', in Reid (ed.), 1972, pp. 394–403.

Reid, Jessie F. (ed.) (1972b), *Reading: Problems and Practices*, London,
Ward Lock Educational.

Rogers, Sinclair (ed.) (1976), *They Don't Speak Our Language*, London,
Edward Arnold.

Romaine, S. and Reid, E. (1976), 'Glottal sloppiness?', *Teaching
English*, 9, 3, Summer 1976, pp. 12–17.

Rosen, Harold (1973), *Language and Class: A Critical Look at the
Theories of Basil Bernstein*, Bristol, Falling Wall Press.

Ruhlen, Merritt (1975), *A Guide to the Languages of the World*, Stanford University Press.

Sarna, N. M. *et al.* (1974), 'Biblical literature', *Encyclopaedia Britannica,
Macropaedia*, 2, pp. 892ff.

Schmidt, Siegfried, J. (1976), *Texttheorie*, Munich, Wilhelm Fink.

Scott, Laueen and Coker, John (1977), 'The language programme in
Aboriginal schools', *Pivot*, 4, 1, pp. 25–7.

Scragg, D. G. (1974), *A History of English Spelling*, Manchester University Press.

Searle, J. R. (1975), 'The logical status of fictional discourse', *New Literary History*, 6, 2, pp. 319–32.

Sebeok, Thomas A. (ed.) (1963–76), *Current Trends in Linguistics*, vols 1–14, The Hague, Mouton.

Sharpe, Margaret C. (1977), 'Alice Springs Aboriginal English', in Brumby and Vaszolyi (eds), 1977, pp. 45–50.

Sharpe, Margaret C. and Sandefur, John (1977), 'A brief description of Roper Creole', in Brumby and Vaszolyi (eds), 1977, pp. 51–60.

Shaw, G. B. (1962), *Androcles and the Lion*, Harmondsworth, Penguin (Shaw alphabet edition).

Shiach, Gordon McGregor (1972), *Teach Them to Speak*, London, Ward Lock Educational.

Sinclair, J. M. and Coulthard, R. M. (1975), *Towards an Analysis of Discourse*, London, Oxford University Press.

Sivertsen, Eva (1960), *Cockney Phonology*, Oslo University Press.

Sjoberg, A. F. (1964), 'Writing, speech and society: some changing inter-relationships', in *Proceedings of the Ninth International Congress of Linguists*, The Hague, Mouton, pp. 892–7.

Sjoberg, A. F. (1966), 'Sociocultural and linguistic factors in the development of writing systems for pre-literate peoples', in W. Bright (ed.), *Sociolinguistics*, The Hague, Mouton, 1966, pp. 260–76.

Smith, Frank (1973), *Psycholinguistics and Reading*, London, Holt, Rinehart & Winston.

Southgate, Vera (1969), *ITA: an Independent Evaluation*, London, Murray.

Speitel, H. H. (1975), 'Dialect', in Davies (ed.), 1975, pp. 34–53.

Stauffer, R. G. (1971), 'Thorndike's "Reading as reasoning": a perspective', in Melnik and Merritt (eds), 1972b, pp. 31–6.

Steinberg, S. H. (1961), *Five Hundred Years of Printing*, Harmondsworth, Penguin, 2nd edition.

Strang, Barbara M. H. (1970), *A History of English*, London, Methuen.

Stubbs, Michael (1976), *Language, Schools and Classrooms*, London, Methuen.

Stubbs, Michael (1978), 'Review of Hawkins *Social Class, the Nominal Group and Verbal Strategies*', *British Journal of Educational Studies*, 26, 2, June 1978, pp. 195–6.

Stubbs, Michael and Delamont, Sara (eds) (1976), *Explorations in Classroom Observation*, London, Wiley.

Thorndike, Edward L. (1917), 'Reading as reasoning: a study of mistakes in paragraph reading', *Journal of Educational Psychology*, 8, 6, June 1917, pp. 323–32. Reprinted in Melnik and Merritt (eds), 1972b, pp. 20–30).

Torrey, Jane W. (1969), 'Learning to read without a teacher: a case study', *Elementary English*, 46, pp. 550–6. Reprinted in Smith, 1973, pp. 147–57.

Tough, Joan (1977), *The Development of Meaning*, London, Allen & Unwin.

Trager, G. L. (1974), 'Writing and writing systems', in Sebeok (ed.), vol. 12, pp. 373–496.

Trudgill, Peter (1974a), *The Social Differentiation of English in Norwich*, London, Cambridge University Press.

Trudgill, Peter (1974b), *Sociolinguistics*, Harmondsworth, Penguin.

Trudgill, Peter (1975), *Accent, Dialect and the School*, London, Edward Arnold.

Tucker, A. N. (1971), 'Orthographic systems and conventions in sub-Saharan Africa', in Sebeok (ed.), vol. 7, pp. 618–53.

Unesco (1953), *The Use of Vernacular Languages in Education*, Monographs on Fundamental Education 8, Paris: Unesco.

Vachek, Josef (1945–9), 'Some remarks on writing and phonetic transcription', *Acta Linguistica*, 5, pp. 86–93. Reprinted in E. P. Hamp *et al.* (eds), *Readings in Linguistics*, University of Chicago Press, 1966, pp. 152–7.

Vachek, Josef (1964), 'On peripheral phonemes of Modern English', *Brno Studies in English*, 4, pp. 7–109.

Vachek, Josef (1966), 'On the integration of the peripheral elements into the system of language', *Travaux Linguistiques de Prague*, 2, pp. 23–38.

Vachek, Josef (1971), 'Review of R. Venezky *The Structure of English Orthography*', *Language*, 47, 1, pp. 212–16.

Vachek, Josef (1973), *Written Language: General Problems and Problems of English*, The Hague, Mouton.

Valdmann, Albert (1968), 'Language standardization in a diglossia situation: Haiti', in Fishman, Ferguson and Das Gupta (eds), 1968, pp. 313–26.

Valdmann, Albert (1973), 'Some aspects of decreolization in Creole French', in Sebeok (ed.), vol. 11, pp. 507–36.

Venezky, Richard L. (1970), *The Structure of English Orthography*, The Hague, Mouton.

Venezky, Richard L. (1974), 'Theoretical and experimental bases for teaching reading', in Sebeok (ed.), vol. 12, pp. 2057–100.

Vernon, M. D. (1971), 'The effect of motivational and emotional factors on learning to read', in Reid (ed.), 1972, pp. 47–64.

Voegelin, C. F. and Voegelin, F. M. (1977), *Classification and Index of the World's Languages*, New York, Elsevier.

Vygotsky, L. S. (1962), *Thought and Language*, Cambridge, Mass., MIT Press.

Wax, M. L. and Wax, R. H. (1971), 'Cultural deprivation as an educational ideology', in E. B. Leacock (ed.), *The Culture of Poverty: a Critique*, New York, Simon & Schuster, pp. 127–39.

Weaver, W. W., Kingston, A. J., and Figa, L. E. (1972), 'Experiments in children's perceptions of words and word boundaries', in A. J. Kingston (ed.), *Toward a Psychology of Reading and Language*, University of Georgia Press, 1977, pp. 188–97.

Wells, Gordon (1977), 'Language use and educational success: a response to Joan Tough's *The Development of Meaning*', *Nottingham Linguistic Circular*, 6, 2, pp. 29–50.

Welmers, W. E. (1971), 'Christian missions and language policies in Africa', in Sebeok (ed.), vol. 7, 1971, pp. 559-69. Reprinted in Fishman (ed.), 1974, pp. 191-203.

Whorf, B. L. (1956), *Language, Thought and Reality*, edited by J. B. Carroll, Cambridge, Mass., MIT Press.

Widdowson, H. G. (1975), *Stylistics and the Teaching of Literature*, London, Longman.

Wijk, Axel (1959), *Regularized English*, Stockholm, Almquist-Wiksell.

Wilkinson, A. (1971), *The Foundations of Language*, London, Oxford University Press.

Wurm, S. A. (1971), 'Language policy, language engineering and literacy in New Guinea and Australia', in Sebeok (ed.), vol. 8, pp. 1025-38; revised version in Fishman (ed.), 1974, pp. 205-22.

Wyld, H. C. (1914, 3rd edition, 1927), *A Short History of English*, London, John Murray.

Zachrison, R. E. (1930), *Anglic, a New Agreed Simplified English Spelling*, Uppsala, Almquist & Wiksell.

Zengler, M. S. (1962), 'Literacy as a factor in language change', *American Anthropologist*, 64, pp. 132-9.

Name index

Abercrombie, D., 23, 129
Albrow, K. H., 5, 43, 57, 63, 66
Alisjahbana, S. T., 64
Andrzejewski, B. W., 101
Ardener, E., 16
Asimov, I., 105

Baratz, J. C. and S. S., 144, 147, 153
Barber, C., 31
Barnes, D., 115
Basso, K., 17
Bell, A. G., 124
Bell, R. T., 16, 112
Bereiter, C., 146
Bernstein, B. B., 111–12, 144f, 148f, 152, 156, 157
Berry, J., 73, 75, 83
Bloomfield, L., 24, 25, 94
Boas, F., 94
Bolinger, D. L., 29
Bowers, J., 14
Brown, G., 119, 121
Brumby, E., 90
Bugarski, R., 124
Bull, W. E., 155
Burns, D. H., 75
Bynon, T., 39

Caxton, W., 51, 107
Chall, J. S., 11
Chomsky, C., 5, 43

Chomsky, N., 16, 43, 66, 158–9
Cipolla, C. M., 27
Clark, J. W., 33, 52
Coker, J., 91
Comrie, B., 83
Cook-Gumperz, J., 111
Cottrell, L., 25
Coulthard, R. M., 115
Creber, J. W. P., 151
Crystal, D., 112

Davie, R., 143
Davies, A., 153, 156
Davy, D., 112
De Camp, D., 31
De Francis, J., 85
Delamont, S., 163
Deutsch, M., 146
Diringer, D., 25, 48, 71, 91
Dittmar, N., 16, 146, 148, 155
Dixon, R. M. W., 90
Downing, J., 11, 22, 99, 123
Dressler, W., 122

Edison, T., 23
Edgerton, W. F., 47
Edwards, A. D., 16, 154
Ekwall, E., 36, 40
Ellis, J., 124
Engelmann, S., 146
Ervin-Tripp, S., 100
Evans, H., 79
Ezard, J., 80

Subject index